16-99

™

✔ KU-537-384

References for the Rest of Us! ®

BESTSELLING BOOK SERIES

Are you intimidated and confused by computers? Do you find that traditional manuals are overloaded with technical details you'll never use? Do your friends and family always call you to fix simple problems on their PCs? Then the For Dummies® computer book series from Hungry Minds, Inc. is for you.

For Dummies books are written for those frustrated computer users who know they aren't really dumb but find that PC hardware, software, and indeed the unique vocabulary of computing make them feel helpless. For Dummies books use a lighthearted approach, a down-to-earth style, and even cartoons and humorous icons to dispel computer novices' fears and build their confidence. Lighthearted but not lightweight, these books are a perfect survival guide for anyone forced to use a computer.

Already, millions of satisfied readers agree. They have made For Dummies books the #1 introductory level computer book series and have written asking for more. So, if you're looking for the most fun and easy way to learn about computers, look to *For Dummies* books to give you a helping hand.

Hungry Minds™

1/01

Networking

FOR

DUMMIES®

5TH EDITION

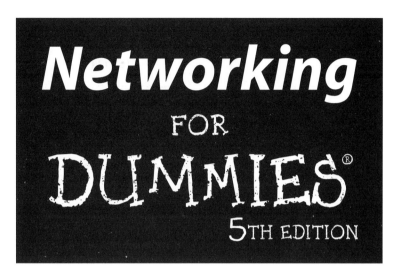

Networking

FOR

DUMMIES®

5TH EDITION

by Doug Lowe

Hungry Minds™

HUNGRY MINDS, INC.

New York, NY ◆ Indianapolis, IN ◆ Cleveland, OH

Networking For Dummies® 5th Edition

Published by
Hungry Minds, Inc.
909 Third Avenue
New York, NY 10022
www.hungryminds.com
www.dummies.com (Dummies Press Web Site)

Library of Congress Control Number: 00-105684

ISBN: 0-7645-0772-9

Printed in the United States of America

10 9 8 7 6 5 4 3

5B/RV/QS/QR/IN

Distributed in the United States by Hungry Minds, Inc.

Distributed by CDG Books Canada Inc. for Canada; by Transworld Publishers Limited in the United Kingdom; by IDG Norge Books for Norway; by IDG Sweden Books for Sweden; by IDG Books Australia Publishing Corporation Pty. Ltd. for Australia and New Zealand; by TransQuest Publishers Pte Ltd. for Singapore, Malaysia, Thailand, Indonesia, and Hong Kong; by Gotop Information Inc. for Taiwan; by ICG Muse, Inc. for Japan; by Intersoft for South Africa; by Eyrolles for France; by International Thomson Publishing for Germany, Austria and Switzerland; by Distribuidora Cuspide for Argentina; by LR International for Brazil; by Galileo Libros for Chile; by Ediciones ZETA S.C.R. Ltda. for Peru; by WS Computer Publishing Corporation, Inc., for the Philippines; by Contemporanea de Ediciones for Venezuela; by Express Computer Distributors for the Caribbean and West Indies; by Micronesia Media Distributor, Inc. for Micronesia; by Chips Computadoras S.A. de C.V. for Mexico; by Editorial Norma de Panama S.A. for Panama; by American Bookshops for Finland.

For general information on Hungry Minds' products and services please contact our Customer Care Department within the U.S. at 800-762-2974, outside the U.S. at 317-572-3993 or fax 317-572-4002.

For sales inquiries and reseller information, including discounts, premium and bulk quantity sales, and foreign-language translations, please contact our Customer Care Department at 800-434-3422, fax 317-572-4002, or write to Hungry Minds, Inc., Attn: Customer Care Department, 10475 Crosspoint Boulevard, Indianapolis, IN 46256.

For information on licensing foreign or domestic rights, please contact our Sub-Rights Customer Care Department at 650-653-7098.

For authorization to photocopy items for corporate, personal, or educational use, please contact Copyright Clearance Center, 222 Rosewood Drive, Danvers, MA 01923, or fax 978-750-4470.

For information on using Hungry Minds' products and services in the classroom or for ordering examination copies, please contact our Educational Sales Department at 800-434-2086 or fax 317-572-4005.

Please contact our Public Relations Department at 212-884-5163 for press review copies or 212-884-5000 for author interviews and other publicity information or fax 212-884-5400.

Hungry Minds™ is a trademark of Hungry Minds, Inc.

About the Author

Doug Lowe has written a whole bunch of computer books, including more than 30 *For Dummies* books, such as *PowerPoint 2000 For Dummies, Internet Explorer 5.5 For Dummies,* and *Microsoft Office 2000 For Dummies Quick Reference.* He lives in that sunny All American City Fresno, California, where the motto is, "Oh No, It Can't Be August Already!" with his wife, three teenaged daughters, and two female golden retrievers. He's one of those obsessive-compulsive decorating nuts who puts up tens of thousands of lights at Christmas and creates computer-controlled Halloween decorations that rival Disney's Haunted Mansion. Maybe his next book should be *Tacky Holiday Decorations For Dummies.*

Dedication

To Debbie, Rebecca, Sarah, and Bethany.

Author's Acknowledgments

The list of thank-yous for this book is long and goes back several years. I'd like to first thank John Kilcullen, David Solomon, Janna Custer, Erik Fafforn, Grag Robertson, and Ray Marshall for all their help with the first edition. Then came the second edition, for which I would like to thank Tim Gallan, Mary Goodwin, and Joe Salmeri. For the third edition, I'd like to thank Jennifer Ehrlich, Constance Carlisle, and Jamey L. Marcum. The fourth edition enlisted the help of Jeanne S. Criswell, Ted Cains, and Jamey L. Marcum.

Whew! For this fifth edition, I'd like to thank project editor Dana Lesh, who did a great job of overseeing all the editorial work that was required to put this book together. I'd also like to thank Rebekah Mancilla, Becky Huehls, Amy Pettinella, and Suzanne Thomas, the covey of copy editors who made sure the i's were crossed and the t's dotted (oops, reverse that!). Thanks also to technical editor Garrett Pease, who made many pertinent suggestions throughout. And, as always, thanks to all the behind-the-scenes people who chipped in with help I'm not even aware of.

Publisher's Acknowledgments

We're proud of this book; please send us your comments through our Online Registration Form located at www.dummies.com.

Some of the people who helped bring this book to market include the following:

Acquisitions, Editorial, and Media Development

Project Editor: Dana Rhodes Lesh

    (Previous Edition: Jeanne S. Criswell)

Acquisitions Editor: Georgette Blau

Copy Editors: Rebecca Huehls, Rebekah Mancilla, Amy Pettinella, Suzanne Thomas

    (Previous Edition: Ted Cains)

Proof Editor: Dwight Ramsey

Technical Editor: Garrett Pease

Editorial Manager: Rev Mengle

Editorial Assistant: Candace Nicholson

Production

Project Coordinator: Leslie Alvarez

Layout and Graphics: Beth Brooks, Jacque Schneider, Julie Trippetti, Jeremey Unger

Proofreaders: Laura Albert, Corey Bowen, Sally Burton, Carl Pierce, Charles Spencer, York Production Services, Inc.

Indexer: York Production Services, Inc.

General and Administrative

Hungry Minds, Inc.: John Kilcullen, CEO; Bill Barry, President and COO; John Ball, Executive VP, Operations & Administration; John Harris, CFO

Hungry Minds Technology Publishing Group: Richard Swadley, Senior Vice President and Publisher; Mary Bednarek, Vice President and Publisher, Networking and Certification; Walter R. Bruce III, Vice President and Publisher, General User and Design Professional; Joseph Wikert, Vice President and Publisher, Programming; Mary C. Corder, Editorial Director, Branded Technology Editorial; Andy Cummings, Publishing Director, General User and Design Professional; Barry Pruett, Publishing Director, Visual

Hungry Minds Manufacturing: Ivor Parker, Vice President, Manufacturing

Hungry Minds Marketing: John Helmus, Assistant Vice President, Director of Marketing

Hungry Minds Online Management: Brenda McLaughlin, Executive Vice President, Chief Internet Officer

Hungry Minds Production for Branded Press: Debbie Stailey, Production Director

Hungry Minds Sales: Roland Elgey, Senior Vice President, Sales and Marketing; Michael Violano, Vice President, International Sales and Sub Rights

◆

The publisher would like to give special thanks to Patrick J. McGovern, without whom this book would not have been possible.

◆

Contents at a Glance

Cartoons at a Glance

By Rich Tennant

"I DON'T KNOW - SOME PARTS OF THE NETWORK SEEM JUST FINE, AND OTHER PARTS SEEM TO BE COMPLETELY OUT OF CONTROL."

page 323

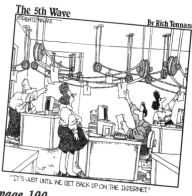

"IT'S JUST UNTIL WE GET BACK UP ON THE INTERNET."

page 199

"AND JUST WHAT THE HECK PART OF THE NETWORK DID YOU SAY YOU'RE FROM?"

page 145

"If it works, it works. I've just never seen network cabling connected with Chinese handcuffs before."

page 77

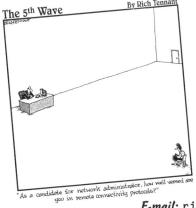

"As a candidate for network administrator, how well versed are you in remote connectivity protocols?"

page 239

I'll tell you this-retraining for client/server isn't going to be easy. Do you know how old some of these dogs are?

page 7

Fax: 978-546-7747
E-mail: richtennant@the5thwave.com
World Wide Web: www.the5thwave.com

Table of Contents

Introduction

- -

*W*elcome to the fifth edition of *Networking For Dummies,* the book that's written especially for people who have this nagging feeling in the back of their minds that they should network their computers but haven't a clue as to how to start or where to begin.

Do you often copy a spreadsheet file to a floppy disk and give it to the person in the next office so that he or she can look at it? Are you frustrated because you can't use the fancy laser printer that's on the financial secretary's computer? Do you wait in line to use the computer that has the customer database? You need a network!

Or maybe you already have a network, but you have just one problem: They promised that the network would make your life easier, but instead, it's turned your computing life upside down. Just when you had this computer thing figured out, someone popped into your office, hooked up a cable, and said, "Happy networking!" Makes you want to scream.

Either way, you've found the right book. Help is here, within these humble pages.

This book talks about networks in everyday — and often irreverent — terms. The language is friendly; you don't need a graduate education to get through it. And the occasional potshot will help unseat the hallowed and sacred traditions of networkdom, bringing just a bit of fun to an otherwise dry subject. The goal is to bring the lofty precepts of networking down to earth where you can touch them and squeeze them and say, "What's the big deal? I can do this!"

About This Book

This isn't the kind of book you pick up and read from start to finish, as if it were a cheap novel. If I ever see you reading it at the beach, I'll kick sand in your face. This book is more like a reference, the kind of book you can pick up, turn to just about any page, and start reading. You have 32 chapters, and each one covers a specific aspect of networking — such as printing on the network, hooking up network cables, or setting up security so that bad guys can't break in. Just turn to the chapter you're interested in and start reading.

Each chapter is divided into self-contained chunks, all related to the major theme of the chapter. For example, the chapter on hooking up the network cable contains nuggets like these:

- What Is Ethernet?
- Three Types of Ethernet Cable
  - The yellow stuff
  - Thinnet
  - Unshielded twisted-pair cable
- Installing Network Cables
  - Getting the tools that you need
  - Attaching a BNC connector to thinnet cable
  - Attaching an RJ-45 connector to UTP cable
- Professional Touches

You don't have to memorize anything in this book. It's a "need-to-know" book: You pick it up when you need to know something. Need to know what 100baseT is? Pick up the book. Need to know how to create good passwords? Pick up the book. Otherwise, put it down and get on with your life.

How to Use This Book

This book works like a reference. Start with the topic you want to find out about. Look for it in the table of contents or in the index to get going. The table of contents is detailed enough that you should be able to find most of the topics you're looking for. If not, turn to the index, where you can find even more detail.

After you've found your topic in the table of contents or the index, turn to the area of interest and read as much as you need or want. Then close the book and get on with it.

Of course, the book is loaded with information, so if you want to take a brief excursion into your topic, you're more than welcome. If you want to know the big security picture, read the whole chapter on security. If you just want to know how to make a decent password, read just the section on passwords. You get the idea.

If you need to type something, you'll see the text you need to type like this: **Type this stuff**. In this example, you type **Type this stuff** at the keyboard and press Enter. An explanation usually follows, just in case you're scratching your head and grunting, "Huh?"

Whenever I describe a message or information that you see on the screen, I present it as follows:

```
A message from your friendly network
```

This book rarely directs you elsewhere for information — just about everything that you need to know about networks is right here. For more information about Windows, try *Windows 98 For Dummies* or *Microsoft Windows Millennium Edition For Dummies,* both by Andy Rathbone (IDG Books Worldwide, Inc.). For more NetWare information, you can get a copy of *Networking With NetWare For Dummies,* 4th Edition, by Ed Tittel, James E. Gaskin, and Earl Follis. And you can find other *For Dummies* books that cover just about every program known to humanity.

What You Don't Need to Read

Much of this book is skippable. I've carefully placed extra-technical information in self-contained sidebars and clearly marked them so that you can steer clear of them. Don't read this stuff unless you're really into technical explanations and want to know a little of what's going on behind the scenes. Don't worry; my feelings won't be hurt if you don't read every word.

Foolish Assumptions

I'm going to make only two assumptions about who you are: *(1)* You're someone who works with a PC, and *(2)* you either have a network or you're thinking about getting one. I hope that you know (and are on speaking terms with) someone who knows more about computers than you do. My goal is to decrease your reliance on that person, but don't throw away his or her phone number quite yet.

Is this book useful for Macintosh users? Absolutely. Although the bulk of this book is devoted to showing you how to link Windows-based computers to form a network, you can find information about how to network Macintosh computers as well.

How This Book Is Organized

Inside this book, you find chapters arranged in six parts. Each chapter breaks down into sections that cover various aspects of the chapter's main subject. The chapters are in a logical sequence, so reading them in order (if you want to read the whole thing) makes sense. But the book is modular enough that you can pick it up and start reading at any point.

Here's the lowdown on what's in each of the six parts.

Part I: The Absolute Basics: A Network User's Guide

The chapters in this part present a layperson's introduction to what networking is all about. This is a good place to start if you're clueless about what a network is. It's also a great place to start if you're a hapless network user who doesn't give a whit about optimizing network performance, but you want to know what the network is and how to get the most out of it.

Part II: Building Your Own Network

Uh-oh. The boss just gave you an ultimatum: Get a network up and running by Friday or pack your things. The chapters in this section cover everything you need to know to build a network, from picking the network operating system to installing the cable.

Part III: Network Management For Dummies

I hope that the job of managing the network doesn't fall on your shoulders, but in case it does, the chapters in this part can help you out. You find out all about backup, security, performance, dusting, mopping, and all the other stuff network managers have to do.

Part IV: Webifying Your Network

After you get your network up and running, the first thing your users do is bang on your door and demand Internet access. The chapters in this part show you how to grant their request. Not only that, but you find out how to set up your own Web server so that you can create a Web site of your own. And you discover how to turn your network into an intranet so that your LAN users can access information on a local Web server.

Part V: More Ways to Network

The chapters in this part present additional information about networking, such as setting up a network in your home, dialing in to your network from another computer while you're away from the office, welcoming Macintosh computers and older MS-DOS computers into your network fold, and setting up a Linux server for your network.

Part VI: The Part of Tens

This wouldn't be a *For Dummies* book without a collection of lists of interesting snippets: ten network commandments, ten network gizmos only big networks need, ten big network mistakes, and more!

Icons Used in This Book

Hold it — technical stuff is just around the corner. Read on only if you have your pocket protector.

Pay special attention to this icon; it lets you know that some particularly useful tidbit is at hand — perhaps a shortcut or a little-used command that pays off big.

Did I tell you about the memory course I took?

Danger Will Robinson! This icon highlights information that may help you avert disaster.

Information specific to NetWare. Skip this stuff if you don't use, or do not plan to use, NetWare.

Windows 2000 Server information is in the vicinity.

You can find information about the latest version of Windows just around the corner.

Where to Go from Here

Yes, you can get there from here. With this book in hand, you're ready to plow right through the rugged networking terrain. Browse through the table of contents and decide where you want to start. Be bold! Be courageous! Be adventurous! And above all, have fun!

Part I

The Absolute Basics: A Network User's Guide

The 5th Wave   By Rich Tennant

I'll tell you this—retraining for client/server isn't going to be easy. Do you know how old some of these dogs are?

In this part . . .

One day the Network Thugs barge into your office and shove a gun in your face. "Don't move until we've hooked you up to the network!" one of them says while the other one rips open your PC, installs a sinister-looking electronic circuit card, closes the PC back up, and plugs a cable into its back. "It's done," they say as they start to leave. "Now . . . don't call the cops. We know who you are!"

If this has happened to you, you'll appreciate the chapters in this part. They provide a gentle introduction to computer networks written especially for the reluctant network user.

What if you don't have a network yet, and you're the one who's supposed to do the installing? Then the chapters in this part clue you in to what a network is all about. That way, you're prepared for the unfortunately more technical chapters contained in Part II.

Chapter 1

Networks Will Not Take Over the World, and Other Network Basics

*C*omputer networks get a bad rap in the movies. In *War Games,* Matthew Broderick plays a nerdy computer-whiz kid who nearly starts World War III by playing a game called "Global Thermonuclear War" on a Defense Department computer. In the *Terminator* movies, a computer network of the future called "Skynet" takes over the planet, builds deadly terminator robots, and sends them back through time to kill everyone unfortunate enough to have the name Sarah Connor. And in *The Matrix*, a vast and powerful computer network enslaves humans and keeps them trapped in a simulation of the real world.

Fear not. These bad networks exist only in the dreams of science fiction writers. Real-world networks are much more calm and predictable. They don't think for themselves, they can't evolve into something you don't want them to be, and they won't hurt you — even if your name is Sarah Connor.

Now that you're over your fear of networks, you're ready to breeze through this chapter. It's a gentle, even superficial, introduction to computer networks, with a slant toward the concepts that can help you use a computer that's attached to a network. This chapter isn't very detailed; the really detailed and boring stuff comes later.

What Is a Network?

A *network* is nothing more than two or more computers connected by a cable so that they can exchange information.

Of course, computers can exchange information in other ways besides networks. Most of us have used what computer nerds call the *sneakernet.* That's where you copy a file to a floppy disk and then walk the disk over to someone else's computer. (The term *sneakernet* is typical of computer nerds' feeble attempts at humor.)

The whole problem with the sneakernet is that it's slow; plus, it wears a trail in your carpet. One day, some penny-pinching computer geeks discovered that connecting computers together with cables was actually cheaper than replacing the carpet every six months. Thus, the modern computer network was born.

You can create a computer network by hooking all the computers in your office together with cables and installing a special *network interface card* (an electronic circuit card that goes inside your computer — ouch!) in each computer so that you have a place to plug in the cable. Then you set up your computer's operating system software to make the network work, and — voilà — you have a working network. That's all there is to it.

Figure 1-1 shows a typical network with four computers. You can see that all four computers are connected with a network cable to a central network device called a *hub.* You can also see that Ward's computer has a fancy laser printer attached to it. Because of the network, June, Wally, and the Beaver can also use this laser printer. (Also, you can see that the Beaver has stuck yesterday's bubble gum to the back of his computer. Although not recommended, the bubble gum shouldn't adversely affect the network.)

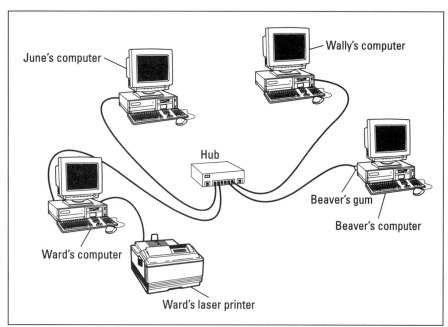

Figure 1-1: A typical network.

Computer networking has its own strange vocabulary. Fortunately, you don't have to know every esoteric networking term. Here are a few basic buzz-words to get you by:

- Networks are often called LANs. *LAN* is an acronym that stands for *local area network*. It's the first *TLA,* or *three-letter acronym*, that you see in this book. You don't need to remember it, or any of the many TLAs that follow. In fact, the only three-letter acronym you need to remember is TLA.

- You may guess that a four-letter acronym is called an *FLA.* Wrong! A four-letter acronym is called an *ETLA,* which stands for *extended three-letter acronym.*

- Every computer connected to the network is said to be *on the network.* The technical term (which you can forget) for a computer that's on the network is a *node.*

- When a computer is turned on and can access the network, the computer is said to be *online.* When a computer can't access the network, it's *offline.* A computer can be offline for several reasons. The computer can be turned off, the user may have disabled the network connection, the computer may be broken, the cable that connects it to the network can be unplugged, or a wad of gum can be jammed into the disk drive.

- ✔ When a computer is turned on and working properly, it's said to be *up*. When a computer is turned off or broken, it's said to be *down*. Turning off a computer is sometimes called *taking it down*. Turning it back on is sometimes called *bringing it up*.

- ✔ Don't confuse local area networks with the Internet. The *Internet* is a huge amalgamation of computer networks strewn about the entire planet. Networking the computers in your home or office so that they can share information with one another and connecting your computer to the worldwide Internet are two entirely separate things. If you want to use your local area network to connect your computers to the Internet, you can consult Chapter 18 for instructions.

Why Bother?

Frankly, computer networks are a bit of a pain to set up. So, why bother? Because the benefits of having a network make the pain of setting one up bearable. You don't have to be a Ph.D. to understand the benefits of networking. In fact, you learned everything you need to know in kindergarten: Networks are all about sharing. Specifically, networks are about sharing three things: files, resources, and programs.

- ✔ **Sharing files:** Networks enable you to share information with other computers on the network. Depending on how you set up your network, you can share files with your network friends in several different ways. You can send a file from your computer directly to a friend's computer by attaching the file to an e-mail message and then mailing it. Or, you can let your friend access your computer over the network so that your friend can retrieve the file directly from your hard drive. Yet another method is to copy the file to a disk on another computer, and then tell your friend where you put the file so that he or she can retrieve it later. One way or the other, the data travels to your friend's computer over the network cable, and not on a floppy disk as it does in a sneakernet.

- ✔ **Sharing resources:** You can set up certain computer resources — such as a hard drive or a printer — so that all the computers on the network can access them. For example, the laser printer attached to Ward's computer in Figure 1-1 is a shared resource, which means that anyone on the network can use it. Without the network, June, Wally, and the Beaver would have to buy their own laser printers.

Hard drives can be shared resources, too. In fact, you must set up a hard drive as a shared resource in order to share files with other users. Suppose Wally wants to share a file with the Beaver, and a shared hard drive has been set up on June's computer. All Wally has to do is copy his file to the shared hard drive in June's computer and tell the Beaver where he put it. Then, when the Beaver gets around to it, he can copy the file from June's computer to his own. (Unless, of course, Eddie Haskell deletes the file first.)

You can share other resources, too, such as modems (which enable you to access the Internet) and CD-ROM or DVD drives (devices that store vast quantities of data and are most useful for large clip-art libraries and encyclopedias and for playing tunes or watching movies while you're supposed to be working).

✔ **Sharing programs:** Rather than keeping separate copies of programs on each person's computer, sometimes putting programs on a drive that everyone shares is best. For example, if you have ten computer users who all use a particular program, you can purchase and install ten copies of the program — one for each computer. Or you can purchase a ten-user license for the program and then install just one copy of the program on a shared drive. Each of the ten users can then access the program from the shared hard drive.

In most cases, however, running a shared copy of a program over the network is unacceptably slow. A more common way of using a network to share programs is to copy the program's installation disks or CDs to a shared network drive. Then you can use that copy to install a separate copy of the program onto each user's local hard drive. For example, Microsoft Office enables you to do this, if you purchase a license from Microsoft for each computer on which you install Office.

The advantage of installing Office from a shared network drive is that you don't have to lug around the installation disks or CDs to each user's computer. And the system administrator can customize the network installation so that the software is installed the same way on each user's computer. (However, these benefits are significant only for larger networks. If your network has fewer than about ten computers, you're probably better off installing the program separately on each computer directly from the installation disks or CDs.)

Remember that purchasing a single-user copy of a program and then putting it on a shared network drive, so that everyone on the network can access it, is illegal. If you have five people who use the program, you need to either purchase five copies of the program or purchase a network license that specifically allows five or more users.

Another benefit of networking is that networks enable computer users to communicate with one another over the network. The most obvious way networks allow computer users to communicate is by passing messages back and forth using e-mail programs or instant messaging programs. But networks also offer other ways to communicate: For example, you can hold online meetings over the network. Network users who have inexpensive video cameras attached to their computers can have video conferences. You can even play a friendly game of Hearts over a network — during your lunch break, of course.

Servers and Clients

The network computer that contains the hard drives, printers, and other resources that are shared with other network computers is called a *server*. This term comes up repeatedly, so you have to remember it. Write it on the back of your left hand.

Any computer that's not a server is called a *client*. You have to remember this term, too. Write it on the back of your right hand.

Only two kinds of computers are on a network: servers and clients. Look at your left hand and then look at your right hand. Don't wash your hands until you have these terms memorized.

The distinction between servers and clients in a network would be somewhat fun to study in a sociology class, because it's similar to the distinction between the haves and the have-nots in society.

✔ Usually, the most powerful and expensive computers in a network are the servers. This fact makes sense because every user on the network shares the server's resources.

✔ The cheaper and less powerful computers in a network are the clients. Clients are the computers used by individual users for everyday work. Because clients' resources don't have to be shared, they don't have to be as fancy.

✔ Most networks have more clients than servers. For example, a network with ten clients can probably get by with one server.

✔ In many networks, a clean line of segregation exists between servers and clients. In other words, a computer is either a server or a client, and not both. A server can't become a client, nor can a client become a server.

✔ Other networks are more progressive, allowing any computer in the network to be a server and allowing any computer to be both server and client at the same time. The network illustrated in Figure 1-1 is this type of network.

Dedicated Servers and Peers

In some networks, a server computer is a server computer and nothing else. This server computer is dedicated solely to the task of providing shared resources, such as hard drives and printers, to be accessed by the network client computers. Such a server is referred to as a *dedicated server* because it can perform no other task besides network services.

Other networks take an alternative approach, enabling any computer on the network to function as both a client and a server. Thus, any computer can share its printers and hard drives with other computers on the network. And while a computer is working as a server, you can still use that same computer for other functions such as word processing. This type of network is called a *peer-to-peer network,* because all the computers are thought of as peers, or equals.

Here are some points to ponder concerning the difference between dedicated server networks and peer-to-peer networks while you're walking the dog tomorrow morning:

✔ Peer-to-peer networking features are built into Microsoft Windows 95, 98, and Millennium Edition (Windows Me). Thus, if your computer runs Windows, you don't have to buy any additional software to turn your computer into a server. All you have to do is enable the Windows server features.

✔ The network server features that are built into Windows 9*x*/Me aren't very efficient because these versions of Windows were not designed primarily to be network servers. If you're going to dedicate a computer to the task of being a full-time server, you should use a special network operating system instead of the standard Windows operating system. A network operating system, also known as a *NOS,* is specially designed to handle networking functions efficiently. The two most commonly used network operating systems are Microsoft's Windows 2000 Server (which used to be known as Windows NT Server) and Novell's NetWare. I describe them both in the next section, "The NOS Choice."

✔ Many networks are both peer-to-peer and dedicated server networks at the same time. These networks have one or more server computers that run Windows 2000 Server or some other NOS, as well as client computers that use the server features of Windows to share their resources with the network.

✔ Besides being dedicated, it's helpful if your servers are also sincere.

The NOS Choice

Most dedicated network servers do not run a desktop version of Windows such as Windows Me or Windows 98. Instead, dedicated network servers usually run a network operating system or NOS. A network operating system is specially designed to efficiently carry out the tasks of coordinating the access to shared network resources among the network client computers.

Although you have several network operating systems to choose from, the two most popular are NetWare and Windows 2000 Server.

- ✔ One of the most popular network operating systems is NetWare, from a company called Novell. NetWare is very advanced but also very complicated. So complicated, in fact, that it has an intensive certification program that rivals the bar exam. The lucky ones that pass the test are awarded the coveted title *Certified Novell Engineer,* or *CNE,* and a lifetime supply of pocket protectors. Fortunately, a CNE is really required only for large networks with dozens or even hundreds of computers attached. Building a NetWare network with just a few computers isn't too difficult.

- ✔ Windows 2000 Server is a special network server version of Windows 2000, which is itself a more advanced version of the popular Windows operating system from Microsoft. Windows 2000 used to be known as Windows NT. Thanks to the familiar Windows interface, Windows 2000 Server is a bit easier to set up and use than NetWare.

    Not wanting to be left out, Microsoft has its own certification program for Windows 2000 specialists. If you pass the full battery of certification tests, you get to wear an MCSE badge, which lets the whole world know that you are a *Microsoft Certified Systems Engineer.*

- ✔ Other network operating system choices include UNIX, Linux, and IBM's OS/2 Warp Server. Apple also makes its own network server operating system called Mac OS X Server, designed specially for Macintosh computers.

What Makes a Network Tick?

To use a network, you don't really have to know much about how it works. Still, you may feel a little bit better about using the network if you realize that it doesn't work by voodoo. A network may seem like magic, but it isn't. The following is a list of the inner workings of a typical network:

- ✔ **Network interface cards:** Inside any computer attached to a network is a special electronic circuit card called a *network interface card.* The TLA for network interface card is *NIC.*

    Using your network late into the evening is not the same as watching NIC at night.

    On newer computers, you can use an external network interface that connects to the computer via the computer's USB port.

- ✔ **Network cable:** The network cable is what physically connects the computers together. It plugs into the network interface card at the back of your computer. Two types of cables are commonly used for networks.

The first type of cable, called *coaxial* (sometimes called just *coax*), is similar to the cable used to bring Nick at Nite to your TV. The cable used for cable TV is not the same as the cable used for computer networks, though. So, don't try to replace a length of broken network cable with TV cable. It won't work. Networks require a higher grade of cable than is used for cable TV.

The other common type of network cable looks like a telephone cable. However, appearances can be deceiving. Many phone systems are wired using a lower grade of cable that won't work for networks. For a computer network, each pair of wires in the cable must be twisted in a certain way. That's why this type of cable is called a *twisted-pair cable.* Standard phone cable doesn't have the right twists.

Of the two cable types, twisted-pair cable is the best kind to use for new networks. Coax cable is found in plenty of older networks, but if you are building a new network, you want to use twisted-pair cable. For the complete lowdown on networking cables, refer to Chapter 10.

✔ **Network hub:** If your network is set up using twisted-pair cable, your network also needs a network hub. A *hub* is a small box with a bunch of cable connectors. Each computer on the network is connected by cable to the hub. The hub, in turn, connects all the computers to each other. If your network uses coax cable, the cable goes directly from computer to computer, so a network hub isn't used.

Instead of hubs, some networks use a faster device known as a *switch.* The term *hub* is often used to refer to both true hubs and switches.

✔ **Network software:** Of course, the software really makes the network work. To make any network work, a whole bunch of software has to be set up just right. For peer-to-peer networking with Windows, you have to play with the Control Panel to get networking to work. And network operating systems such as Windows 2000 Server or Novell's NetWare require a substantial amount of tweaking to get them to work just right. For more information about choosing which network software to use for your network, refer to Chapter 8. To find out what you need to know to configure the software so that your network runs smoothly, refer to Chapters 12 through 16.

It's Not a Personal Computer Anymore!

If I had to choose one point that I want you to remember from this chapter more than anything else, it's this: Once you hook up your personal computer (PC) to a network, it's not a personal computer anymore. You are now part of a network of computers, and in a way, you've given up one of the key things that made PCs so successful in the first place: independence.

I got my start in computers back in the days when mainframe computers ruled the roost. *Mainframe computers* are big, complex machines that used to fill entire rooms and had to be cooled with chilled water. My first computer was a water-cooled Binford Power-Proc Model 2000. Argh, argh, argh. (I'm not making up the part about the water. A plumber was frequently required to install a mainframe computer. In fact, the really big ones were cooled by liquid nitrogen. I am making up the part about the Binford 2000.)

Mainframe computers required staffs of programmers and operators just to keep them going. They had to be carefully managed. A whole bureaucracy grew up around managing mainframes.

Mainframe computers used to be the dominant computer in the workplace. Personal computers changed all that. Personal computers took the computing power out of the big computer room and put it on the user's desktop, where it belongs. PCs severed the tie to the centralized control of the mainframe computer. With a PC, a user could look at the computer and say, "This is mine . . . all mine!" Mainframes still exist, but they're not nearly as popular as they once were.

Networks are changing everything all over again. In a way, it's a change back to the mainframe computer way of thinking. True, the network isn't housed in the basement and doesn't have to be installed by a plumber. But you can no longer think of your PC as your own. You're part of a network, and like the mainframe, the network has to be carefully managed.

Here are a few ways in which a network robs you of your independence:

- You can't just indiscriminately delete files from the network. They may not be yours.

- Just because Wally sends something to Ward's printer doesn't mean it immediately starts to print. The Beave may have sent a two-hour print job before that. Wally just has to wait.

- You may try to retrieve an Excel spreadsheet file from a network drive, only to discover that someone else is using it. Like Wally, you just have to wait.

- If you copy that 600MB database file to a server's drive, you may get calls later from angry coworkers complaining that no room is left on the server's drive for their important files.

- Someone may pass a virus to you over the network. You may then accidentally infect other network users.

- If you want to access a file on Ward's computer but Ward hasn't come in and turned his computer on yet, you have to go into his office and turn it on yourself. To add insult to injury, you have to know Ward's password if

> Ward decided to password-protect his computer. (Of course, if you're the Beave, you probably already know Ward's password and everyone else's too, for that matter. If you don't, you can always ask Eddie Haskell.)
>
> ✔ If your computer is a server, you can't just turn it off when you're finished using it. Someone else may be accessing a file on your hard drive or printing on your printer.
>
> ✔ Why does Ward always get the best printer? If *Leave It to Beaver* were made today, I bet the good printer would be on June's computer.

The Network Manager

Because so much can go wrong, even with a simple network, designating one person as the *network manager* (sometimes also called the *network administrator* or *supervisor*) is important. This way, someone is responsible for making sure that the network doesn't fall apart or get out of control.

The network manager doesn't have to be a technical genius. In fact, some of the best network managers are complete idiots when it comes to technical stuff. What's important is that the manager be organized. The manager's job is to make sure that plenty of space is available on the file server, the file server is backed up regularly, new employees can access the network, and so on.

The network manager's job also includes solving basic problems that the users themselves can't solve and knowing when to call in an expert when something really bad happens.

> ✔ Part III of this book is devoted entirely to the hapless network manager. So if you're nominated, read that section. If you're lucky enough that someone else is nominated, celebrate by buying him or her a copy of this book.
>
> ✔ In small companies, picking the network manager by drawing straws is common. The person who draws the shortest straw loses and becomes manager.
>
> ✔ Of course, the network manager can't really be a complete technical idiot. I was lying. (For those of you in Congress, that means I was "testifying.") I exaggerated to make the point that organizational skills are more important than technical skills. The network manager needs to know how to do various maintenance tasks. This knowledge requires at least a little technical know-how, but the organizational skills are more important.

What Have They Got That You Don't Got?

With all this stuff to worry about, you may begin to wonder if you're smart enough to use your computer after it's attached to the network. Let me assure you that you are. If you're smart enough to buy this book because you know that you need a network, you're more than smart enough to use the network after it's put in. You're also smart enough to install and manage a network yourself. This isn't rocket science.

I know people who use networks all the time. And they're no smarter than you are. But they do have one thing that you don't have: a certificate. And so, by the powers vested in me by the International Society for the Computer Impaired, I present you with the certificate in Figure 1-2, confirming that you've earned the coveted title, Certified Network Dummy, better known as *CND*. This title is considered much more prestigious in certain circles than the more stodgy CNE or MSCE badges worn by real network experts.

Congratulations, and go in peace.

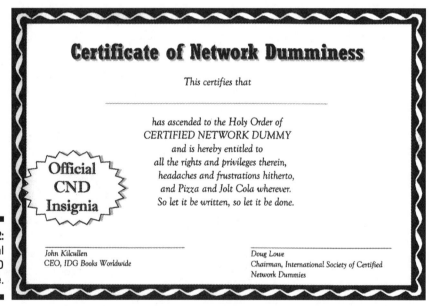

Certificate of Network Dumminess

This certifies that

_____

has ascended to the Holy Order of
CERTIFIED NETWORK DUMMY
and is hereby entitled to
all the rights and privileges therein,
headaches and frustrations hitherto,
and Pizza and Jolt Cola wherever.
So let it be written, so let it be done.

Official
CND
Insignia

John Kilcullen
CEO, IDG Books Worldwide

Doug Lowe
Chairman, International Society of Certified
Network Dummies

Figure 1-2:
Your official
CND
certificate.

Chapter 2

Life on the Network

∙ ∙

In This Chapter

▶ Using local resources and network resources

▶ Playing the name game

▶ Logging on to the network

▶ Mapping network drives

▶ Using shared folders

▶ Using a network printer

▶ Logging off the network

∙ ∙

*A*fter you hook up your PC to a network, it's not an island anymore —
separated from the rest of the world like some kind of isolationist fanatic
waving a "Don't tread on me" flag. The network connection changes your PC
forever. Now your computer is a part of a "system," connected to "other computers" on the "network." You have to worry about annoying network details,
such as using local and shared resources, logging in and accessing network
drives, using network printers, logging off, and who knows what else.

Oh, bother.

This chapter brings you up to speed on what living with a computer network
is like. Unfortunately, this chapter gets a little technical at times, so you may
need your pocket protector.

Distinguishing between Local Resources and Network Resources

In case you didn't catch this in Chapter 1, one of the most important differences between using an isolated computer and using a network computer is
the distinction between *local resources* and *network resources*. Local resources
are things such as hard drives, printers, modems, and CD-ROM drives that are
connected directly to your computer. You can use local resources whether

you're connected to the network or not. Network resources are the hard drives, printers, modems, and CD-ROM drives that are connected to the network's server computers. You can use network resources only after your computer is connected to the network.

The whole trick to using a computer network is to know which resources are local resources (they belong to you) and which are network resources (they belong to the network). In most networks, your C drive is a local drive. And if a printer is sitting next to your PC, it's probably a local printer. You can do anything you want with these resources without affecting the network or other users on the network (as long as the local resources aren't shared on the network).

✔ You can't tell just by looking at a resource whether it's a local resource or a network resource. The printer that sits right next to your computer is probably your local printer, but then again, it may be a network printer. The same holds for hard drives: The hard drive in your PC is probably your own, but it may be a network drive, which can be used by others on the network.

✔ Because dedicated network servers are full of resources, you may say that they aren't only dedicated (and sincere) but also resourceful. (Groan. Sorry, this is yet another in a tireless series of bad computer-nerd puns.)

What's in a Name?

Just about everything on a computer network has a name: The computers themselves have names, the people that use the computers have names, and the hard drives and printers that can be shared on the network have names. Knowing all the names that are used on your network isn't essential, but you do need to know some of them.

✔ Every person who can use the network has a *user identification* (*user ID* for short). You need to know your user ID in order to log on to the network. You also need to know the user IDs of your buddies, especially if you want to steal their files or send them nasty notes. You can find more information about user IDs and logging on in the section "Logging On to the Network" later in this chapter.

✔ Letting the folks on the network use their first names as their user IDs is tempting, but not a good idea. Even in a small office, you eventually run into a conflict. (And what about that Mrs. McCave — made famous by Dr. Seuss when she had 23 children and named them all Dave?) I suggest that you come up with some kind of consistent way of creating user IDs. For example, you may use your first name plus the first two letters of your last name. Then Wally's user ID would be `wallycl` and Beaver's would be `beavercl`. Or you may use the first letter of your first name followed by your complete last name. Then Wally's user ID would be `wcleaver` and Beaver's would be `bcleaver`. (Note that in most networks, capitalization does matter in the user name. Thus, `bcleaver` is different from `BCleaver`.)

✔ Every computer on the network must have a unique computer name. You don't have to know the names of all the computers on the network, but it helps if you know your own computer's name and the names of any server computers you need to access. The computer's name is often the user ID of the person who uses the computer most often. Sometimes the names indicate the physical location of the computer, such as `office-12` or `back-room`. Server computers often have names that reflect the group that uses the server most, like `acctng-server` or `cad-server`.

Then again, some network nerds like to assign techie-sounding names like `BL3K5-87a`.

Or you may want to use names from science fiction movies. `HAL`, `Colossus`, `M5`, and `Data` come to mind. Cute names like `Herbie` are not allowed. (However, `Tigger` and `Pooh` are entirely acceptable. Recommended, in fact. Tiggers like networks.)

✔ Network resources such as hard drives and printers have names, too. For example, a network server may have two printers, named `laser` and `inkjet` (to indicate the type of printer), and two hard drives, named C drive and D drive.

✔ In NetWare, names of hard drives are called *volume names.* Often, they are names such as SYS1, SYS2, and so on. NetWare administrators frequently lack sufficient creativity to come up with more interesting volume names.

✔ Networks that use a network operating system such as Windows 2000 Server or Novell's NetWare have a user ID for the network administrator. If you log on using the administrator's user ID, you can do anything you want: add new users, define new network resources, change Wally's password — anything. The supervisor's user ID is usually something very clever, such as `ADMINISTRATOR`.

Logging On to the Network

To use network resources, you must connect your computer to the network, and you must go through a super-secret process called *logging on.* The purpose of logging on is to let the network know who you are so that it can decide if you're one of the good guys.

Logging on is a little bit like cashing a check: The process requires two forms of identification. The first form is your *user ID,* the name by which the network knows you. Your user ID is usually some variation of your real name, like "Beave" for "The Beaver." Everyone who uses the network must have a user ID.

Your *password* is a secret word that only you and the network know. If you type the correct password, the network believes you are who you say you are. Every user has a different password, and the password should remain a secret.

In the early days of computer networking, you had to type a logon command at a stark MS-DOS prompt and then supply your user ID and password. Nowadays, the glory of Windows is that you get to log on to the network through a special network logon dialog box, which appears when you start your computer, as shown in Figure 2-1.

Figure 2-1: You have to enter your user ID and password to access the network.

If you're stuck using an old MS-DOS based computer, you may still have to type a logon command to access your network. Your network administrator can cheerfully show you how to do this. (If he or she grumbles, offer a jelly doughnut.)

Here are some more logon points to ponder:

✔ The terms *user name* and *logon name* are sometimes used instead of user ID. They mean the same thing.

✔ As long as we're talking about words that mean the same thing, *log in* and *log on* mean the same thing.

✔ As far as the network is concerned, you and your computer aren't the same thing. Your user ID refers to you, not to your computer. That's why you have a user ID and your computer has a computer name. You can log on to the network using your user ID from any computer that's attached to the network. And other users can log on at your computer using their own user IDs.

When others log on at your computer using their own user IDs, they can't access any of your network files that are protected by your password. However, they *are* able to access any local files that you haven't protected. So be careful which people you allow to use your computer.

✓ If you are logging on to a Windows NT or Windows 2000 Server network, the logon dialog box will include a field in which you can enter the domain name you want to log on to. Hopefully, a suitable default value will appear for the domain name so that you can safely ignore this field. If not, your network administrator will be happy to tell you how to enter this information.

✓ For NetWare networks, the logon dialog box may indicate the tree and context you are using to log on. Hopefully, your network administrator will have already configured the tree and context to the correct values. If not, he or she will tell you how to set the correct tree and context values. (On older NetWare networks, you may be asked to enter the name of the NetWare Login Server. Again, your network administrator will tell you what name to enter.)

✓ Your computer may be set up so that it logs you on automatically whenever you turn it on. In that case, you don't have to type your user ID and password. This setup makes the task of logging on more convenient, but takes the sport out of it. And it's a terrible idea if you're the least bit worried about bad guys getting into your network or personal files.

✓ Guard your password with your life. I'd tell you mine, but then I'd have to shoot you.

Understanding Shared Folders

Before Network (B.N.), your computer probably had just one hard drive, known as C drive. Maybe two, C and D. In any case, these drives are physically located inside your PC. They are your local drives.

Now that you're on a network, you probably have access to drives that aren't located inside your PC but are located instead in one of the other computers on the network. These network drives can be located on a dedicated server computer or, in the case of a peer-to-peer network, on another client computer.

In some cases, you can access an entire network drive over the network. But in most cases, you can't access the entire drive. Instead, you can access only certain folders (*directories* in old MS-DOS lingo) on the network drives. Either way, the shared drives or folders are known in Windows terminology as *shared folders*.

Shared folders can be set up with restrictions on how you may use them. For example, you may be granted full access to some shared folders so that you can copy files to or from them, delete files on them, create or remove folders on them, and so on. On other shared folders, your access may be limited in certain ways. For example, you may be able to copy files to or from the shared folder, but not delete files, edit files, or create new folders. You may also be asked to enter a password before you can access a protected folder. The amount of disk space you are allowed to use on a shared folder may also be limited. For more information about file-sharing restrictions, refer to Chapter 13.

Keep in mind that in addition to accessing shared folders that reside on other people's computers, you can also designate your computer as a server to enable other network users to access folders that you share. To learn how to share folders on your computer with other network users, refer to Chapter 4.

Welcome to the Network 'Hood

 Windows enables you to access network resources, such as shared folders, by opening the Network Neighborhood icon that resides on your desktop. When you first open the Network Neighborhood, you're greeted by icons that represent the computers that are connected to your local network workgroup, plus an icon representing the entire network, as shown in Figure 2-2.

Figure 2-2:
The
Network
Neighbor-
hood lists
the
computers
in your
network.

If you are using Windows Millennium Edition, the Network Neighborhood is known as My Network Places. Other than the name change, My Network Places works the same as the Network Neighborhood. Throughout the rest of this chapter, I use the term *Network Neighborhood* to refer to both the Network Neighborhood in Windows 95 or 98 and My Network Places in Windows Me.

Network Neighborhood is also known as My Network Places in Windows 2000.

To access shared folders that reside on another computer, open the icon that represents the computer in the Network Neighborhood. This action displays the folders that are designated as shared folders on that computer, as shown in Figure 2-3.

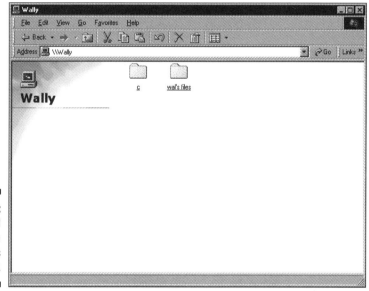

Figure 2-3:
Shared
folders on
Wally's
computer.

If the computer you want to access isn't listed in the Network Neighborhood window, open the Entire Network icon. Doing so allows you to access other computers that are available on your network.

As Figure 2-3 shows, Wally has designated two shared folders on his computer: one, named *c*, is his entire C drive. The other, named *wal's files,* is a folder containing files he wants to share. You can open either of these folders and then access the files within them as if they were located on your local drives.

You can also access the Network Neighborhood from any Windows application program. For example, suppose that you're working with Microsoft Word and would like to open a document file that has been stored in a shared folder on your network. All you have to do is choose the File➪Open command to bring up an Open dialog box. Near the top of the Open dialog box is a list box labeled *Look In.* From this list, choose the Network Neighborhood icon shown in Figure 2-4 to access network computers. Then, locate the document file that you want to open on the network.

Figure 2-4:
You can access the Network Neighborhood from any Windows program.

Here are a few points to ponder concerning the Network Neighborhood:

- ✔ Viewing the resources that are available on the network by way of the Network Neighborhood is also known as *browsing the network*. Unfortunately, browsing the network through the Network Neighborhood might be painfully slow if a large number of computers are connected to your local network workgroup.

- ✔ A trick known as *mapping* lets you access your favorite shared network folders quickly without having to browse the entire network. For more information, see the next section, titled "Mapping Network Drives."

Mapping Network Drives

If you find yourself accessing a particular shared folder frequently, you may want to use a special trick called *mapping* to access the shared folder more efficiently. Mapping assigns a drive letter to a shared folder. Then you can use the drive letter to access the shared folder as if it were a local drive. In this way, you can access the shared folder from any Windows program without having to navigate through the Network Neighborhood.

For example, you can map a shared folder named \Wal's Files to drive G on your computer. Then, to access files stored in the shared \Wal's Files folder, you would look on drive G.

To map a shared folder to a drive letter, follow these steps:

1. **Use the Network Neighborhood to locate the shared folder you want to map to a drive.**

   If you're not sure how to do this, refer to the section "Welcome to the Network 'Hood" earlier in this chapter.

2. **Right-click the shared folder and then choose the Map Network Drive command from the pop-up menu that appears.**

   This action summons the Map Network Drive dialog box, shown in Figure 2-5.

Figure 2-5:
Mapping a
network
drive.

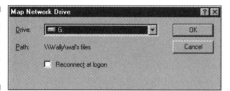

3. **Change the drive letter in the Drive drop-down list if you want to.**

   You probably don't have to change the drive letter that Windows selects (in Figure 2-5, drive G). But if you're picky, you can select the drive letter from the Drive drop-down list.

4. **If you want this network drive to be automatically mapped each time you log on to the network, check the Reconnect at Logon option.**

   If you leave the Reconnect at Logon option unchecked, the drive letter is available only until you shut Windows down or log off the network. If you check this option, the network drive automatically reconnects each time you log on to the network.

   Be sure to check the Reconnect at Logon option if you use the network drive often.

5. **Click OK.**

   That's it! You're done.

 Your network administrator may have already set up your computer with one or more mapped network drives. If so, you can ask him or her to tell you which network drives have been mapped. Or you can just open My Computer and have a look. (Mapped network drives are listed in My Computer using the icon shown in the margin.)

   ✔ Assigning a drive letter to a network drive is called *mapping the drive,* or *linking the drive* by network nerds. "Drive H is mapped to a network drive," they say.

✔ The drive letter that you use to map a drive on a network server doesn't have to be the same drive letter that the server uses to access the file. For example, suppose that you use drive H to link to the server's C drive. (This is confusing, so have another cup of coffee.) In this scenario, drive H on your computer is the same drive as drive C on the server computer. This shell game is necessary for one simple reason: You can't access the server's C drive as drive C because your computer has its own drive C! You have to pick an unused drive letter and map or link it to the server's C drive.

✔ Network drive letters don't have to be assigned the same way for every computer on the network. For example, a network drive that is assigned drive letter H on your computer may be assigned drive letter Q on someone else's computer. In that case, your drive H and the other computer's drive Q are really the same drive. This can be very confusing. If your network is set up this way, put pepper in your network administrator's coffee.

✔ Accessing a shared network folder through a mapped network drive is much faster than accessing the same folder via the Network Neighborhood. That's because Windows has to browse the entire network to list all available computers whenever you open the Network Neighborhood window. In contrast, Windows does not have to browse the network at all to access a mapped network drive.

Four Good Uses for a Shared Folder

After you know which shared network folders are available, you may wonder what you're supposed to do with them. Here are four good uses for a network folder.

Use it to store files that everybody needs

A shared network folder is a good place to store files that more than one user needs to access. Without a network, you have to store a copy of the file on everyone's computer, and you have to worry about keeping the copies synchronized (which you can't do, no matter how hard you try). Or you can keep the file on a disk and pass it around. Or you can keep the file on one computer and play musical chairs — whenever someone needs to use the file, he or she goes to the computer that contains it.

With a network, you can keep one copy of the file in a shared folder on the network, and everyone can access it.

Dealing with programs that don't like to share

If you're trying to share a file that's accessed by an older program — for example, an ancient DOS version of a spreadsheet program like Lotus 1-2-3 — you may have a problem. You have to make sure that two people don't try to update the file at the same time. For example, suppose that you retrieve a spreadsheet file and start to work on it and then another user retrieves the same file a few minutes later. That user won't see the changes you've made so far because you haven't saved the file on the drive yet. Now, suppose you finish making your changes and you save the file while the other user is still staring at the screen. Guess what happens when the other user saves his or her changes a few minutes later? All the changes you made are gone, lost forever in the Black Hole of Unprotected Concurrent Access.

The root cause of this problem is that older programs don't *reserve* the file while they're working on it. As a result, other programs aren't prevented from working on the file at the same time. The result is a jumbled mess. Fortunately, programs that are designed to work with Windows 95 or later are much more understanding about networks, so they do reserve files when you open them. These programs are much safer for network use.

Use it to store your own files

You can also use a shared network folder as an extension of your own hard drive storage. For example, if you've filled up all the free space on your hard drive with pictures, sounds, and movies that you've downloaded from the Internet, but the network server has billions and billions of gigabytes of free space, you have all the drive space you need. Just store your files on the network drive!

Here are a few guidelines for storing files on network drives:

- ✔ Using the network drive for your own files works best if the network drive is set up for private storage that other users can't access. That way, you don't have to worry about the nosy guy down in Accounting who likes to poke around in other people's files.

- ✔ Don't overuse the network drive. Remember that other users have probably filled up their own hard drives, so they want to use the space on the network drive, too.

- ✔ Before you store personal files on a network drive, make sure that you have permission. A note from your mom will do.

Use it as a pit stop for files on their way to other users

"Hey, Wally, could you send me a copy of last month's baseball stats?"

"Sure, Beave." But how? If the baseball stats file resides on Wally's local drive, how does Wally send a copy of the file to Beaver's computer? Wally can do this by copying the file to a network folder. Then Beaver can copy the file to his local hard drive.

Here are some tips to keep in mind when you use a network drive to exchange files with other network users:

- ✔ Don't forget to delete files that you've saved to the network folder after they've been picked up! Otherwise, the network folder quickly fills up with unnecessary files.

- ✔ Creating a directory on the network drive specifically intended for holding files en route to other users is a good idea. Call this directory PITSTOP or something similar to suggest its function.

- ✔ Most e-mail programs also let you deliver files to other users. This is called "sending a file attachment." The advantage of sending a file via e-mail is that you don't have to worry about details like where to leave the file on the server and who's responsible for deleting the file.

Use it to back up your local hard drive

If enough drive space is available on the file server, you can use it to store backup copies of the files on your hard drive. Just copy the files that you want to back up to a shared network folder.

Obviously, copying all your data files to the network drive can quickly fill up the network drive. You'd better check with the network manager before you do it. The manager may have already set up a special network drive that is designed just for backups. And, if you're lucky, your network manager may be able to set up an automatic backup schedule for your important data so you don't have to remember to back it up manually.

Hopefully, your network administrator also routinely backs up the contents of the network server's disk to tape. That way, if something happens to the network server, the data can be recovered from the backup tapes.

Using a Network Printer

Using a network printer is much like using a network hard drive. You can print to a network printer from any Windows program by choosing File⇨Print to call up a Print dialog box from any program and choosing a network printer from the list of available printers.

Keep in mind, however, that printing on a network printer isn't exactly the same as printing on a local printer. When you print on a local printer, you're the only one who is using that printer. But when you print to a network printer, you're sharing that printer with other network users. This complicates things in several ways:

- ✔ If several users print to the network printer at the same time, the network has to keep the print jobs separate from one another. If it didn't, the result would be a jumbled mess, with your 168-page report being mixed up with the payroll checks. That would be bad. Fortunately, the network takes care of this situation by using a fancy feature called *print spooling.*

- ✔ Invariably, when I get in line at the hardware store, the person in front of me is trying to buy something that doesn't have a product code on it. I end up standing there for hours waiting for someone in Plumbing to pick up the phone for a price check. Network printing can be like that. If someone sends a two-hour print job to the printer before you send your half-page memo, you have to wait. Network printing works on a first-come, first-served basis, unless you know some of the tricks that I discuss in Chapter 3.

- ✔ Before you were forced to use the network, your computer probably had just one printer attached to it. Now, you may have access to a local printer and several network printers. You may want to print some documents on your cheap (oops, I mean local) inkjet printer but use the network laser printer for really important stuff. To do that, you have to find out how to use your programs' functions for switching printers.

- ✔ Network printing is really too important a subject to squeeze into this chapter. So Chapter 3 goes into this topic in more detail.

Logging Off the Network

After you finish using the network, you should log off. Logging off the network makes the network drives and printers unavailable. Your computer is still physically connected to the network (unless you cut the network cable with pruning shears — bad idea! Don't do it!), but the network and its resources are unavailable to you.

✔ After you turn off your computer, you're automatically logged off the network. After you start your computer, you have to log in again. Logging off the network is a good idea if you're going to leave your computer unattended for a while. As long as your computer is logged in to the network, anyone can use it to access the network. And because unauthorized users can access it under your user ID, you get the blame for any damage they do.

✔ In Windows, you can log off the network by clicking the Start button and choosing the Log Off command. This process logs you off the network without restarting Windows. (In some versions of Windows 95, you must choose the Start⇨Shut Down command to log off the network.)

Chapter 3

Using a Network Printer

*I*f you come to hate anything about using a network, it's using a network printer. Oh, for the good ol' days when your slow but simple dot-matrix printer sat on your desk right next to your computer for you, and nobody else but you, to use. Now you have to share the printer down the hall. It may be a neat printer, but now you can't watch it all the time to make sure that it's working.

Now you have to send your 80-page report to the network printer, and when you go check on it 20 minutes later, you discover that it hasn't printed yet because someone else sent an 800-page report before you. Or the printer's been sitting idle for 20 minutes because it ran out of paper. Or your report just disappeared into Network-Network Land.

What a pain. This chapter can help you out. It clues you in to the secrets of network printing and gives you some Network Pixie Dust (NPD) to help you find those lost print jobs. (This chapter may also convince you to spend $69 of your own money to buy your own little inkjet printer so that you won't have to mess around with the network printer!)

What's So Special about Network Printing?

Why is network printing such a big deal? In Chapter 2, I talk about sharing network drives and folders and show that sharing is really pretty simple. After everything is set up right, using a network drive is hardly different from using a local drive.

The situation would be great if sharing a printer were just as easy. But it isn't. The problem with network printing is that printers are slow and finicky devices. They run out of paper. They eat paper. They run out of toner or ink. And sometimes they just croak. Dealing with all these problems is hard enough when the printer is right next to the computer on your desk, but using the printer that's accessed remotely via a network is even harder.

A printer in every port

Before I delve into the details of network printing, I want to review some printing basics. A *port* is a connection on the back of your computer. You use ports to connect devices to the computer. You plug one end of a cable into the port and plug the other end of the cable into a connector on the back of the device that you want to connect. Most computers have two devices connected to ports: a printer and a mouse. Some computers have other devices, such as a modem or a scanner.

Ports come in two varieties: *parallel* and *serial.* A parallel port is the type that is most often used for printers. Certain types of older printers used serial port connections, but most of these printers have long since been used to make beehives. The serial port is mostly used nowadays to connect a mouse or a modem to the computer. (Actually, serial ports are making a comeback in the form of a new, improved version called a *USB.* See the sidebar "Hop on the Universal Serial Bus" for more information.)

Another type of port that your computer may or may not have is a SCSI port. *SCSI* (pronounced *skuzzy*), which stands for *Small Computer System Interface,* is a special type of high-speed parallel port that's used mostly to connect disk drives, tape drives, CD-ROM drives, and other devices, such as scanners, to your computer. Because you don't use the SCSI port to connect a printer, you can ignore it for now.

Here are some additional points to ponder concerning the mysteries of printer ports:

- After the introduction of the first IBM Personal Computer way back in 1492, the names LPT1, LPT2, and LPT3 were assigned to the parallel ports (LPT stands for "Line Printer"). The first parallel port (and the only parallel port on most computers) is LPT1. LPT2 and LPT3 are the second and third parallel ports. Even today, Windows uses these same names.

- LPT1 has a pseudonym: PRN. The names LPT1 and PRN both refer to the first parallel port and are used interchangeably.

- COM1, COM2, COM3, and COM4 are the names used for the four serial ports. (COM stands for *communications*, a subject that the people who came up with names like LPT1 and COM1 needed to study more closely.)

- Hopefully, the name assigned to each port on your computer is printed next to the port's connector on the back of your computer. If not, you have to check your computer's manual to find out which port is which.

Hop on the Universal Serial Bus

In 1997, a new type of serial bus called the *Universal Serial Bus,* or *USB,* became available on new computers. The idea behind the USB is to eventually replace most, if not all, of the external connections required by your computer.

Think about all the external devices that you may have to connect to a typical computer: keyboard, monitor, mouse, printer, and perhaps a scanner, modem, video camera, speakers, and maybe even an external CD-ROM or tape drive. Each of these devices needs its own type of cable, and it's up to you to figure out which of the many receptacles on the back of your computer to plug each cable into.

Now, with USB, you can replace all of these components (except the monitor) with USB-compatible devices and plug them all into USB ports. If your computer doesn't have enough USB ports, you can purchase an inexpensive USB hub, which you can plug USB devices into. Or, you can daisy-chain many USB devices to each other. For example, you can plug your keyboard into the USB port on the back of your computer, and you can plug your mouse into a USB port located on your keyboard.

Besides saving you the hassle of untangling a multitude of cables and connectors, USB devices also automatically reconfigure themselves after you attach them to your computer. You no longer have to fuss with IRQ settings or other configuration details. You can even add or remove USB devices without turning off your computer or restarting Windows.

You can also use the USB to connect to the network without having to install a separate network interface card inside your computer by using a USB Ethernet adapter.

Printer configuration

All you have to do to use a printer is plug it into the parallel port (or the USB port) on the back of your computer, right? Nope. You must also configure Windows to work with the printer. To do this, you must install a special piece of software called a *printer driver,* which tells Windows how to print to your printer.

Each type of printer has its own type of printer driver. Drivers for the most common printers come with Windows. For printers that are more exotic — or for newer printers that weren't available at the time you purchased Windows — the printer manufacturer supplies the driver on a disk that comes with the printer.

To find out what printers are already configured for your computer, click the Start button and then choose the Settings⊅Printers command. The Printers folder appears, as shown in Figure 3-1.

Figure 3-1:
The Printers
folder.

The Printers folder shows an icon for each printer installed on your computer. In the case of Figure 3-1, only one printer has been installed: a Hewlett-Packard LaserJet 4L. If you have more than one printer installed on your computer, you see a printer icon for each printer.

You can configure a new printer for your computer by double-clicking the Add Printer icon. Doing so starts the Add Printer Wizard, which adds a printer driver for a new printer to your computer. For more information about using this Wizard, see the section "Adding a Network Printer" later in this chapter.

Spooling and the print queue

Printers are far and away the slowest part of any computer. As far as your computer's central processing unit (CPU) is concerned, the printer takes an eternity to print a single line of information. To keep the CPU from twiddling its microscopic thumbs, computer geeks invented *spooling*.

Spooling is really pretty simple. Suppose that you use Microsoft Word to print a 200-page report. Without spooling, Word would send the report directly to the printer. You'd have to play Solitaire until the printer finished printing.

With spooling, Word doesn't send the report directly to the printer. Instead, Word sends the report to a disk file. Because the disk drives are so much faster than printers, you have to wait only a few seconds for the print job to finish. After your 200-page report is sent to the spool file, you can continue to use Word for other work, even though the printer hasn't actually finished your report yet.

Suppose you turn right around and send another 200-page report to the printer, while the printer is still busy printing the first 200-page report. The second report must wait for the printer to finish the first report. The place where the report waits is called the *print queue.* Print queue is the computer-nerd term for the line in which your print job has to wait while other print jobs that reached the line sooner are printed. Your print job isn't actually printed until it gets to the front of the line; that is, until it gets to the front of the queue.

Here are a few more spooling tidbits:

- ✔ The people who invented network printing way back in the 1960s thought that calling the line that print jobs wait in a *line* would be uncool. The Beatles and anything British were popular back then, so they picked the British-sounding word *queue* instead.

- ✔ Although considered rude, cutting to the front of the queue is possible. You find out how to do that later in this chapter. This trick is good to know — especially if you're the only one who knows.

- ✔ Brits always use too many letters. They like to throw extra letters into words like *colour*. The word *queue* is pronounced like "cue," not "cue-you." "Cue-you" is spelled "queueue," and is often used by Certified Network Dummies as an insult.

- ✔ Believe it or not, the word *spool* is actually an acronym — a five-letter acronym, or EETLA ("Expanded Extended Three-Letter Acronym") to be precise. Brace yourself, because this acronym is really nerdy: Spool stands for "Simultaneous Peripheral Output On-Line."

What is a print job?

I've used the term *print job* several times without explaining what it means, so you're probably already mad at me. I'd better explain before it's too late. A print job is a collection of printed pages that are kept together and treated as a set. If you print a 20-page document from Word, the entire 20-page printout is a single print job. Every time you use Word's Print command (or any other program's Print command), you create a print job.

How does the network know when one print job ends and the next one begins? Because the programs that do the printing send out a special code at the end of each Print command that says, "This is the end of the print job. Everything up to this point belongs together, and anything I print after this point belongs to my next print job."

Analogy alert! You can think of this code as the little stick you use at the grocery-store checkout stand to separate your groceries from the groceries that belong to the person in line behind you. The stick tells the clerk that all the groceries in front of the stick belong together, and the groceries behind the stick belong to the next customer.

When you print over a network, you can do lots of neat stuff with print jobs. You can tell the print server to print more than one copy of your job. You can tell it to print a full-page banner at the beginning of your job so that your job will be easy to find in a big stack of print jobs. Or you can tell it to stop printing when your job gets to the front of the line so that you can change from plain paper to preprinted invoices or checks. You handle these tricks from the standard Windows Print dialog boxes.

Adding a Network Printer

Before you can print to a network printer, you have to configure your computer to access the network printer that you want to use. From the Start menu, choose Settings⇨Printers to open the Printers folder. If your computer is already configured to work with a network printer, an icon for the network printer appears in the Printers folder (see the icon in the margin). You can tell a network printer from a local printer by the shape of the printer icon. Network printer icons have a pipe attached to the bottom of the printer.

If you don't have a network printer configured for your computer, you can add one by using the Add Printer Wizard. Open the Add Printer icon in the Printers folder to start the Add Printer Wizard. When the Wizard asks whether you want to add a local or a network printer, choose network. Then, when the Wizard

asks you to type the path for the network printer, click the Browse button. A
dialog box similar to the one in Figure 3-2 appears, showing the computers and
shared resources available on your Network Neighborhood.

Figure 3-2:
The Add
Printer
Wizard
wants to
know which
network
printer you
want to use.

Sniff around in this dialog box until you find the printer you want to use from
your computer. Click this printer and then click OK to return to the Add
Printer Wizard.

If you are using a printer that is attached directly to the network rather than
to a print server, do not click the Browse button. Instead, type the complete
network printer name when the Add Printer Wizard asks for it. If you don't
know what name to use, ask your network administrator.

Next, the Wizard copies the correct printer driver for the network printer to
your computer. Depending on the operating system that your computer uses
and the Windows version that you use, you may be asked to insert your
Windows CD-ROM so that Windows can locate the driver files, or you may
have to insert the driver disk that came with the printer. In many cases, however, Windows copies the driver files directly from the server computer that
the printer is attached to, so you won't have to bother with the Windows CD
or the printer's driver disks.

Finally, the Add Printer Wizard asks for a name that you want to give to the
network printer and whether you want to designate the printer as your
default printer, as shown in Figure 3-3. Type a name that distinguishes the
printer from other printers that you may have installed on your computer,
and then click Next to continue. As its final duty, the Add Printer Wizard
offers to print a test page so that you can make sure that the network connection and printer configuration are working properly.

Figure 3-3:
Choosing a
name for a
network
printer.

Using a Network Printer

After you have installed the network printer in Windows, printing to the network printer is a snap. You can print to the network printer from any Windows program by using the File⇨Print command to summon the Print dialog box. For example, Figure 3-4 shows the Print dialog box for WordPad — the free word processing program that comes with Windows. Near the top of this dialog box is a drop-down list titled Name, which lists all the printers that are installed on your computer. Choose the network printer from this list and then click OK to print your document. That's all there is to it!

Figure 3-4: A
typical Print
dialog box.

Playing with the Print Queue

After you send your document to a network printer, you usually don't have to worry about it. You just go to the network printer, and — voilà! — your printed document is waiting for you.

That's what happens in the ideal world. In the real world where you and I live, all sorts of things can happen to your print job between the time you send it to the network printer and the time it actually prints:

✔ You discover that someone else already sent a 50-trillion-page report ahead of you that isn't expected to finish printing until the national debt is completely paid off.

✔ The price of framis valves goes up $2 each, rendering foolish the recommendations you made in your report.

✔ Your boss calls and tells you that his brother-in-law will be attending the meeting, so won't you please print an extra copy of the proposal for him. Oh, and a photocopy won't do. Originals only, please.

✔ You decide to take lunch, so you don't want the output to print until you get back.

Fortunately, your print job isn't totally beyond your control just because you've already sent it to the network printer. You can easily change the status of jobs that you've already sent. You can change the order in which jobs print, hold a job so that it won't print until you say so, or cancel a job altogether.

You can probably make your network print jobs do other tricks, too — such as shake hands, roll over, and play dead. But the basic tricks — hold, cancel, and change the print order — are enough to get you started.

Using Windows Print Queue Tricks

To play with the printer queue, choose Settings⇨Printers from the Start menu and then open the icon for the printer that you want to manage. A window similar to the one shown in Figure 3-5 appears. If you happen to be Wally, you can see the bad news: Some user named Beave has slipped in a 166-page report from Microsoft Word before your little 1-page memo.

Figure 3-5: Managing a print queue.

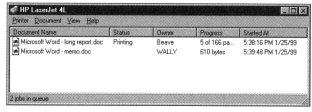

To manipulate the print jobs that appear in the print queue or in the printer itself, use the following tricks:

- ✔ To temporarily stop a job from printing, select the job and choose the Document⇨Pause Printing command. Choose the same command again to release the job.

- ✔ To delete a print job, select the job and choose the Document⇨ Cancel Printing command.

- ✔ To stop the printer, choose the Printer⇨Pause Printing command. To resume, choose the command again.

- ✔ To delete all print jobs, choose the Printer⇨Purge Print Documents command.

- ✔ To cut to the front of the line, drag the print job that you want to print to the top of the list.

Note that depending on how your network is set up, you may not be able to mess with other users' print jobs. Sigh.

The best thing about Windows printer management is that it shelters you from the details of working with different network operating systems. Whether you print on a NetWare printer, a Windows NT printer, or a Windows 95/98 or Windows Me shared printer, the Printer window icon manages all print jobs in the same way.

What to Do When the Printer Jams

The only three sure bets in life: The original *Star Wars* movies are better than the prequels, old actors like Harrison Ford always play across from leading ladies that are twenty years younger, and the printer always jams shortly after your job reaches the front of the queue.

What do you do when you walk in on your network printer while it's printing all 133 pages of your report on the same line?

1. **Start by yelling "Fire!"**

   No one comes to your rescue if you yell "Printer!"

2. **Find the printer's online button and press it.**

   This step takes the printer offline so that the server stops sending infor-mation to it and the printer stops. This doesn't cure anything, but it stops the noise. If you must, turn the printer off.

3. **Pull out the jammed paper and reinsert the good paper into the printer. Nicely.**

4. **Press the online button so that the printer resumes printing.**

If the printer completely crumbles up one or more pages of your document, you can reprint just the pages that were messed up by calling up the Print dialog box from the program you used to print the document and selecting the pages you want to reprint. If the printer ate the entire print job, you'll have to reprint the entire thing. (If you're using Windows 2000, you can use the Print Queue to restart the print job from the first page.)

Chapter 4

Becoming a Server

· ·

· ·

*A*s you probably know, networks consist of two types of computers: client computers and server computers. In the economy of computer networks, *client computers* are the consumers — the ones who use network resources such as shared printers and disk drives. *Servers* are the providers — the ones that offer their own printers and hard drives to the network so that the client computers can use them.

This chapter shows you how to turn your humble Windows client computer into a server computer so that other computers on your network can use your printer and any folders that you decide you want to share. In this way, your computer functions as both a client and a server computer at the same time. Your computer is a client when you send a print job to a network printer or when you access a file stored on another server's hard drive. Your computer is a server when someone else sends a print job to your printer or accesses a file stored on your computer's hard drive.

If you are using Windows Millennium Edition, you can use the Home Networking Wizard to share your files and printers. For more information, see Chapter 21.

Enabling File and Printer Sharing

Before you can share your files or your printer with other network users, you must set up a Windows 9*x*/Me feature known as *File and Printer Sharing*. Without this feature installed, your computer can be a network client but not a server.

If you are lucky, the File and Printer Sharing feature is already set up on your computer. To find out, double-click the My Computer icon on your desktop. Select the icon for your C drive and then click File in the menu bar to reveal the File menu. If the menu includes a Sharing command, then File and Printer Sharing is already set up, so you can skip the rest of this section. If you can't find a Sharing command in the File menu, then you have to install File and Printer Sharing before you can share a file or a printer with other network users.

To install File and Printer Sharing on your computer, follow these steps:

1. **From the Start menu, choose Settings⇨Control Panel.**

   The Control Panel comes to life.

2. **Double-click the Network icon.**

   The Network dialog box appears, as shown in Figure 4-1.

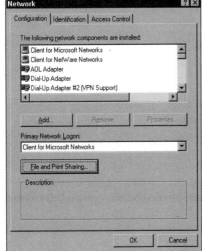

Figure 4-1:
The
Network
dialog box.

3. **Click the File and Print Sharing button.**

   This action summons the File and Print Sharing dialog box, as shown in Figure 4-2.

Figure 4-2:
The File and
Print
Sharing
dialog box.

4. **Click the File and Print Sharing options you want to enable for your computer.**

   The first option enables you to share your files with other network users; the second allows you to share your printer. To share both your files and your printer, check both options.

5. **Click OK to dismiss the File and Print Sharing dialog box.**

   You return to the Network dialog box.

6. **Click OK to dismiss the Network dialog box.**

   The Network dialog box vanishes, and a Copy Progress dialog box appears to let you know that Windows is copying the files required to enable File and Print Sharing. If you're prompted to insert the Windows CD-ROM, do so with a smile.

   After all the necessary files have been copied, you see a dialog box informing you that you must restart your computer for the new settings to take effect.

7. **Click Yes to restart your computer.**

   Your computer shuts down and then restarts. Your computer may take a minute or so to restart, so be patient. When your computer comes back to life, you're ready to share files or your printer.

While you are in the Network dialog box, do not mess around with any of the other network settings. You can safely change the File and Print Sharing options, but you should leave the rest of the settings on the Network dialog box well enough alone.

Sharing a Hard Drive or Folder

To enable other network users to access files that reside on your hard drive, you must designate either the entire drive or a folder on the drive as a shared drive or folder. If you share an entire drive, other network users can access all the files and folders on the drive. If you share a folder, network users can access only those files that reside in the folder you share. (If the folder you share contains other folders, network users can access files in those folders, too.)

I recommend against sharing an entire hard drive, unless you want to grant everyone on the network the freedom to sneak a peek at every file on your hard drive. Instead, you should share just the folder or folders that contain the specific documents that you want others to be able to access. For example, if you store all your Word documents in the My Documents folder, you can share your My Documents folder so that other network users can access your Word documents.

To share a folder, follow these steps:

1. **Double-click the My Computer icon on your desktop.**

   The My Computer window comes to center stage.

2. **Select the folder that you want to share.**

   Click the icon for the drive that contains the folder that you want to share, and then find the folder itself and click it.

3. **Choose the File⇨Sharing command.**

   The Properties dialog box for the folder that you want to share appears. Notice that the sharing options are grayed out as long as the Not Shared option is selected.

4. **Click the Shared As option.**

   After you click this option, the rest of the sharing options come alive, as shown in Figure 4-3.

   If you prefer, you can skip Steps 2 through 4. Instead, just right-click the folder you want to share and then choose Sharing from the pop-up menu that appears.

Figure 4-3:
The Sharing options come to life when you click the Shared As option.

My Documents Properties

General | Web Sharing | Sharing |

- ○ Not Shared
- ● Shared As:
  - Share Name: MYDOCUMENTS
  - Comment:

Access Type:
- ○ Read-Only
- ● Full
- ○ Depends on Password

Passwords:
- Read-Only Password:
- Full Access Password: ********

[OK]   [Cancel]   [Apply]

5. **Change the Share Name if you don't like the name that Windows proposes.**

   The *Share Name* is the name that other network users use to access the shared folder. You can use any name you want, but the name can be no more than 12 characters in length. Uppercase and lowercase letters are treated the same in a share name, so the name My Documents is the same as MY DOCUMENTS.

Windows proposes a share name for you based on the actual folder name. If the folder name is 12 or fewer characters, the proposed share name is the same as the folder name. But if the folder name is longer than 12 characters, Windows abbreviates it. For example, the name Multimedia Files becomes MULTIMEDIA F.

If the name that Windows chooses doesn't make sense or seems cryptic, you can change the share name to something better. For example, I would probably use MEDIA FILES instead of MULTIMEDIA F.

6. **Type a Comment for the folder if you want.**

   The Comment field lets you provide more information about the shared folder.

7. **Use the Access Type settings to indicate the level of access that you want to allow other users to have.**

   You have three options for the Access Type settings:

   - **Read Only:** Network users can open files in the shared folder, but they can't change, rename, delete, or create new files in the shared folder.

   - **Full:** Network users can open, modify, rename, delete, and create new files in the shared folder.

   - **Depends on Password:** You can grant some users read-only access, while other users who know the right password get full access.

8. **If you want to protect the folder with a password, type the password in the password field.**

   If you selected Read Only in Step 7, you can type a password in the Read-Only Password field. Then, anyone who attempts to access the folder has to type the password before Windows allows him or her to read the files in the folder.

   If you selected Full in Step 7, you can type a password in the Full-Access Password field. Again, Windows requires that anyone who wants to access the folder must first type the correct password.

   If you selected Depends on Password in Step 7, you can type a password in both the Read-Only Password and Full-Access Password fields. Then, a user is granted read-only or full access to the folder depending on which password that the user types.

9. **Click OK.**

   If you typed a password in either password field in Step 8, Windows displays the dialog box shown in Figure 4-4 so that you can confirm the passwords. Type each password again and then click OK.

   The Properties dialog box vanishes, and a hand is added to the icon for the folder to show that the folder is shared, as shown in the margin.

Figure 4-4:
Windows
asks you to
confirm your
passwords.

Password Confirmation ☒
Please reenter your passwords to confirm they are correct.   OK
                                                              Cancel
┌ Passwords: ──────────────────────────────────
│ Read-Only Password: [   ]
│
│ Full Access Password: [   ]
└──

If you change your mind and decide that you want to stop sharing a folder, double-click the My Computer icon, select the folder or drive that you want to stop sharing, and choose the File⇨Sharing command to summon the Properties dialog box. Click the Not Shared option and then click OK.

Sharing a Printer

Sharing a printer is much more traumatic than sharing a hard drive. When you share a hard drive, other network users access your files from time to time. When they do, you hear your drive click a few times, and your computer may hesitate for a half-second or so. The interruptions caused by other users accessing your drive are sometimes noticeable, but rarely annoying.

But when you share a printer, your co-worker down the hall is liable to send a 40-page report to your printer just moments before you try to print a 1-page memo that has to be on the boss's desk in two minutes. The printer may run out of paper or, worse yet, it may jam during someone else's print job — and you'll be expected to attend to the problem.

Although these interruptions can be annoying, sharing your printer makes a lot of sense in some situations. If you have the only decent printer in your office or workgroup, everyone is going to be bugging you to let them use it anyway. You may as well share the printer on the network. At least this way, they won't be lining up at your door asking you to print their documents for them.

To designate your printer as a shared printer, follow the bouncing ball through these steps:

1. **From the Start menu, choose the Settings⇨Printers command.**

   The Printers folder appears, as shown in Figure 4-5. In this example, the Printers folder lists a single printer, named HP LaserJet 4L.

2. **Select the printer that you want to share.**

   Click the icon for the printer to select the printer.

Figure 4-5:
The Printers
folder.

3. **Choose the File⇨Sharing command.**

   You're right: This doesn't make sense. You're sharing a printer, not a file, but the Sharing command is found under the File menu. Go figure.

   When you choose the File⇨Sharing command, the Properties dialog box for the printer appears.

4. **Click the Shared As option.**

   Figure 4-6 shows the Printer Properties dialog box that appears after you click the Shared As option.

5. **Change the Share Name if you don't like the name suggested by Windows.**

   Other computers use the share name to identify the shared printer, so choose a meaningful or descriptive name.

6. **Type a Comment for the printer if you want.**

   The comment field lets you provide more information about the shared printer.

7. **If you want to password-protect the printer, type a password in the Password field.**

   If you leave the Password field blank, any network user can access your printer. If you type a password in the Password field, anyone who tries to access your printer is asked to enter the password.

HP LaserJet 4L Properties

| Graphics | Fonts | | Device Options |
| General | Details | Sharing | Paper |

○ Not Shared

⦿ Shared As:

Share Name: HP

Comment:

Password:

OK   Cancel   Apply

Figure 4-6:
The
Properties
dialog box
for a shared
printer.

8. Click OK.

You return to the Printers folder, where a hand is added to the printer icon, as shown in the margin, to show that the printer is now a shared network printer.

To take your shared printer off the network so that other network users can't access it, follow the above procedure through Step 3 to call up the Printer Properties dialog box. Check Not Shared instead of Shared As and then click OK. The hand disappears from the printer icon to indicate that the printer is no longer shared.

Chapter 5

Mr. McFeeley's Guide to E-mail

· ·

· ·

Do you often return to your office after a long lunch to find your desk covered with those little pink "While You Were Out" notes and your computer screen plastered with stick-on notes?

If so, maybe the time has come for you to bite the bullet and find out how to use your computer network's electronic mail, or *e-mail,* program. Most computer networks have one. If yours doesn't, bug the network manager until he or she gets one.

This chapter introduces you to what's possible with a good e-mail program. So many e-mail programs are available that I can't possibly show you how to use all of them, so I'm focusing on Microsoft Outlook, the e-mail program that comes with Microsoft Office. Other e-mail programs are similar.

E-mail and Why It's So Cool

E-mail is nothing more than the computer-age equivalent of Mr. McFeeley, the postman from *Mr. Rogers' Neighborhood.* E-mail enables you to send messages to and receive messages from other users on the network. Instead of writing the messages on paper, sealing them in an envelope, and then giving them to Mr. McFeeley to deliver, e-mail messages are stored on disk and electronically delivered to the appropriate user.

Sending and receiving e-mail

To send an e-mail message to another network user, you must activate the e-mail program, compose the message by using a text editor, and provide an address, which is usually the network user ID of the user that you want the message sent to. Most e-mail programs also require that you create a short comment that identifies the subject of the message.

When you receive a message from another user, the e-mail program copies the message to your computer and then displays it on-screen so you can read it. You can then delete the message, print it, save it to a disk file, or forward it to another user. You can also reply to the message by composing a new message to be sent back to the user who sent the original message.

Here are some additional thoughts about sending and receiving e-mail:

- ✔ When someone sends a message to you, most e-mail programs immediately display a message on your computer screen or make a sound to tell you to check your e-mail. If your computer isn't on the network when the message is sent, then you're notified the next time that you log on to the network.

- ✔ Most e-mail programs can be set up to check for new e-mail automatically when you log on to the network.

- ✔ Most e-mail programs enable you to attach a file to your text message. You can use this feature to send a word-processing document, a spreadsheet, or a program file to another network user.

- ✔ Most e-mail programs enable you to keep a list of users that you commonly send e-mail to in an address book. That way you don't have to retype the user ID every time.

- ✔ Most programs also enable you to address a message to more than one user — the electronic equivalent of a carbon copy. Some programs also enable you to create a list of users and assign a name to this list. Then you can send a message to each user in the list by addressing the message to the list name. For example, June may create a list including Ward, Wally, and Beaver, and call the list Boys. To send e-mail to all the boys on her family network, she simply addresses the message to Boys.

- ✔ Some e-mail programs can handle your Internet e-mail as well as your LAN e-mail.

Understanding the mail server

E-mail programs rely on a network server computer that is set up as a mail server, which works kind of like an electronic post office where messages are stored until they can be delivered to the recipient. A network server that is used as a mail server doesn't have to be dedicated to this purpose, although this is sometimes true for larger networks. In smaller networks, a network file and print server can also act as the mail server.

Here are some details that you should know about mail servers:

✔ Windows NT and NetWare come with basic mail server programs that let you set up an e-mail system for your network. For more advanced e-mail functions, you can purchase and install a separate mail server, such as Microsoft Exchange Server. (Unfortunately, the mail server that comes with Windows 2000 is considerably more difficult to set up and use than the one that comes with Windows NT.)

✔ Disk space on a mail server is often at a premium. Be sure to delete unneeded messages after you read them.

✔ Managing the mail server can become one of the most time-consuming tasks of managing a network. Be prepared to spend time managing user accounts, fixing broken message folders, and tinkering with various settings and options.

Microsoft Outlook

Because it is a part of Microsoft Office, Microsoft Outlook is one of the most popular programs for accessing e-mail. Although many other e-mail programs are available, most of them work much like Outlook for the basic chores of reading and creating e-mail messages.

Internet Explorer 4 and later (which is included with Windows 98 and Windows Me) comes with a scaled-back version of Outlook called *Outlook Express.* Outlook Express is designed to work only with e-mail that you send and receive over the Internet, not for e-mail that you exchange with other users over a local area network. As a result, Outlook Express is generally not used as an e-mail program for network users. (However, if each network user has an Internet connection and an Internet e-mail account, Outlook Express works fine.)

The following sections describe some basic procedures for using Microsoft Outlook to send and receive e-mail.

Sending e-mail

To send an e-mail message to another network user, start Microsoft Outlook by choosing Microsoft Outlook from the Start⇨Programs menu. Outlook appears in its own window, as shown in Figure 5-1.

Figure 5-1:
Microsoft
Outlook.

 To create a message to send to another user, click the New Mail Message button. A window appears in which you may type the e-mail address of the recipient (usually the recipient's network user ID), the subject of the message, and then the message itself.

Figure 5-2 shows a message that has been composed and is now ready to be delivered.

Figure 5-2:
Creating an
e-mail
message.

After you finish typing the message, click the Send button. The message is delivered to the user listed in the To field.

Here are a few additional points about sending e-mail:

✔ The recipient must run Outlook or another e-mail program on his or her computer to check for incoming e-mail. When the recipient runs his or her e-mail program, your message is delivered.

✔ You can keep a personalized address list using the Address Book, which is available from the Tools menu in Outlook.

✔ You can use Outlook to send e-mail to other users of your local network and to send to and receive e-mail from Internet users. However, a modem or some other type of connection to the Internet is necessary to send e-mail to an Internet e-mail address.

Reading your e-mail

To read e-mail sent to you by other users, simply start Microsoft Outlook by choosing it from the Start⇨Programs menu. After you start Outlook, the program automatically checks to see if you have any new e-mail and automatically checks for new messages on a regular basis. Any new messages that you receive appear in the main Outlook window, highlighted with boldface type. In addition, Outlook plays a special sound to inform you whenever you receive new e-mail.

To read a message that has been sent to you, just double-click the message in the Outlook main window. The text of the message appears in a separate window.

After you read the message, you have several options for handling it:

✔ If the message is worthy of a reply, click the Reply button. A new message window appears, enabling you to compose a reply. The new message is automatically addressed to the sender of the original message, and the text of the original message is inserted at the bottom of the new message.

✔ If the message was addressed to more than one recipient, the Reply to All button lets you send a reply that is addressed to all the recipients listed on the original message.

✔ If the message was intended for someone else, or if you think that someone else should see it (maybe it contains a juicy bit of gossip), click the Forward button. A new message window appears, enabling you to type the name of the user that you want the message forwarded to.

✔ If you want a hard copy of the message, click the Print button.

✔ If the message is unworthy of even filing, click the Delete button. Poof! The message is whisked away to a folder called Deleted Items. (You can use the Edit⇨Empty "Deleted Items" Folder command to permanently delete everything in the Deleted Items folder.)

✔ If you have more than one message waiting, you can read the next message in line by clicking the Next button.

Electronic Scheduling

Scheduling software takes advantage of the communication features of e-mail to enable you to schedule meetings with other network users. You give the scheduling program a list of the people that you want at the meeting, as well as when and where you want the meeting to occur. The program takes your information and checks the people's schedules to see whether they can make the meeting. If so, the scheduling program notifies everyone of the meeting by sending an e-mail note. If not, the scheduling program suggests an alternate meeting time.

Outlook includes an excellent group-scheduling function that makes it easy to schedule meetings. Here are a few final points on scheduling software:

✔ Most scheduling programs keep track of room usage so that they don't schedule two meetings at the same place and time.

✔ For scheduling software to work, everyone must use it religiously. If Bob forgets to tell the scheduling program about his Friday golf match, the program may well schedule a meeting for him on Friday morning.

✔ Scheduling software is most appropriate for large offices. Purchasing and maintaining the software for an office of three isn't worth the money.

Electronic Conferencing

Electronic Conferencing software lets you hold online meetings with two or more participants. One of the most popular conferencing programs is Microsoft's NetMeeting. Here are some of the more interesting features of NetMeeting:

✔ **Chat:** Two or more users can type messages to one another. Unlike e-mail messages, any chat message you type appears immediately on the other users' computers.

✔ **Whiteboard:** This is a drawing area in which all the participants in a conference can doodle, much like a networked version of Windows Paint.

✔ **File transfer:** You can send files to other NetMeeting users.

✔ **Application sharing:** Other NetMeeting users can see on their screens an application that you're running on your computer. You can also share applications so that several NetMeeting users can work together on a single document over the Internet.

✔ **Voice conference:** If your computer is equipped with a sound card and microphone, you can have a voice conference with another user whose computer also has a sound card and microphone.

✔ **Video conference:** Similarly, if you have attached a video camera to your computer, you can engage in a video conference with other NetMeeting users who also have video cameras on their computers. Video cameras have become quite affordable. However, be advised that a video conference can quickly bog down your network's performance.

E-mail Etiquette

Communicating with someone via e-mail is different from talking with that person face-to-face or over the telephone. You need to be aware of these differences, or you may end up insulting someone without meaning to. Of course, if you do mean to insult someone, pay no attention to this section.

The following paragraphs summarize the salient points of e-mail etiquette:

✔ Always remember that e-mail isn't as private as you'd like it to be. It's not that difficult for someone to electronically steam open your e-mail and read it. So be careful about what you say, to whom you say it, and about whom you say it.

✔ Don't forget that all the rules of social etiquette and office decorum apply to e-mail, too. If you wouldn't pick up the phone and call the CEO of the company, don't send him or her e-mail, either.

✔ When you reply to someone else's e-mail, keep in mind that the person you're replying to may not remember the details of the message that he or she sent to you. Providing some context for your reply is polite. Most e-mail systems (including Outlook) do this for you by automatically tacking on the original message at the end of the reply. If yours doesn't do this, be sure to provide some context, such as including a relevant snippet of the original message in quotation marks, so that the recipient knows what you're talking about.

✔ E-mail doesn't have the advantage of voice inflections. This limitation can lead to all kinds of misunderstandings. You have to make sure that people know when you're joking and when you mean it. E-mail nerds have developed a peculiar way to convey tone of voice: They string together symbols on the computer keyboard to create smileys. Table 5-1 shows some of the more commonly used (or abused) smileys.

Table 5-1	Commonly Used and Abused Smileys
Smiley	**What It Means**
: -)	Just kidding
; -)	Wink
: - (	Bummer
: - 0	Well, I never!
: - x	My lips are sealed.

☞ If you don't get it, tilt your head to the left and look at the smiley sideways.

☞ E-mail nerds also like to use shorthand abbreviations for common words and phrases, like FYI for "For Your Information" and ASAP for "As Soon As Possible." Table 5-2 lists the more common ones.

Table 5-2	Common E-mail Abbreviations
Abbreviation	**What It Stands For**
BTW	By the Way
FWIW	For What It's Worth
IMO	In My Opinion
IMHO	In My Humble Opinion
IOW	In Other Words
PMJI	Pardon Me for Jumping In
ROFL	Rolling on the Floor, Laughing
ROFL,PP	Rolling on the Floor Laughing, Peeing My Pants
TIA	Thanks in Advance
TTFN	Ta Ta for Now (quoting Tigger)
TTYL	Talk to You Later
<g>	Grin
<bg>	Big Grin
<vbg>	Very Big Grin

✔ Note that the abbreviations referring to gestures or facial expressions are typed between a less-than sign and a greater-than sign: <g>. Other gestures are spelled out, like <sniff>, <groan>, or <sigh>.

✔ You're not able to italicize or underline text on many e-mail programs (although you can do so in Exchange, Outlook, or Outlook Express). Type an asterisk before and after a word you *wish* you could italicize. Type an underscore _before_ and _after_ a word that you'd like to underline.

✔ Be aware that if you do use italics, underlining, or any other formatting features that are available in Exchange, Outlook, or Outlook Express, the person receiving your mail may not be able to see the formatting if they use a different e-mail program.

✔ Capital letters are the electronic equivalent of SHOUTING. TYPING AN ENTIRE MESSAGE IN CAPITAL LETTERS CAN BE VERY ANNOYING AND CAN CAUSE YOU TO GET THE ELECTRONIC EQUIVALENT OF LARYNGITIS.

✔ Don't be gullible about hoaxes and chain letters. If you receive an e-mail with a warning about some new virus that wipes out your hard drive if you sneeze near your computer or an e-mail that claims that you'll make eleven billion dollars if you forward the message to ten of your best friends, just delete the e-mail. Don't forward it.

✔ Frequently sending e-mail with large attachments can be annoying.

Chapter 6

Help! The Network's Down!

. . . .

In This Chapter

▶ Checking the obvious things

▶ Finding out whether or not you have a network problem

▶ Restarting the network

▶ Fixing common network problems

▶ Caring for and feeding your network guru

. . . .

*F*ace it: Networks are prone to break.

They have just too many "C" parts. Cables. Connectors. Cards. All these parts must be held together in a delicate balance; the network equilibrium is all-too-easy to disturb. Even the best-designed computer networks sometimes act as if they're held together with baling wire and chewing gum.

To make matters worse, networks breed suspicion. After your computer is attached to a network, you're tempted to blame the network every time something goes wrong, regardless of whether the problem has anything to do with the network. You can't get columns to line up in a Word document? Must be the network. Your spreadsheet doesn't add up? The @#$% network's acting up again.

This chapter doesn't even begin to cover everything that can go wrong with a computer network. If it did, you'd take this book back and demand a refund after you got about 40 pages into "Things that can go wrong with IPX.COM."

Instead, this chapter focuses on the most common things that can go wrong with a network that an ordinary network user (that's you) can fix. And best of all, I point you in the right direction when you come up against a problem that you can't fix yourself.

When Bad Things Happen to Good Computers

What do you do when your computer goes on the blink? Here are some general ideas for identifying the problem and deciding whether you can fix it yourself:

1. **Make sure that your computer and everything attached to it is plugged in.**

   Computer geeks love it when a user calls for help and they get to tell the user that the computer isn't plugged in. They write it down in their geek logs so that they can tell their geek friends about it later. They may even want to take your picture so that they can show it to their geek friends. (Most "accidents" involving computer geeks are a direct result of this kind of behavior.)

2. **Make sure that your computer is properly connected to the network.**

3. **Note any error messages that appear on the screen.**

4. **Try the built-in Windows network troubleshooter.**

   For more information, see the section "Using the Windows Troubleshooter" later in this chapter.

5. **Do a little experimenting to find out whether the problem is indeed a network problem or just a problem with your computer.**

6. **Try restarting your computer.**

7. **Try restarting the entire network.**

   See the section "How to Restart the Network" later in this chapter.

8. **If none of these steps corrects the problem, scream for help.**

   Have a suitable bribe prepared to encourage your network guru to work quickly. (You can find a handy list of suitable bribes at the end of this chapter.)

My Computer's Dead!

If your computer seems totally dead, here are some things to check:

- Is it plugged in?
- If your computer is plugged into a surge protector or a power strip, make sure that the surge protector or power strip is plugged in and turned on. If the surge protector or power strip has a light, it should be glowing.

✔ Make sure that the computer's On/Off switch is turned on. This sounds too basic to even include here, but many computers are set up so that the computer's actual power switch is always left in the On position and the computer is turned on or off by means of the switch on the surge protector or power strip. Many computer users are surprised to find out that their computers have On/Off switches on the back of the cases.

✔ If you think your computer isn't plugged in but it looks like it is, listen for the fan. If the fan is turning, the computer is getting power and the problem is more serious than an unplugged power cord. (If the fan isn't running, but the computer is plugged in and power is on, the fan may be out to lunch.)

✔ If the computer is plugged in, turned on, and still not running, plug a lamp into the outlet to make sure that power is getting to the outlet. You may need to reset a tripped circuit breaker or replace a bad surge protector. Or you may need to call the power company.

Surge protectors have a limited life span. After a few years of use, many surge protectors continue to provide electrical power for your computer, but the components that protect your computer from power surges no longer work. If you are using a surge protector that is more than two or three years old, replace the old surge protector with a new one.

✔ The monitor has a separate power cord and switch. Make sure that the monitor is plugged in and turned on. (The monitor actually has two cables that must be plugged in. One runs from the back of the monitor to the back of the computer; the other is a power cord that comes from the back of the monitor and must plug into an electrical outlet.)

✔ Your keyboard, monitor, mouse, and printer are all connected to the back of your computer by cables. Make sure that these cables are all plugged in securely.

✔ Make sure that the other ends of the monitor and printer cables are plugged in properly, too.

✔ Most monitors have knobs that you can use to adjust the contrast and brightness of the monitor's display. If the computer is running but your display is dark, try adjusting these knobs. They may have been turned all the way down.

Ways to Check Your Network Connection

Network gurus often say that 95 percent of all network problems are cable problems. The cable that connects your computer to the rest of the network is a finicky beast. It can break at a moment's notice, and by "break," I don't necessarily mean "to physically break in two." Sure, sometimes the problem with the cable is that Eddie Haskell got to it with pruning shears. But cable problems aren't usually visible to the naked eye.

✔ If your network uses *twisted-pair cable* (the cable that looks something like phone wire and is sometimes called "10baseT," "UTP," or "Cat-5" cable), you can quickly tell whether the cable connection to the network is good by looking at the back of your computer. A small light is near where the cable plugs in. If this light is glowing steadily, the cable is good. If the light is dark or if it's flashing intermittently, you have a cable problem.

If the light is not glowing steadily, try removing the cable from your computer and reinserting it. This action may cure the weak connection.

✔ Detecting a cable problem in a network that's wired with *coaxial cable*, the kind that looks like cable-TV cable, is more difficult. The connector on the back of the computer forms a T. The base end of the T plugs into your computer. One or two coaxial cables plug into the outer ends of the T. If you use only one coaxial cable, you must use a special plug called a *terminator* instead of a cable at the other end of the T. If you can't find a terminator, try conjuring one up from the twenty-first century. **Warning:** Do not do this if your name happens to be Sarah Connor.

Don't unplug a coaxial cable from the network while the network is running. Data travels around a coaxial network the way the baton travels around the track in a relay race. If one person drops it, the race is over. The baton never gets to the next person. Likewise, if you unplug the network cable from your computer, the network data never gets to the computers that are "down the line" from your computer.

Well, actually, Ethernet — see Chapter 10 — isn't dumb enough to throw in the towel at the first sign of a cable break. You can disconnect the cable for a few seconds without permanently scattering network messages across the galaxy, and you can disconnect the T connector itself from the network card so long as you don't disconnect the cables from the T connector. But don't attempt either action unless you have a good reason and a really good bribe for the network manager, who is sure to find out that you've been playing with the cables.

✔ Some networks are wired so that your computer is connected to the network with a short (six feet or so) patch cable. One end of the patch cable plugs into your computer, and the other end plugs into a cable connector mounted on the wall. Try quickly disconnecting and reconnecting the patch cable. If that doesn't do the trick, try to find a spare patch cable that you can use.

If you can't find a spare patch cable, try borrowing a fellow network user's patch cable. If the problem goes away when you use your neighbor's patch cable, you can assume that your patch cable has gone south and needs to be replaced. The good news is that you can purchase a replacement patch cable from your local computer store for about $15.

✔ If you come in late at night while no one is around, you can swap your bad patch cable with someone else's good cable, and no one will ever know. The next day, that particular neighbor will want to borrow this book from you so that he or she can find out what's wrong with the network. The day after that, someone else will need the book. You may never get your book back. You'd better buy a copy for everyone now.

Notice: Neither the author nor the publisher endorses such selfish behavior. We mention it here only so that you'll know what happened when one day someone down the hall has a network problem, and you suddenly have a network problem the next day.

✔ In some networks, computers are connected to one another via a small box called a *hub*. The hub is prone to cable problems, too — especially those hubs that are wired in a "professional manner" involving a rat's nest of patch cables. Don't touch the rat's nest. Leave problems with the rat's nest to the rat — er, that is, the network guru.

A Bunch of Error Messages Just Flew By!

Did you notice any error messages on your computer screen when you started your computer? If so, write them down. They are invaluable clues that can help the network guru solve the problem.

If you see error messages when you start up your computer, keep the following points in mind:

✔ Don't panic if you see lots of error messages fly by. Sometimes a simple problem that's easy to correct can cause a plethora of error messages when you start your computer. The messages may look as if your computer is falling to pieces, but the fix may be very simple.

✔ If the messages fly by so fast that you can't see them, press your computer's Pause key. Your computer comes to a screeching halt, giving you a chance to catch up on your error-message reading. After you've read enough, press the Pause key again to get things moving. (On some computers, the Pause key is labeled "Hold." On computers that don't have a Pause key, pressing Ctrl+Num Lock or Ctrl+S does the same thing.)

✔ If you missed the error messages the first time, restart your computer and watch them again.

✔ Better yet, press F8 when you see the message `Starting Windows`. This displays a menu that allows you to select from several startup options, including one that processes each line of your `CONFIG.SYS` file separately so that you can see the messages displayed by each command before proceeding to the next command.

The Windows Networking Troubleshooter

Windows 98 comes with a built-in troubleshooter that can often help you pin down the cause of a network problem. To use it, click the Start button and then choose Help. Click Troubleshooting and then click Windows 98 Troubleshooters. Finally, click Networking to start the Networking Troubleshooter as shown in Figure 6-1. Answer the questions asked by the troubleshooter and click Next to move from screen to screen. The Networking Troubleshooter can't solve all networking problems, but it does point out the causes of the most common problems.

Figure 6-1:
The
Windows 98
Networking
Trouble-
shooter.

Windows Millennium Edition includes a similar troubleshooter that is more oriented toward home networks. To access it, click the Start button and then choose Help. Click the Troubleshooting link, and then click the Home Networking & Network Problems link. Finally, click the Home Networking Troubleshooter link to start the troubleshooter.

Windows 95 also has a network troubleshooter, but it is not as thorough.

Time to Experiment

If you can't find some obvious explanation for your troubles — like the computer's unplugged — you need to do some experimenting to narrow down the possibilities. Design your experiments to answer one basic question: Is this a network problem or a local computer problem?

Here are some ways you can narrow down the cause of the problem:

✔ Try performing the same operation on someone else's computer. If no one on the network can access a network drive or printer, something is probably wrong with the network. On the other hand, if you're the only one having trouble, the problem is with your computer alone. Your computer may not be reliably communicating with the network or configured properly for the network, or the problem may have nothing to do with the network at all.

✔ If you're able to perform the operation on someone else's computer without problems, try logging on to the network with someone else's computer, using your own user ID. Then see whether you can perform the operation without error. If you can, the problem is probably on your computer rather than on the server computer. Your network guru will want to know.

✔ If you can't log on at another computer, try waiting for a bit. Your account may be temporarily locked out. If you can't log on in an hour, call the network administrator and offer a doughnut.

✔ Try the operation without using the network. Log off the network by using the Start⇨Logoff command. Then try the operation again.

If the symptoms of the problem remain the same whether your computer is logged on to the network or not, then the problem is probably not with the network.

How to Restart Your Computer

Sometimes trouble gets your computer so tied up in knots that the only thing you can do is reboot. In some cases, your computer just starts acting weird. Strange characters appear on the screen, or Windows goes haywire and won't let you exit a program. Sometimes your computer gets so confused that it can't even move. It just sits there, like a deer staring at oncoming headlights. It won't move, no matter how hard you press the Esc key or the Enter key. You can move the mouse all over your desktop, or you can even throw it across the room, but the mouse pointer on the screen stays perfectly still.

When your computer starts acting strange, you need to reboot. If you must reboot, you should do so as cleanly as possible. Try the following steps:

1. Save your work if you can.

Use the File⇨Save command, if you can, to save any documents or files that you were editing when things started to go haywire. If you can't use the menus, try clicking the Save button in the toolbar. If that doesn't work, try pressing Ctrl+S — the standard keyboard shortcut for the Save command.

2. **Close any running programs if you can.**

Use the File➪Exit command or click the Close button in the upper-right corner of the program window. Or press Alt+F4.

3. **Choose the Start➪Shut Down command from the taskbar.**

The Shut Down Windows dialog box appears.

4. **Select the Restart option and then click OK.**

Your computer restarts itself.

If restarting your computer doesn't seem to fix the problem, you may need to turn your computer all the way off and then turn it on again. To do so, follow the previous procedure until Step 4. Choose the Shut Down option instead of the Restart option and then click OK. Depending on your computer, Windows either turns off your computer or displays a message that says you can now safely turn off your computer. If Windows doesn't turn the computer off for you, flip the On/Off switch to turn your computer off. Wait a few seconds and then turn the computer back on.

Here are a few things to try if you have trouble restarting your computer:

✔ If your computer refuses to respond to the Start➪Shut Down command, try pressing the Ctrl, Alt, and Delete keys at the same time. This is called the "three-finger salute." It's appropriate to say "Queueue" as you do it.

When you press Ctrl+Alt+Delete, Windows 9*x* and later versions attempt to display a dialog box that enables you to close any running programs or shut down your computer entirely. Unfortunately, sometimes Windows 9*x* becomes so confused that it can't display the restart dialog box, in which case pressing Ctrl+Alt+Delete may restart your computer.

✔ If Ctrl+Alt+Delete doesn't do anything, you've reached the last resort. The only thing left to do is press the Reset button on your computer.

Pressing the Reset button (or in Windows 3.1, Windows for Workgroups, or MS-DOS, pressing Ctrl+Alt+Delete) is a drastic action that you should take only after your computer becomes completely unresponsive. Any work you haven't yet saved to disk is lost. (Sniff.) (If your computer doesn't have a Reset button, turn the computer off, wait a few moments, and then turn the computer back on again.)

✔ If at all possible, save your work before restarting your computer. Any work you haven't saved is lost. Unfortunately, if your computer is totally tied up in knots, you probably can't save your work. In that case, you have no choice but to push your computer off the digital cliff.

How to Restart the Network

If you think the network is causing your trouble, you can restart the network to see whether the problem goes away.

Restarting a NetWare or Windows 2000 server is not a good idea unless your network administrator has shown you how to do it and has given you permission to do so. If you don't know what you're doing, you may not be able to get the server running again. In that case, you have to tuck your tail between your legs, call the network administrator, and apologize profusely for messing with the network when you know you shouldn't have.

Here is the basic procedure for restarting a network. Keep in mind that for NetWare or Windows 2000 servers, you may need to take additional steps to get things going again. Check with your network administrator to be sure.

1. **Have all users log off the network and turn off their computers.**

2. **After you're sure the users have logged off the network and shut down their computers, shut down the network server (assuming that you have a dedicated server).**

   You want to do this behaving like a good citizen if possible — decently and in order. If you use Novell NetWare, type **down** on the server's keyboard and then reboot the server. For Windows NT or Windows 2000 Server, use the Start⇨Shut Down command.

3. **Reboot the server computer or turn it off and then on again. Watch the server start up to make sure that no error messages appear.**

4. **Turn on each computer one at a time, making sure that each computer starts up without error.**

Remember the following when you consider restarting the network:

- ✔ Restarting the network is even more drastic than restarting your individual computer. Make sure that everyone saves his or her work and logs off the network before you do it! You can cause major problems if you blindly turn off the server computer while users are logged on.

- ✔ Obviously, restarting the network is a major inconvenience to every network user. Better offer treats.

- ✔ Restarting the network is a job for the network guru. Don't do it yourself unless the network guru isn't around, and even then, do it only after asking his or her permission in writing, preferably in triplicate.

The Care and Feeding of Your Network Guru

Your most valuable asset when something goes wrong with the network is your network guru. If you're careful to stay on good terms with your guru, you're way ahead of the game when you need his or her help.

Make an effort to solve the problem yourself before calling in the cavalry. Check the network connection. Try rebooting. Try using someone else's computer. The more information that you can provide the guru, the more appreciation you get.

Be polite, but assertively tell your guru what the problem is, what you tried to do to fix it, and what you think may be causing the problem (if you have a clue). Say something like this:

"Hi, Joe. I've got a problem with the network: I can't log in from my computer. I tried a few things to try to figure out the problem. I was able to log in from Wally's computer using my user ID, so I think the problem may be just with my computer.

"To be sure, I checked some other things. The green light on the back of my computer where the network cable plugs in is glowing, so I don't think it's a cable problem. I also rebooted my computer, but I still couldn't log on. My guess is that something may be wrong with my computer's network driver, but maybe we should try restarting the server first."

Blow into your guru's ear like that, and he or she will follow you anywhere. (Of course, that may be an undesirable result.)

Here are a few other ways you can be nice to your computer guru, if you are so inclined:

- ✔ Always remember your manners. No one likes to be yelled at, and even computer geeks have feelings (believe it or not). Be polite to your network guru, even if you're mad or you think the problem is his or her fault. This suggestion may sound obvious, but you want your guru to like you.

- ✔ Don't call your guru every time the slightest little thing goes wrong. Computer experts hate explaining that the reason the computer is only printing in capital letters is that you pressed the Caps Lock key.

- ✔ Read the manual. It probably won't help, but at least your guru thinks you tried. Gurus like that.

✔ Humor your network guru when he or she tries to explain what's going on. Nod attentively when she describes what the bindery is or when he says something is wrong with the File Allocation Table. Smile appreciatively when she tries to simplify the explanation by using a colorful metaphor. Wink when he thinks that you understand.

✔ Mimic your guru's own sense of humor, if you can. For example, most computer geeks like the old *Saturday Night Live* routine with the copier guy. So say something like, "It's Joe, fixin' the network. Crimpin' the cable. Jumpin' Joe, the Net-o-Rama, rentin' an apartment at eight oh two dot three Ethernet Lane. Captain Joe of the Good Ship NetWare, goin' down with the server." Don't worry if it's not funny. He'll think it is.

Computer Bribes for Serious Network Trouble

A *For Dummies* book wouldn't be complete without a bribe list. You probably know already about the common foodstuffs most computer gurus respond to: Cheetos, Doritos, Jolt Cola, Diet Coke (I wish they made Diet Jolt — twice the caffeine, and twice the NutraSweet), Twinkies, and so on.

Bribes of this sort are suitable for small favors. But if you're having a serious problem with your network, you may need to lay it on a bit thicker. More serious bribes include the following:

✔ Computer games, especially 3D shoot-em-ups, such as Quake III.

✔ Videotapes of any Pink Panther, Monty Python, or Mel Brooks movies.

✔ T-shirts, hats, or coffee mugs with strange stuff written on them. Shirts, hats, or mugs from computer companies are even better.

✔ *Star Trek* paraphernalia. A high percentage of computer gurus are also Trekkies, or as they sometimes prefer to be called, Trekkers. Most of them like the original *Star Trek, The Next Generation,* and *Deep Space Nine.* Most don't care for *Voyager.*

If you want to really impress a guru, use the three-letter acronyms for each series: *TOS* for The Original Series, *TNG* for *The Next Generation,* and *DS9* for *Deep Space Nine.* (*VOY* is for *Voyager,* but because nobody likes *Voyager,* it doesn't matter.)

✔ Digitized sounds. You can never have enough digitized sounds. Anything from a Pink Panther movie ("Do you have a *rheum?*"), *Saturday Night Live* ("All right, have a beer, make some copies, havin' a party!"), or *Home Improvement* ("Say, Al, do you suppose they call these coping saws because they're good at handling stress?") will do. Clips from a favorite *Star Trek* show are good bribes, too.

Don't give your guru a digitized recording of the famous "I've fallen and I can't get up" line. He or she already has five of those.

You can find an ample supply of digitized sounds on the Internet. If you don't have access to the Internet, getting it may be worth the cost just for the constant supply of bribes that these files can provide.

✔ MP3 files of songs that computer geeks like. Anything by the Monkees will do. At the time I wrote this, the best place to get MP3 files was Napster (`www.napster.com`). But Napster was in the middle of a major court battle, so they may not be around by the time you read this.

Part II
Building Your Own Network

The 5th Wave   By Rich Tennant

"If it works, it works. I've just never
seen network cabling connected with
Chinese handcuffs before."

In this part . . .

You discover how to build a network yourself, which includes planning it and installing it. And you find out what choices are available for cable types, network operating systems, and all the other bits and pieces that you have to contend with.

Yes, some technical information is included in these chapters. But fear not! I bring you tidings of great joy! Lo, a working network is at hand, and you — yea, even you — can design it and install it yourself.

Chapter 7

The Bad News: You Have to Plan Ahead

*O*kay, so you're convinced that you need to network your computers. What now? Do you stop by Computers-R-Us on the way to work, install the network before morning coffee, and expect the network to be fully operational by noon?

I don't think so.

Networking your computers is just like any other worthwhile endeavor: To do it right requires a bit of planning. This chapter helps you think through your network before you start spending money. It shows you how to come up with a networking plan that's every bit as good as the plan that a network consultant would charge $1,000 for. See? This book is already saving you money!

Making a Network Plan

If you pay a consultant or a company that specializes in network design to study your business and prepare a networking plan, the result is a 500-page proposal with the sole purpose, aside from impressing you with bulk, of preventing you from understanding just exactly what the consultant is proposing.

The truth is, you don't have to be a computer science major to make a good network plan. Despite what computer consultants want you to think, designing a small computer network isn't rocket science. You can do it yourself. Just follow these simple guidelines:

- ✔ Don't rush through the planning phase. The most costly networking mistakes are the ones that you make before you install the network. Think things through and consider alternatives.

- ✔ Write down the network plan. The plan doesn't have to be a fancy, 500-page document. (If you want to make it look good, pick up a ½-inch, three-ring binder. The binder is big enough to hold your network plan with room to spare.)

- ✔ Ask someone else to read your network plan before you buy anything; preferably, ask someone who knows more about computers than you do.

Taking Stock

One of the most challenging parts of planning a network is figuring out how to work with the computers that you already have. In other words, how do you get from here to there? Before you can plan how to get "there," you have to know where "here" is. In other words, you have to take a thorough inventory of your current computers.

What you need to know

You need to know the following information about each of your computers:

- ✔ **The processor type and, if possible, its clock speed.** Hope that all your computers are 500 MHz Pentium IIIs or better. But in most cases, you find a mixture of computers, some new, some old, some borrowed, some blue. You might even find a few archaic pre-Pentium computers.

  You can't usually tell what kind of processor that a computer has just by looking at the computer's case. Most computers, however, display the processor type when you turn them on or reboot them. If the information on the startup screen scrolls too quickly for you to read it, try pressing the Pause key to freeze the information. After you finish reading it, press the Pause key again so that your computer can continue booting.

- ✔ **The size of the hard drive and the arrangement of its partitions.** In Windows, you can find out the size of your computer's hard drive by opening the My Computer window, right-clicking the drive icon, and choosing the Properties command from the shortcut menu that appears. Figure 7-1 shows the Properties dialog box for a 38.1GB hard drive that has 33.5GB of free space.

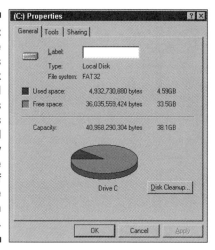

Figure 7-1:
The Properties dialog box for a hard drive shows the drive's total capacity and the amount of free space available on the drive.

If your computer has more than one hard drive, Windows lists an icon for each drive in the My Computer window. Jot down the size and amount of free space available on each of the drives.

For old computers that run MS-DOS instead of Windows, you can use the CHKDSK command to display the size of your hard drives and the amount of free space available.

✔ **The amount of memory.** In Windows, you can find out this information easily enough by right-clicking the My Computer desktop icon and choosing the Properties command. The amount of memory on your computer appears in the dialog box that appears. For example, Figure 7-2 shows the System Properties dialog box for a computer running Windows 98 Second Edition with 128MB of RAM.

If you're working with an older DOS-based computer, you have to fuss with two different kinds of memory: conventional and extended. Use the CHKDSK command to find out how much conventional memory that your computer has. If you have DOS Version 4.0 or later, you can type **MEM** to find out how much extended memory that your computer has.

Some ancient 8088 or 286 computers have an antiquated type of memory known as *expanded memory.* Expanded memory doesn't affect the network much, so don't worry about it. You don't want to fuss with these computers on your network, anyway. They're hard to configure and generally not worth the effort.

✔ **The operating system version.** If you are running Windows 95 or 98, you can determine the version by checking the System Properties dialog box. For example, Figure 7-2 shows the System Properties dialog box for a computer running Windows 98 Second Edition. (The actual Windows version for this computer is 4.10.2222.A.)

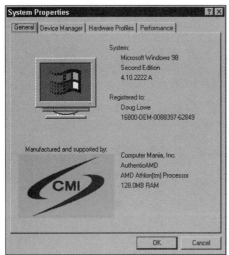

Figure 7-2:
The System
Properties
dialog box
for a
computer
running
Windows 98
Second
Edition with
128MB of
RAM.

For an older, DOS-based computer, you can determine the DOS version by typing **VER** at a DOS prompt. If any of your computers are running a DOS version lower than 3.3, you should upgrade them: DOS versions older than 3.3 have poor network support.

In Windows 3.*x,* you can determine the Windows version by choosing the Help⇨About command from Program Manager.

Once upon a time, Microsoft offered a networked version of its original Windows operating system, known as Windows for Workgroups. Windows for Workgroups was sophisticated for its time, but if you still have any computers running Windows for Workgroups, you really should upgrade them to Windows 98 before you put in a network or expand an existing network. Networking with Windows 98 is much easier than networking with Windows for Workgroups.

✔ **What kind of printer, if any, is attached to the computer.**

✔ **What software is used on the computer.** Microsoft Office? WordPerfect? Lotus 1-2-3? Make a complete list, and include version numbers.

✔ **Any other devices connected to the computer.** A CD drive? Scanner? Zip or Jazz drive? Tape drive? Video camera?

Programs that gather information for you

Gathering information about your computers is a lot of work if you have more than a few computers to network. Fortunately, several available software programs can automatically gather the information for you. These programs inspect various aspects of a computer, such as the CPU type and speed, amount of RAM, and the size of the computer's hard drives. Then they show the information on the screen and give you the option of saving the information to a hard drive file or printing it.

Windows 98 and Windows Me come with just such a program, which is called Microsoft System Information. Microsoft System Information gathers and prints information about your computer. You can start Microsoft System Information by choosing Start⇨Programs⇨Accessories⇨System Tools⇨ System Information.

When you fire up Microsoft System Information, you see a window similar to the one shown in Figure 7-3. Initially, Microsoft System Information displays basic information about your computer, such as your version of Microsoft Windows, the processor type, the amount of memory on the computer, and the free space on each of the computer's hard drives. You can obtain information that is more detailed by clicking Hardware Resources, Components, Software Environment, or Applications in the left side of the window.

Figure 7-3:
Microsoft
System
Information
displays
information
about your
computer.

If you have Windows 95 instead of Windows 98 or Windows Me, don't panic. You may have Microsoft System Information anyway: Microsoft includes it with Office. To start Microsoft System Information from any of the Office programs (Word, Excel, or PowerPoint), choose the Help⇨About command. When the About dialog box appears, click the System Info button.

MS-DOS 6 (including 6.0, 6.2, and 6.22) includes a similar program called *MSD,* which stands for *Microsoft Diagnostics.* To run it, just type **MSD** at a DOS command prompt and press Enter.

Considering Why You Need a Network, Anyway

An important step in planning your network is making sure that you understand why you want the network in the first place. Here are some of the more common reasons for needing a network, all of them quite valid:

- My coworker and I exchange files using a floppy disk just about every day. With a network, we could trade files without using the floppies.

- I don't want to buy everyone a laser printer when I know the one we have now just sits there taking up space most of the day. So wouldn't buying a network be better than buying a laser printer for every computer?

- Someone figured out that we're destroying seven trees a day by printing interoffice memos on paper, so we want to save the rainforest by setting up an e-mail system.

- Business is so good that one person typing in orders eight hours each day can't keep up. With a network, I can have two people entering orders, and I won't have to pay either one overtime.

- My brother-in-law just put in a network at his office, and I don't want him to think I'm behind the times.

Make sure that you identify all the reasons why you think you need a network, and then write them down. Don't worry about winning the Pulitzer Prize for your stunning prose. Just make sure that you write down what you expect a network to do for you.

If you were making a 500-page networking proposal, you'd place the description of why a network is needed in a tabbed section labeled "Justification." In your ½-inch network binder, file the description under "Why."

As you consider the reasons why you need a network, you may conclude that you don't need a network after all. That's okay. You can always use the binder for your stamp collection.

Making Three Basic Network Decisions That You Can't Avoid

When you plan a computer network, you're confronted with three inescapable network decisions. You can't install the network until you make these decisions. The decisions are weighty enough that I devote a separate section in this chapter to each one.

I haven't introduced a new TLA (three-letter acronym) in a while, so I call these basic network decisions *BNDs*, which stands for — you guessed it — "basic network decisions."

What network operating system should you use?

You have many network operating systems from which to choose, but from a practical point of view, your choices are limited to the following:

- ✔ Novell NetWare — the most popular network operating system for large networks. NetWare requires that you dedicate at least one computer to act as a network server, and it can be a challenge for a novice user to install. With NetWare, the client computers can run DOS or any version of Windows. Plus, you can easily connect Macintosh computers to a NetWare network.

- ✔ Windows NT Server, or the more recent version known as Windows 2000 Server. Windows NT/2000 Server is a special version of Windows that, like NetWare, requires that you dedicate one or more computers to act as network servers. Windows NT/2000 Server is best used when all the client computers run some version of Windows — preferably Windows 95 or 98. However, you can make Windows NT Server work with DOS and Macintosh client computers.

- ✔ If you don't want to dedicate a computer to function as a server, you can build the entire network using Windows 95, 98, Windows Me, or Windows 2000 Professional on your client computers.

- ✔ You can start with a simple peer-to-peer network using Windows 95/98, Windows Me, or Windows 2000 Professional now and then upgrade to NetWare or Windows NT/2000 Server later. All the networks listed in this section use the same cable, network interface cards, hubs, and so on. Changing from one to another is a matter of reconfiguring the software. (Of course, to change from a peer-to-peer network to NetWare or Windows NT/2000 Server, you must have a dedicated server computer.)

- ✔ Chapter 8 describes the advantages and disadvantages of each of these systems so that you can decide which is the best choice for your network.

What arrangement of server computers should you use?

A peer-to-peer network built with Windows 95/98, Windows Me, or Windows 2000 Professional does not require you to use dedicated server computers. This fact doesn't mean that dedicated server computers can and should be used only with NetWare or Windows NT/2000 Server. On the contrary, if you can possibly afford it, a dedicated server computer is almost always the way to go, no matter what network operating system you use.

- ✔ Using a dedicated server computer, even on a peer-to-peer network, makes the network faster, easier to work with, and more reliable. Consider what happens when the user of a server computer, which doubles as a workstation, decides to turn the computer off, not realizing that someone else is accessing files on his or her hard drive.

- ✔ You don't necessarily have to use your biggest and fastest computer as your server computer. I've seen networks where the slowest computer on the network is the server. This is especially true when the server is mostly used to share a printer.

- ✔ When you plan your server configuration, you must also plan how your data and program files will be dispersed on the network. For example, will all users have copies of Microsoft Office on their local drives, or will one copy of Office be stored on the server drive? (Within the limits of your software license, of course.)

- ✔ Planning your server configuration also means assigning network drive letters for computers requiring you to map drive letters to network drives. As much as possible, be consistent about your network drive mappings so that a particular network drive is accessed by using the same drive letter from every computer.

- ✔ Server configuration is heady enough to merit its own chapter: Chapter 9.

How should you cable the network?

The third basic networking decision is how to connect your computers.

- ✔ The most popular way to cable your network is to use twisted-pair cable, also known as UTP cable. An alternative is to use coaxial cable, also known as thinnet cable. However, UTP is easier to install, easier to fix if something should go wrong, and allows for faster transfer speeds. Because of these advantages, I recommend you use UTP for all new networks. (For information about the differences between UTP and thinnet cable, refer to Chapter 1.)

- ✔ You must also pick the network interface cards to install into each computer. Using the same card in each computer is best, although you can also mix and match them. The card that you select must be compatible with the cable you select. For example, if you opt to use twisted-pair cable, make sure all of your network cards work with twisted-pair cable.

- ✔ If you use twisted-pair cable, you also need one or more network hubs.

✔ You have to decide where and how to route the cable so that it reaches each of the computers that you need to network, what type of wall jacks to use, and how to manage the cables where they come together at the network hubs. As you plan the cabling, you need to draw a floor plan showing the location of each computer and the route of the cables.

✔ I give you the gory details of network cabling in Chapter 10.

Using a Network Starter Kit — Networks to Go

For me, one of the most fun parts of building a network is going to my local computer store and filling a shopping cart full of stuff. I love to wander the aisles and pick out a network hub, network interface cards, cables, connectors, and other goodies.

If shopping isn't your bag, you can buy in a single box all the pieces you need to network two or three computers. A typical network starter kit for two computers includes two Ethernet network interface cards, a small hub, two twisted pair cables with connectors already attached (so that you can connect both computers to the hub), and instructions for hooking everything up. A kit of this sort costs between $50 and $1500, depending on where you purchase it, who manufactures the individual components in the kit, and whether the kit works at 10Mbps or 100Mbps.

The starter kit accommodates the first two computers in your network. For each additional computer that you want to connect, you need to purchase an add-on kit that contains a network interface card and a cable.

Here are a couple of additional points to ponder concerning network starter kits:

✔ The cable that comes with the starter kit is generally 25 feet long. This is usually enough cable to connect computers that are located in the same room. If the computers are in separate rooms, you probably need additional network cable.

✔ The hub that comes with twisted-pair starter kits usually has ports for connecting as many as four or five computers. If you know you need to network more than that, you should probably purchase the hub and other network components separately.

Looking at a Sample Network Plan

Consider a typical family business: Cleavers' Baseball Card Emporium, which buys and sells valuable as well as worthless baseball cards and other baseball memorabilia.

The Cleavers' computer inventory

The Cleavers have four computers:

- ✔ Ward's computer is a brand-new 750 MHz Pentium III with 128MB of RAM and a 40GB hard drive. Ward runs Microsoft Windows 98 Second Edition and Office 2000 for spreadsheet analysis (Excel) and occasional word processing (Word). He also has a high-speed laser printer.

- ✔ June's computer is a 200 MHz Pentium III with 64MB of RAM and an 8GB hard drive. June runs Windows 95 and does most of the company's word processing with an old version of Word for Windows. She has a little inkjet printer that she bought at a garage sale for $20, but it doesn't work well, so she would like to use Ward's laser printer to print letters.

- ✔ Wally's computer is a 486 with 4MB of RAM, a 300MB hard drive, and Windows 3.1.

- ✔ The Beaver has a 133MHz Pentium computer with 16MB of RAM, a 2GB hard drive, and a built-in Ethernet port. The computer originally belonged to Eddie Haskell, but Beave traded a Joe DiMaggio, a Wade Boggs, and a Sammy Sosa for it. The Beaver keeps the company's inventory records on his computer by using a database program that he created himself using Java.

Why the Cleavers need a network

The Cleavers want to network their computers for two simple reasons:

- ✔ So that everyone can access the laser printer.
- ✔ So that everyone can access the inventory database.

Without the second reason, the Cleavers wouldn't need a network. They can share the laser printer by purchasing a simple printer-sharing switch that would enable all four computers to access the printer (see the sidebar "Stupid stuff about printer switches"). But to give everyone access to the inventory database requires a network.

Stupid stuff about printer switches

If your only reason for networking is to share a printer, there may be a cheaper way: Buy a switch box instead of a network. Switch boxes let two or more computers share a single printer. Instead of running a cable directly from one computer to the printer, you run cables from each computer to the switch box and then run one cable from the switch box to the printer. Only one of the computers has access to the printer at a time; the switch decides which one.

You can find two kinds of printer switches:

✔ **Manual printer switches:** These have a knob on the front that enables you to select which computer is connected to the printer. When you use a manual switch, you first must make sure that the knob is set to your computer before you try to print. Turning the knob while someone else is printing probably will cost you a bag of doughnuts.

✔ **Automatic printer switches:** These have a built-in electronic ear that listens to each computer. When it hears one of the computers trying to talk to the printer, the electronic ear automatically connects that computer to the printer. The switch also has an electronic holding pen called a *buffer* that can hold printer output from one computer if another computer is using the printer. Automatic switches aren't foolproof, but they work most of the time.

Naturally, a good automatic switch costs more than a manual switch. For example, a manual switch that can enable four computers to share one printer costs about $20. A decent automatic switch to enable four computers to share a printer can set you back about $75. Still, that's a lot cheaper and easier to set up than a full-blown network.

The network operating system

The Cleavers aren't computer whizzes, so they opt for a simple peer-to-peer network operating system based on Windows. This network operating system enables them to share the printer and the hard drive containing the inventory database — so it adequately meets their needs.

After Ward decides that a Windows network is the way to go, he realizes that Wally's computer just won't cut the mustard. Ward considered upgrading Wally's computer by adding more memory, but he decided instead to sell the computer at a garage sale and buy Wally a brand new laptop computer that runs Windows 98 Second Edition.

The server configuration

Because the Cleavers can't afford a separate computer to use as a server, two of the computers do double duty as both clients and servers. Ward's computer is set up as a client/server so that everyone can access his printer, and the Beaver's computer is set up as a client/server so that everyone can access the inventory database.

After the network is up and running, Ward considers moving the inventory database from the Beaver's computer to his own computer. That way, only one server computer has to be managed. Because Ward doesn't use his computer often, he probably won't mind the small reduction in performance as other users access his hard drive. (Of course, because Ward is both company CEO and the head of the household, he won't consider trading his high-powered computer with June, who uses her computer six or seven hours every day. Sigh.)

Network cabling

For simplicity's sake, the Cleavers opt to wire their network with twisted-pair cable. All four computers are located in the spacious den, so the floor plan presents no unusual wiring problems. The hub can be placed on a desk next to any of the four computers.

Fortunately, only three of the computers need networking cards, because Beave's computer has a built-in network port. To simplify shopping, the Cleavers decide to purchase a network starter kit for Ward's and June's computer. They also purchase a laptop Ethernet card to go with Wally's brand-new laptop computer. The Cleavers can have their network up and running in no more than a few hours.

Chapter 8

Choosing Your Weapon (Or, Which Network Should You Use?)

In This Chapter

▶ Considering Novell NetWare

▶ Considering Windows NT Server and Windows 2000 Server

▶ Considering other server operating systems, including OS/2, UNIX, Linux, and the Mac OS X Server

▶ Considering peer-to-peer networking with Windows

*O*ne of the basic choices that you must make before you go too far is to decide which network operating system to use as the foundation for your network. This chapter provides an overview of the advantages and disadvantages of the most popular network operating systems.

Novell NetWare

NetWare is one of the most popular network operating systems, especially for large networks. You can use NetWare to build networks of thousands of computers. But you can also use NetWare for small networks consisting of just a few computers.

Novell currently sells three versions of NetWare: 3.2, 4.2, and 5.1. NetWare 5.1, the latest and greatest version, is naturally the best of the three. It sports a number of advanced features that make it suitable for larger networks. NetWare 4.2 is suitable for smaller networks. Novell continues to sell NetWare 3.2 mainly because the managers of many existing NetWare 3.*x* networks don't want to upgrade to a newer version.

I don't get a penny for promoting *Networking With NetWare For Dummies*

If you think NetWare is the networking system for you, be sure to get a copy of *Networking With NetWare For Dummies,* 4th Edition, by Ed Tittel, James E. Gaskin, and Earl Follis (IDG Books Worldwide). This is a great book that shows you how to install, use, and manage your network and keep your sanity.

I thought I should get, like, a two percent commission or something for promoting *Networking With NetWare For Dummies,* 4th Edition, here, but no such luck. Bummer. Get the book anyway.

What's so great about NetWare?

Throughout this book, I pound NetWare a bit for being overly complicated. However, a lot can be said in favor of NetWare. NetWare can be complicated to set up and administer, but it's still the most popular network operating system in use. There must be something good to say about it! So here goes:

- ✔ When Novell set out to design NetWare way back in the 1980s, the company recognized that the old DOS operating system just didn't cut it for networking. Rather than live with the limitations of DOS, Novell decided to bypass DOS altogether. NetWare file servers don't run DOS or Windows; instead, NetWare itself is the operating system for the file server. This frees NetWare from the many built-in limitations of DOS and Windows.

- ✔ Because NetWare servers don't run DOS or Windows, NetWare servers must be dedicated servers. In other words, you can't have a NetWare server double as a user's workstation. This setup costs more because you must purchase a separate server computer. However, the arrangement is more efficient because the server computer can concentrate on servicing the network.

- ✔ Clients on a NetWare network can include computers running DOS, Windows, OS/2, or the Mac OS. If you have a mix of PCs and Macintoshes, NetWare may be your best choice.

- ✔ The NetWare file server uses a more efficient structure for organizing files and directories than DOS or Windows.

- ✔ All versions of NetWare provide features for System Fault Tolerance (SFT), which keeps the network running even if a hardware failure occurs.

- ✔ NetWare is very reliable and stable. Although NetWare can be difficult to set up, after you get a NetWare server up and running and configured the way you want, the server will pretty much take care of itself with little maintenance.

Do you have the savvy to install NetWare?

How do you know if you have what it takes to contend with NetWare? Try this little self-test. If you know all (or most) of the answers to these questions, you probably have enough computer savvy to figure out NetWare. If you don't, don't feel bad. As the Good Book says (sort of), "Some are prophets, some are evangelists, some are teachers, some are NetWare administrators, some are Computer Dummies. . . ."

1. What command do you use to copy all the files, including files in subdirectories, from drive A to the current directory?

   A. FDISK

   B. DELETE A:*.*

   C. FORMAT C:

   D. XCOPY A:*.* /S

2. Which of these files is processed every time you start your computer?

   A. LETSGETGOING.BAT

   B. GETUPYOULITTLESLEEPYHEAD
       .COM

   C. YOURANG.LURCH

   D. AUTOEXEC.BAT

3. Which of the following bribes are appropriate when enlisting the help of a computer guru?

   A. Cheetos

   B. Doritos

   C. Doughnuts

   D. All of the above

4. Who is the most dangerous man in all of France?

   A. Jacques Cousteau

   B. Marcel Marceau

   C. Big Bird

   D. Chief Inspector Jacques Clouseau

If you answered D to three or more of these questions, you probably have the savvy to install NetWare yourself, unless the question you missed was #3, in which case you don't have a prayer.

Network Directory Service (also known as NDS)

In the original versions of NetWare, information about the resources available on each server and the users that could log on was stored in a special file called the *bindery* on the server. Each server's bindery contained information only about the resources on that particular server. The bindery meant that, as a user, you had to log on separately to each server that contained the resources that you wanted to use. NetWare 3.2 still works this way.

With NetWare versions 4.2 and 5, the bindery has been replaced by a feature called the *Network Directory Service,* or *NDS.* NDS is like a super bindery for the entire network. With NDS, you don't have to log on to individual servers. Instead, you can log on to the network just once to gain access to any of the network's resources.

NDS isn't particularly important for small networks with only one server. For large networks with dozens of servers, though, NDS is a major improvement because it dramatically simplifies management of the servers. For example, suppose your network had ten servers running NetWare 3.2. Each time a new user is added to the network, you have to add user ID and other information to each of the ten servers. With NDS, you have to add the new user information just once.

NetWare 4.2

Although not the most current version of NetWare, NetWare 4.2 is still widely used, especially for smaller networks. NetWare 4 was the first version of NetWare to use the Network Directory Service (NDS) to simplify the task of managing networks with more than one server. You can use 4.2 for small networks with just a dozen or so users, or you can use it with huge networks with thousands of users and dozens of servers.

Novell claims that NetWare 4.2 can run on any 386-based computer with at least 16MB of RAM and 55MB of free drive space. This may be possible, but I sure don't want to try it. A more realistic minimum setup for a NetWare 4.2 server computer is something like this:

- ✔ Pentium processor, at least 100MHz
- ✔ 32MB of RAM (64MB is better)
- ✔ 2GB of drive space

This setup gives you enough computing horsepower, RAM, and drive space to make NetWare run decently for a small network, with a dozen or fewer clients. For a larger network, you'll want more RAM and drive space and probably a faster processor.

NetWare 5.1

NetWare 5.1 is the newest version of NetWare, and it provides several major improvements over NetWare 4.2. Here are just a few of the new features of NetWare 5.1:

✔ A graphical user interface based on Java, which lets you administer the server in a more friendly manner that resembles Windows.

✔ Better support for TCP/IP, the networking protocol used for the Internet.

✔ Advanced operating system features, such as memory protection, virtual memory, and better multiprocessor support — up to 32 processors in a single server. (If you don't know what any of that means, count your blessings.)

✔ Files can be as large as 8 terabytes (that's 8,000GB), and NetWare 5 can support billions of files on a single hard drive.

NetWare 5.1 requires a beefier server computer than NetWare 4.2 does. A NetWare 5.1 server requires at least a Pentium processor, 128MB of RAM, and 1.3MB of free hard drive space. You probably want an even more powerful computer than that for your NetWare 5.1 server. Here's a recommended minimum configuration:

✔ 500MHz Pentium II processor

✔ 256MB RAM

✔ 10GB free hard drive space

The price of the NetWare 5.1 server software varies depending on how many client computers your network has. Unfortunately, you can't buy NetWare client licenses one at a time. Instead, you purchase the NetWare software, which enables you to use it for five users. Then, you purchase licenses that allow you to connect additional users of 5, 10, 25, 50, 100, 250, or 500 at a time. If your network has six users, you must purchase the five-user server plus a five-user connection license.

Table 8-1 shows the prices for NetWare 5.1 as of June 2000. (The pricing for NetWare 4.2 is a bit less.) As you can see, the price that you pay for NetWare depends on how many users the server will support. You start by purchasing the base operating system, which supports up to five users. Then, you purchase additional client licenses (Novell calls them "Additive Licenses") to enable the server to support more users.

For example, suppose you want to set up a NetWare 5.1 server to support 30 users. You would purchase the NetWare 5.1 5-user system for $995 and the 25-user Additive License for $2,750, for a total of $3,745. For 30 users, that amounts to a cost of about $125 per user.

With NetWare, the more users that a server will support, the less the per-user cost. For a server that will support 500 or more users, NetWare costs about $55 per user. But for a five-user network, NetWare 5.1 costs $199 per user.

Table 8-1	NetWare 5.1 Pricing
Product	*Price*
NetWare 5.1 Server with 5 client connections	$995
5 additional users	$995
10 additional users	$1,430
25 additional users	$2,750
50 additional users	$4,125
100 additional users	$6,995
250 additional users	$13,495
500 additional users	$26,995

NetWare 5.1 is also available in a special Small Business edition, which includes the basic NetWare 5 operating system, plus a collection of goodies designed to make networking easier for small businesses. Among the extras you get with NetWare for Small Business are the following:

✔ GroupWise 5.5, an e-mail and group scheduling program that is similar to Microsoft Outlook

✔ Novell Internet Connection Expert (NICE), a tool for connecting your server to the Internet

✔ BorderManager, a suite of security programs for safeguarding your network's Internet access

✔ Oracle 8.04, a powerful server-based database program

✔ A full complement of Netscape programs for accessing the Internet and creating your own Web site

One of the best features of NetWare for Small Business is that it lets you purchase client licenses one user at a time. NetWare for Small Business costs $1,295 and allows up to five users to connect to the server. But after that initial purchase, you can buy add-on client licenses one at a time for just $70 each.

Meanwhile, back at the BackOffice

Windows NT Server and Windows 2000 Server are designed to work with a family of products from Microsoft called *Microsoft BackOffice*. BackOffice includes a variety of server programs that are designed to support basic business functions, such as database access and e-mail support. Here are the pieces that make up BackOffice:

✔ Microsoft SQL Server, a database program

✔ Microsoft Exchange Server, Microsoft's e-mail server

✔ Microsoft Site Server for creating advanced Internet Web sites

✔ Microsoft SNA Server to connect to mainframe computers

✔ Microsoft System Management Server to manage large networks

Microsoft's Server Operating Systems

When it comes to network operating systems, Microsoft played second fiddle to Novell for the longest time. However, Microsoft gained a lot of ground on NetWare with the introduction of Windows NT Server 4 in 1996. Microsoft currently offers two versions of its flagship server operating system: Windows NT Server 4 and Windows 2000 Server. Windows 2000 Server is the newer and more advanced version. However, because Windows 2000 Server is so new, many companies have chosen to stay with Windows NT Server 4, at least for awhile.

Windows NT Server 4

Windows NT Server 4 sports the same user interface as Windows 95, so if you already know your way around Windows 95, NT Server 4 will seem familiar. Unlike Windows 95, however, NT Server 4 includes a number of advanced networking features that make it suitable for use as a network server for small or large networks.

Windows NT Server 4 comes with a bunch of free Internet tools. These tools enable you to connect to the Internet and set up your own Internet Web site. In addition, you can use the Internet tools to set up an Intranet, which is simply a Web site that can be accessed only from the computers that are on your LAN.

Here's a summary of the more pertinent features of NT:

✔ The server processor must be at least a 486, with at least 16MB of memory. Yeah, right. I wouldn't use it on anything smaller than a 200MHz Pentium with 64MB of RAM.

✔ Some of the file-system limits are

- Max number of users: unlimited
- Number of volumes: 25
- Max size of a volume: 17,000GB
- Max hard drive space for server: 408,000GB
- Largest file: 17 billion GB (Wow! That's more than the maximum hard drive space for a server, which is impossible!)
- Max amount of RAM in server: 4GB
- Max number of open files: unlimited

✔ Microsoft has a pricing structure that is similar to Novell's: You purchase the operating system along with a certain number of client licenses, and then add additional licenses to accommodate additional users. For NT Server, you buy the server with 5 client licenses for $809 or 25 client licenses for $1,619. Then you can add additional client licenses for $39.95 apiece, or you can buy client licenses 25 at a time for $699 (which works out to $32.95 per client).

✔ For networks with 50 or fewer PCs, Microsoft offers a special version of NT Server called *Microsoft BackOffice Small Business Server,* also known as *SBS.* SBS includes Windows NT Server and selected BackOffice features (including SQL Server and Exchange Server) and a set of wizards that simplifies the task of administering a small network. The base price for five users is $1,499, and you can add additional users in groups of five ($299) or twenty ($999). (At the time I wrote this, Microsoft was readying a new version of Small Business Server to work with Windows 2000 Server.)

Windows 2000 Server

The most current server operating system from Microsoft is Windows 2000 Server. Windows 2000 Server builds on the strengths of Windows NT Server 4, adding new features that make Windows 2000 Server faster, easier to manage, more reliable, and easier to use for large and small networks alike.

The most significant new feature of Windows 2000 Server is called *Active Directory,* which provides a single directory of all network resources and enables program developers to incorporate the directory into their programs. Active Directory integrates various directory services, such as Novell's NDS and NT's own directory services, and enables you to manage all the directory information on your network using a single interface that resembles the Internet's World Wide Web.

NTFS drives

NT Server can use hard drives that are formatted in the same way as standard Windows and MS-DOS drives. (The technical term for this type of drive formatting is *FAT*, which stands for File Allocation Table.) But for better performance, Windows NT Server enables you to format your hard drives using a different type of disk format, called *NTFS* (for NT File System). NTFS drives have the following advantages over FAT drives:

✔ NTFS drives can be larger than FAT drives. FAT uses 32-bit disk addresses, which means that the largest hard drive can be 4GB. NTFS uses 64-bit disk addresses, which can theoretically support drives that are several million times larger than the biggest drives made today.

✔ NTFS is much more efficient at using the space on your hard drive. As a result, NTFS can cram more data onto a given hard drive than FAT.

✔ NTFS drives provide better security features than FAT drives. NTFS stores security information on disk for each file and directory. In contrast, FAT has only rudimentary security features.

✔ NTFS drives are more reliable because NTFS keeps duplicate copies of important information, such as the location of each file on the hard drive. If a problem develops on an NTFS drive, Windows NT Server can probably correct the problem without losing any data. In contrast, FAT drives are prone to losing information.

Windows 2000 Server comes in three versions:

✔ **Windows 2000 Server** is the basic server, designed for small- to medium-sized networks. It includes all the basic server features, including file and print sharing, and acts as an Internet Web and e-mail server.

✔ **Windows 2000 Advanced Server** is the next step up, designed for larger networks. Advanced Server can support server computers that have up to 8GB of memory (not hard drive — RAM!) and four integrated processors instead of the single processor that desktop computers and most server computers have.

✔ **Windows 2000 Datacenter Server** is Microsoft's most ambitious operating system yet. It can support servers that have as many as 32 processors with up to 64GB of RAM and is specially designed for large database applications. (At the time I wrote this, Windows 2000 Datacenter Server was not yet released but was expected within a few months.)

The pricing for Windows 2000 Server is similar to the pricing for Windows NT Server. You must purchase a server license for each Windows 2000 Server computer, which includes a certain number of client licenses. You must purchase extra client licenses for additional users. Table 8-2 lists the prices for the various types of Windows 2000 Server and client licenses.

Table 8-2	Windows 2000 Server
Product	*Price*
Windows 2000 Server, 5 clients	$999
Windows 2000 Server, 10 clients	$1,199
Windows 2000 Advanced Server, 25 clients	$3,999
Client license 5 pack	$199
Client license 20 pack	$799

Other Server Operating Systems

Although NetWare and Windows NT/2000 Server are the most popular choices for network operating systems, they're not the only available choices. The following sections briefly describe four other server choices: IBM's OS/2 Warp Server, Banyan VINES, UNIX, and Linux.

For Macintosh users, Apple offers a special server operating system called Mac OS X Server. For more information about Mac OS X Server, refer to Chapter 25.

OS/2 Warp Server

IBM's OS/2 Warp Server is one operating system that you shouldn't overlook; it's comparable in many ways to both NetWare and NT Server. OS/2 Warp Server offers advanced file- and print-server features and supports DOS, Windows 3.*x*, Windows 95 and 98, and Macintosh client computers.

One of OS/2 Warp Server's biggest limitations is its lack of a global directory service, such as NetWare's NDS or Microsoft's Active Directory.

Banyan VINES

VINES is a sophisticated network operating system that has been around for more than a decade, and is used in many large corporations. However, unless you already know a lot about VINES, I suggest you steer clear.

UNIX

UNIX originally began its life as a time-sharing operating system for minicomputers, but it has since become a popular server operating system for medium- to large-sized networks. For some types of network servers, such as those that require high-performance database access, UNIX is the server operating system of choice.

Unlike other server operating systems, UNIX comes in different variations from several vendors. No single version of "true" UNIX exists. Instead, many different versions look somewhat alike but are not completely compatible. The best known version of UNIX is available from a company called Santa Cruz Operation, or SCO.

Linux

Perhaps the most interesting operating system available today is Linux. Linux is a free operating system that is based on UNIX. Linux was started by Linus Torvalds, who thought it would be fun to write a version of UNIX in his free time — as a hobby. He enlisted help from hundreds of programmers throughout the world, who volunteered their time and efforts via the Internet. Today, Linux is a full-featured version of UNIX; its users consider it to be as good or better than Windows. In fact, almost as many people now use Linux as use Macintosh computers.

Linux offers the same networking benefits of UNIX and can be an excellent choice as a server operating system.

Apple Mac OS X Server

All the other server operating systems I describe in this chapter run on Intel-based PCs with Pentium or Pentium-compatible processors. But what about Macintosh computers? After all, Macintosh users need networks, too. For Macintosh networks, Apple offers a special network server operating system known as Mac OS X server. Mac OS X Server has all the features you'd expect in a server operating system: file and printer sharing, Internet features, e-mail, and so on. For more information, refer to Chapter 25.

Peer-to-Peer Networking with Windows

If you're not up to the complexity of NetWare or Windows 2000, you may want to opt for a simple peer-to-peer network based on Windows.

Advantages of peer-to-peer networks

The main advantage of a peer-to-peer network is that it is easier to set up and use than a NetWare or NT/2000 network, mainly because peer-to-peer relies on the networking features that are built into Windows. After you install Windows on a computer, all you have to do is adjust a few configuration settings to get your network up and running.

Another advantage of peer-to-peer networks is that they can be less expensive than server-based networks. Here are some of the reasons that peer-to-peer networks are inexpensive:

- ✔ Peer-to-peer networks don't require you to use a dedicated server computer. Any computer on the network can function as both a network server and a user's workstation. (However, you can configure a computer as a dedicated server if you want to. Doing so results in better performance but negates the cost benefit of not having a dedicated server computer.)

- ✔ Peer-to-peer networks are easier to set up and use, which means that you can spend less time figuring out how to make the network work and keep it working. And, as Einstein proved, time is money (hence his famous equation, E=M\$^{2}).

- ✔ Then there's the cost of the server operating system itself. Both NetWare and Windows 2000 Server can cost as much as \$200 per user. And the total cost increases as your network grows larger, although the cost per user drops. For a peer-to-peer Windows server, you pay for Windows once. There are no additional charges based on the number of users on your network.

Drawbacks of peer-to-peer networks

Yes, peer-to-peer networks are easier to install and manage than NetWare or NT, but they do have their drawbacks:

- ✔ Because peer-to-peer networks are Windows-based, they're subject to the inherent limitations of Windows. Windows is designed primarily to be an operating system for a single-user, desktop computer rather than function as part of a network, so Windows can't manage a file or printer server as efficiently as a real network operating system.

- ✔ If you don't set up a dedicated network server, someone (hopefully, not you) may have to live with the inconvenience of sharing his or her computer with the network. With NetWare or NT/2000 Server, the server computers are dedicated to network use so that no one has to put up with this inconvenience.

- ✔ Although a peer-to-peer network may have a lower cost per computer for smaller networks, the cost difference between peer-to-peer networks and NetWare or NT/2000 is less significant in larger networks (say, 20 or more clients).

- ✔ Peer-to-peer networks do not work well when your network starts to grow. Peer-to-peer servers just don't have the security or performance features required for a growing network.

Windows 98 Second Edition

Windows 98 Second Edition (also known as Windows 98 SE), the current version of Windows at the time of this writing, includes everything you need to set up a peer-to-peer network. If all your computers run Windows 98 (or Windows 95), you only have to purchase network cards and cable to build a network.

Here are the more salient features of Windows 98 networking:

- ✔ Windows 98 automatically detects most networking cards and configures itself to work with them.

- ✔ Windows 98 enables you to access the network through a desktop icon called Network Neighborhood. Using it is child's play.

- ✔ Windows 98 can connect to other Windows 98 or Windows 95 computers as well as to Windows NT Server or NetWare servers.

- ✔ Windows 98 includes a great Hearts game that you can play with other network users.

Windows Millennium Edition

Windows Millennium Edition, also known as Windows Me, is an update of Windows 98 that is designed especially for home users. One of the best features of Windows Me is the Home Networking Wizard, which simplifies the task of setting up a small network in your home. For more information about using the Home Networking Wizard, see Chapter 21.

Windows NT Workstation 4

Although Windows NT is usually considered a server operating system, Microsoft also peddles a desktop version of NT called Windows NT Workstation 4. NT Workstation 4 sports the user-friendly Windows 95 user interface and costs only about $50 more than Windows 98. NT Workstation offers many advantages over Windows 95 or 98 — the most important advantage being that NT Workstation does not crash as often as Windows 9*x*/Me and that NT Workstation supports the NTFS file system and improved security.

Windows 2000 Professional

Windows 2000 also comes in a desktop version, known as Windows 2000 Professional. Windows 2000 Pro incorporates the Windows 98 User Interface, so it's even easier to use than Windows NT 4 Workstation.

One of the main advantages of using Windows 2000 Professional as a peer-to-peer network server is the Windows 2000 security system. Windows 2000 Pro lets you implement user-based security rather than share-based security. In other words, with Windows 2000 Pro, you can set up user accounts that require users to log on to access the network.

Chapter 9

Planning Your Servers

· ·

In This Chapter

▶ Deciding whether to use dedicated servers

▶ Making sure that you provide enough disk space

▶ Storing programs and data files on a server

▶ Using a separate print server

▶ Buying a reliable server computer

· ·

*O*ne of the key decisions you must make when networking your computers is how you make use of server computers. Even if you use a peer-to-peer network system, such as Windows 98, you must still deal with the question of servers.

This chapter helps you to make the best use of your network server, first by convincing you to use a dedicated server if possible and then by suggesting ways to use the server efficiently.

To Dedicate or Not to Dedicate

In case you haven't noticed, I'm a big believer in dedicated server computers, even if you use a peer-to-peer network. Yes, one of the strengths of a simple Windows peer-to-peer network is that you can use any computer on the network as both a server computer and a user's workstation. Does that mean you should make every computer a server? No way.

You give up a lot when your desktop computer doubles as a network server:

🖝 Every time someone accesses data on your hard drive, your own work is temporarily suspended. If the data on your hard drive is popular, you become annoyed with the frequent delays.

🖝 You lose the sense of privacy that comes with having your own computer. Remember that nasty memo about your boss? You'd better not leave it lying around on your hard drive . . . someone else may lift it off the network.

You can set up your hard drive so that you have some private space where other users can't snoop about. But make sure that you set it up right and remember to store confidential files in private space. And make sure that you know more about the networking software than anyone else in the office. Someone who knows more about networking than you do can probably figure out a way to thwart your security measures.

✔ You lose the independence of having your own computer. You have to leave your computer on all day even when you're not using it because someone else may be. Do you want to turn off your computer because the noise it makes interrupts your afternoon nap? You can't. Do you want to delete some unnecessary files to free up some hard drive space? You can't — at least, not if the files don't belong to you.

✔ Your computer isn't immune to damage caused by other network users. What if someone accidentally deletes an important file on your hard drive? What if someone copies a 100MB file onto your hard drive while you aren't looking, so that no free space is available when you try saving the spreadsheet that you've been working on all afternoon? Or what if someone infects your hard drive with a virus?

I hope that you're convinced. If you can at all afford it, set aside a computer for use as a dedicated server. Beg, borrow, or steal a computer if you must.

Here are a few other thoughts to consider about using dedicated servers:

✔ Peer-to-peer networks enable you to adjust certain configuration options for network servers. If you use a computer as both a server and a client, you must balance these options so that they provide reasonable performance for both server and client functions. But if you dedicate the computer as a server, you can skew these options in favor of the server functions. In other words, you're free to tweak the server's configuration for peak network performance. You can find details for doing this in Chapter 14.

✔ As a general rule, try to limit the number of servers on your network. Having one server sharing a 40GB drive is better than two servers each sharing a 20GB drive. The fewer servers you have on your network, the less time you have to spend administering them.

✔ In a larger network, you may want to use two dedicated server computers: one as a file server and the other as a print server. This improves the performance for file operations and network printing. (As an alternative, you can use a network-ready printer so that you don't have to tie up a server computer for printing.)

✔ If you're the greedy type, offer to donate your old 100MHz Pentium computer as the network server if the company will purchase a new 750MHz Pentium III computer for your desktop.

Actually, this idea has merit: The file server doesn't have to be the fastest computer on the block, especially if it's mostly used to store and retrieve word processing, spreadsheet, and other types of files instead of being used for intensive database processing.

How Much Disk Space Do You Need?

The general rule for a network is that you can never have enough disk space. No matter how much you have, you eventually run out. Don't delude yourself into thinking that 20GB is twice as much space as you may ever need. Make that space available to the network, and it fills up in no time.

What then? Should you just keep adding a new hard drive to your file server every time you run out of space? Certainly not. The key to managing network disk space is just that — managing it. Someone has to sign on the dotted line that he or she promises to keep tabs on the network disk and let everyone know when it's about to burst its seams. And every network user must realize that disk storage on the server is a precious resource — to be used judiciously and not squandered.

Here are a few additional tips that can help you make the best use of your server disk space:

✔ If you use Windows 98 for the server computer, consider activating the Windows DriveSpace feature on the shared network drive. To set up DriveSpace properly, you must first quote from *Wayne's World:* Say "Ex-squeeze me," and DriveSpace politely compresses the data on your hard drive so that its capacity is effectively doubled. The only trouble with compressing your data is that it slows down the server a bit. For the best server performance, you're better off purchasing a larger hard drive and not compressing it.

Both Windows NT/2000 and NetWare also allow you to use compression to extend disk space on your servers.

✔ Encourage all network users to remember that their computers have local hard drives in addition to the network drives. Just because you have a network doesn't mean that everything has to be stored on a network drive!

✔ If you use Windows NT/2000 or NetWare for your file server, you can set up quotas to limit the amount of disk space each network user can use.

✔ Don't try to cut costs by using *diskless clients.* Some networks are set up so that the clients have no local drives at all. For this to work, a special chip is required in the network interface card so that the computer can boot without a hard drive. Diskless clients are cheaper, but they force the user to store everything on the network. In addition, they bog down the network because routine disk accesses, such as locating program files, have to travel across the network cable.

What to Put on a File Server

Of course, the only way to predict how much network disk space that you need is to plan what files you're going to store on the server. You need enough space to accommodate the network itself, shared data files, private data files, and shared application programs.

The network itself

You can't make all the space on the network server's hard drive available to network users; you have to reserve some of it for the network operating system itself. Setting aside a few gigabytes of drive space for the network operating system, print spool files, sealing wax, and other fancy stuff is not unreasonable.

A network can take up an amazing amount of drive space. Check out these numbers:

- NetWare 4.2 requires about 105MB.
- NetWare 5.1 consumes about 1.3GB.
- Windows NT Server needs about 125MB.
- Windows 2000 Server swallows about 1GB.
- Both Windows 98 and Windows Me chew up about 200MB.

Shared data files

Allow sufficient space on the file server for the data files that network users share. One large database file, or hundreds, or even thousands of small word processing or spreadsheet files may take up most of this space. Either way, don't skimp on space here.

Estimate the amount of space that you need for shared files. The only way you can estimate this is to add up the size of the files that must be shared. Now, double the result. If you can afford to, double it again.

Private data files

Every user wants access to network disk space for private file storage — perhaps because their own drives are getting full, they want the security of knowing that their files are backed up regularly, or they just want to try out the network.

You have two approaches to providing this private space:

✔ Create a folder for each network user on a shared network drive. For example, the Cleavers set up the following folders for private storage:

- Ward   \WARD

- June   \JUNE

- Wally   \WALLY

- Beaver   \BEAVER

Now, just tell each network user to store private files in his or her own folder. The problem with this setup is that these folders aren't really private; nothing keeps Beaver from looking at the files in Wally's directory.

To make these directories more secure, you can password-protect them by using the security features in your network operating system.

✔ Create a separate network drive mapping for each private folder. For example, you can map drive P to each network user's private directory. Then you can tell each user to store private files on his or her P drive. For Wally, the P drive refers to the \WALLY folder, but for Beaver, the P drive refers to \BEAVER. This setup keeps Beaver out of Wally's files.

The net effect (groan, sorry) of this setup is that each user seems to have a separate P drive on the server. In reality, these drives are merely folders on the server drive.

Estimating the disk space required for private file storage is more difficult than estimating space for shared file storage. After your users figure out that they have seemingly unlimited private storage on the network server, they start filling it up. That's why it's a good idea to set up user disk quotas on NetWare and Windows NT/2000 servers.

Shared programs

If several users use the same application program, consider purchasing a network version of the program and storing the program file on the network server. The advantage of sharing the program rather than storing a separate copy of the program on each user's local drive is that you have to manage only one copy of the software. For example, if a new version of the software comes out, you have to update just the copy on the server rather than separate copies on each workstation.

The network version of most programs enables each network user to set the program's options according to his or her preferences. Thus, one user may run the program using the default setup with boring colors, while another user may prefer to change the screen colors so that the program displays magenta text on a cyan background. Stalin probably would have outlawed network versions.

Many application programs create temporary files that you're not aware of and don't normally need to worry about. When you use these programs on a network, be sure to configure them so that the temporary files are created on a local drive rather than on a network drive. This configuration not only gives you better performance, but also ensures that one user's temporary files don't interfere with another's.

Planning Your Network Drive Mapping

If you plan to use mapped drive letters to access network drives, you should scope out which drive letters you will use. Here are some general rules to follow:

- ✔ Be consistent. If a network drive is accessed as drive Q from one workstation, map it as drive Q from all workstations that access the same drive. Don't have one user referring to a network drive as drive Q and another using the same drive but with a different letter.

- ✔ Use drive letters that are high enough to avoid conflicts with drive letters that are used by local drives. For example, suppose that one of your computers has three disk partitions, a CD-ROM drive, and a CD-RW drive. This computer would already have drive letters C through G assigned. I usually start network drive assignments with drive M and continue with N, O, P, and so on.

  Novell NetWare usually begins drive assignments at drive F.

- ✔ If you use DriveSpace on a Windows 98 server computer, be aware that DriveSpace uses up drive letters, which can affect your network drive letter assignments. To protect yourself, start your network before you install DriveSpace so that DriveSpace can find its way around your network drive assignments. And always wear a helmet and safety goggles when using DriveSpace.

- ✔ For Windows client computers, keep in mind that drive letter mapping isn't a requirement. Users can access any shared network drive via the Network Neighborhood icon that appears on the Windows desktop.

Sharing CD-ROM Drives

CD-ROM drives have become standard equipment on desktop computers, but if your computer is the only one in the office with a CD-ROM drive, you may have users waiting in line to borrow time on your computer so that they can use your CD-ROM drive.

Fortunately, all the network operating systems described in this book enable you to set up a CD-ROM drive as a shared network drive so that users throughout the network can access it. In fact, sharing a CD-ROM drive is no different than sharing a regular disk drive.

But an annoying problem crops up when you share a desktop computer's CD-ROM drive with other network users. Imagine that you're using your CD-ROM drive for important work, such as playing the hot game you just bought last night, when some clown down in sales wants to access the master price list CD just sent in from corporate headquarters. You get an annoying message that says something like `Please Insert the Master Price List CD in Drive D`. And that won't be the last of it, either. You're going to be pestered by annoying interruptions like this all day long.

If you're going to share a CD-ROM drive, make sure that it's located on a dedicated server computer and the CD-ROM is dedicated to a particular drive. For example, if corporate headquarters really does send you a CD containing the master price list and the network users need to access this CD frequently, dedicate an entire CD-ROM drive just for this CD. Then you won't have to contend with annoying messages about changing the drives.

If you have more than one CD to be shared, just install more than one CD-ROM drive in the server computer. With the cost of CD-ROM drives being so low — good ones cost under $100 — this solution isn't unrealistic. If you share more than a few CDs, you can even buy special CD-ROM *towers* with stacks of CD-ROM drives built in. For example, you can purchase a CD-ROM tower with seven 40-speed CD-ROM drives for under $1,000. These towers are self-contained servers with network software built in, so you can connect them directly to your network.

An alternative to a CD-ROM tower is a *jukebox*. A jukebox is a single CD-ROM drive that can hold several discs and automatically swaps discs as they are accessed. Jukeboxes are less expensive than towers, but they're slower; whenever a user accesses a disc that isn't currently in the CD-ROM drive, the jukebox must switch discs. If two users simultaneously access two discs, the jukebox spends a lot of time shuttling discs back and forth. (To avoid this problem, you can get jukeboxes that have more than one CD reader built in — for more money, of course.)

If you don't want to fuss with shared CD-ROM drives, CD-ROM towers, or jukeboxes, you can always just copy the entire contents of your most popular CD-ROM discs to the server's hard drive.

Sharing a rewritable CD drive (CD-RW) is a little more complicated than sharing a read-only CD-ROM drive. Windows itself does not support the write/rewrite features of CD-RW drives, so you have to use special software that comes with the CD-RW drive to write or rewrite data on a CD-RW drive. Most CD-RW software does not support networks. But some programs, such as Adaptec's DirectCD program, do support networks. With DirectCD, you can share a CD-RW drive and then use the network to write data to the drive. (For more information, visit Adaptec's Web site at www.adaptec.com.)

Using a Separate Print Server

If you have a larger network (say, a dozen or more computers) and shared printing is one of the main reasons that you're networking, you may want to consider using two dedicated server computers — one as a file server and the other as a print server. By using separate server computers for file and print sharing, you improve the overall performance of your network.

Here are some thoughts to keep in mind when you use a separate print server:

- ✔ If the printer is used exclusively for text output, the print server can be the slowest computer on the network and you still won't notice any performance delay. If you do a lot of graphics printing on a high-quality laser printer, however, don't use a dog computer for the print server. I've seen ten-minute print jobs slowed to an hour or more by a cheap print server.

- ✔ As an alternative to dedicating a separate computer to use as a print server, you can connect most printers directly to the network via an inexpensive print server device. The most commonly used device of this type is called the *HP JetDirect,* made by Hewlett-Packard (the same folks who make all those great printers). An external HP JetDirect is a small box that contains an Ethernet port (RJ-45 for twisted-pair, BNC for thinnet, or both) and a parallel port to which you can attach a printer. Internal HP JetDirect cards are designed to be installed in Hewlett-Packard printers, enabling you to connect the printer directly to the network. You can get a single-printer external HP JetDirect for about $150.

Buying a Server Computer

If you have a spare computer lying around that you can use as a server, great. Most of us don't have spare computers in the closet, though. If you plan to buy a new computer to use as a network server, here are some tips for configuring it properly:

- ✔ A network server computer doesn't need to have the latest in large-screen color monitors and supercharged graphics cards. An ordinary 14- or 15-inch monitor with an inexpensive video card will do.

✔ On the other hand, don't scrimp on the processor and memory. Buy the fastest Pentium II or Pentium III processor that you can afford and equip it with at least 128MB of RAM; 256MB is better. Every last byte of extra memory can be put to good use on a server.

✔ Buy the biggest hard drive that you can afford. The price of hard drive storage has dropped so much in recent years that you can easily outfit a server computer with at least 5GB of hard drive storage. I've seen 10GB drives advertised for under $100, and you can get a 40GB drive for under $300.

✔ While you're at it, buy SCSI drives instead of IDE drives. SCSI offers much better performance for network servers, where several users are accessing the drive simultaneously. SCSI is more expensive than IDE, but the performance benefit is worth the increased cost. For more information about the benefits of SCSI over IDE, see Chapter 14.

✔ Have the computer built in a tower-style case that has plenty of room for expansion — several free bays for additional hard drives and a more-than-adequate power supply. You want to make sure that you can expand the server when you realize that you didn't buy enough drive space.

Keeping the Power On

One feature that people often overlook when setting up a network server is the power. You can simply plug the server computer into the wall, or you can plug it into a surge protector to smooth out power spikes before they damage your computer. Using a surge protector is a good idea, but an even better idea is to connect your server computer to a device called an *uninterruptible power supply,* or UPS.

Inside the UPS box is a battery that is constantly charged and some electronics that monitor the condition of the power coming from the wall outlet. If a power failure occurs, the battery keeps the computer running. The battery can't run the computer forever, but it can keep your computer running long enough — anywhere from ten minutes to more than an hour, depending on how much you paid for the UPS — to shut things down in familiar Presbyterian fashion (decently and in order). For most small networks, a UPS that keeps you going for ten minutes is enough. You just want to make sure that any disk in progress (I/O) has time to finish. A decent UPS that is capable of protecting a single server computer can be had for about $150.

Here are a few additional thoughts about UPS:

- ✔ Using a UPS can prevent you from losing data when a power outage occurs. Without a UPS, your server computer can be shut down at the worst of times, such as while your computer is updating the directory information that tracks the location of your files. With a UPS, the computer can stay on long enough for such meticulous operations to be completed safely.

- ✔ In a true UPS, power is always supplied to the computer from the battery; the current from the wall outlet is used only to keep the battery charged. Most inexpensive UPS devices are actually *stand-by power supplies (SPSs)*. An SPS runs the computer from the wall-outlet current but switches to battery within a few gazillionths of a second if a power failure occurs. With a true UPS, you have no delay between the power failure and the battery takeover, so a true UPS does a better job than an SPS of protecting your computer against power outages, brownouts, and other minor power glitches. SPSs are less expensive than UPSs, though, so they're more commonly used.

- ✔ The ultimate power-failure protection is to attach a UPS to every computer on the network. That gets a bit expensive, though. At the very least, you should protect the server.

- ✔ If a power outage occurs and your server is protected by a UPS, get to the server as quickly as you can, log everyone off, and shut down the server. You should also go to each computer and turn off the power switch. Then, when power is restored, you can restart the server, restart each workstation, and assess the damage.

- ✔ Better yet, get a UPS that can be connected to the server computer through a serial port, a USB port, or a network port. Then configure the UPS to automatically power down the server should the power fail.

Location, Location, and Location

The final network server consideration that I need to address in this chapter is where to put the server. In the old days, you put the network server in a room with glass windows all around, paid a full-time lab technician in a white coat to tend to its every need, and gave it a name like ARDVARC or SHADRAC.

Nowadays, the most likely location for a file server is in the closet. Nothing says that the server has to be in a central location; it can be in the closet down at the end of the hall, atop the filing cabinets in the storage room, or in the corner office. The server can be almost anywhere, as long as it's near an electrical outlet and a network cable can be routed to it.

Of course, a print server is different. Ideally, the print server should be near the printer, which should be in an accessible location with storage space for paper and toner (for laser printers), a place to leave printouts that belong to other users, and a box to drop wasted paper so that it can be recycled.

Some bad locations for the server:

- ✔ In the attic. Too dusty.
- ✔ In the bathroom. Too much moisture.
- ✔ In the kitchen. Your computer gurus raid your refrigerator every time you call them. They start showing up spontaneously "just to check."
- ✔ In your boss's office. You don't want him or her to think of you every time the server beeps.

The good news is that you still get to name your server computer. You can call it something boring like SERVER1, or you can give it an interesting name like BERTHA or SPOCK.

Chapter 10

Oh, What a Tangled Web We Weave: Cables, Adapters, and Other Stuff

*I*f you've ever installed an underground sprinkler system, you won't have any trouble cabling your network. Working with network cable is a lot like working with sprinkler pipe: You have to use the right size pipe (cable), the right valves and headers (hubs and repeaters), and the right sprinkler heads (network interface cards).

Network cables have one compelling advantage over sprinkler pipes: You don't get wet when they leak.

This chapter tells you far more about network cables than you probably need to know. I introduce you to *Ethernet,* the most common system of network cabling for small networks. Then you find out how to work with the cables used to wire an Ethernet network. You also find out how to select the right network interface cards, which enable you to connect the cables to your computers.

What Is Ethernet?

Ethernet is a standardized way of connecting computers to create a network. You can think of Ethernet as a kind of municipal building code for networks: It specifies what kind of cables to use, how to connect the cables together, how long the cables can be, how computers transmit data to one another using the cables, and more.

You may have heard of two other popular network building codes: Token Ring and ARCnet. Ethernet is more commonly used than Token Ring because Ethernet is less expensive. Ethernet is used more than ARCnet because ARCnet is slower.

TECHNICAL STUFF

Worthless filler about network topology

A networking book wouldn't be complete without the usual textbook description of the three basic *network topologies*. The first type of network topology is called a *bus*, in which network nodes (that is, computers) are strung together in a line, like this:

A bus is the simplest type of topology but it has some drawbacks. If the cable breaks somewhere in the middle, the break splits the network into two.

The second type of topology is called a *ring*:

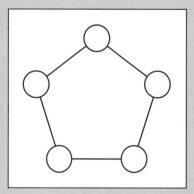

A ring is very much like a bus except with no end to the line: The last node on the line is connected to the first node, forming an endless loop.

The third type of topology is called a *star:*

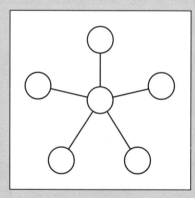

In a star network, all the nodes are connected to a central hub. In effect, each node has an independent connection to the network, so a break in one cable doesn't affect the others.

Ethernet networks are based on a bus design. However, fancy cabling tricks make an Ethernet network appear to be wired like a star when twisted-pair cable is used.

Some people treat Ethernet, Token Ring, and ARCnet like religions that they're willing to die for. To a Lord of the Token Ring, Ethernet is like an evil troll. Ethernet fanatics often claim that you can hear evil messages if you send data backward through a Token Ring network. Ethernet and Token Ring fanatics both treat ARCnet users as if they were a cult — possibly due to reports of ARCnet disciples giving away flowers at airports. Don't engage an Ethernet, Token Ring, or ARCnet Pharisee in a discussion about the merits of his or her network beliefs over the opponents' beliefs. It's futile.

Without regard to the technical merits of Ethernet, Token Ring, or ARCnet, the fact is that the vast majority of small networks use Ethernet. You can purchase inexpensive Ethernet components at just about any computer store, and you can even purchase Ethernet cable and connectors at many hardware warehouse stores. Because Ethernet is inexpensive and readily available, it is really the only choice for new networks — small as well as large.

Here are a few interesting tidbits about Ethernet standards:

✔ Ethernet is a set of standards for the infrastructure on which a network is built. All the network operating systems that I discuss in this book — NetWare, Windows NT Server, Windows 2000 Server, Windows 95/98, and Windows Me — can operate on an Ethernet network. If you build your network on a solid Ethernet base, you can change network operating systems later.

✔ Ethernet is often referred to by network gurus as 802.3 (pronounced *eight-oh-two-dot-three*), which is the official designation used by the *IEEE* (pronounced *eye-triple-e*), a group of electrical engineers who wear bow ties and have nothing better to do than argue about inductance all day long. This situation is a good thing, though, because if not for them, you wouldn't be able to mix and match Ethernet components made by different companies.

✔ Standard Ethernet transmits data at a rate of 10 million bits per second, or 10Mbps. Because 8 bits are in a byte, that translates into roughly 1.2 million bytes per second. In practice, Ethernet can't move information that fast because data must be transmitted in packages of no more than 1,500 bytes, called *packets*. So 150KB of information has to be split into 100 packets.

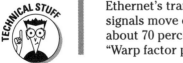

Ethernet's transmission speed has nothing to do with how fast electrical signals move on the cable. The electrical signals themselves travel at about 70 percent of the speed of light, or as Captain Picard would say, "Warp factor point-seven-oh. Engage."

> ✔ A newer version of Ethernet, called *Fast Ethernet,* moves data ten times as fast as normal Ethernet. Because Fast Ethernet moves data at a whopping 100Mbps and uses twisted-pair cabling, it's often called *100BaseT* (and sometimes *100BaseTx*). Fast Ethernet is a tad more expensive than standard 10 Mbps Ethernet, but I recommend that you use 100BaseT cables and components for all new networks.
>
> ✔ An even faster version of Ethernet, known as *Gigabit Ethernet,* is also available. Gigabit Ethernet components are expensive, though, so they are usually used to create a high-speed network backbone.

Three Types of Ethernet Cable

You can construct a 10Mbps Ethernet network by using one of three different types of cable: *thick coaxial cable* (called *yellow cable* because it's usually yellow), *thin coaxial* cable (called *thinnet* because it's thinner than the yellow stuff or *cheapernet* because it's cheaper than the yellow stuff), or *twisted pair cable,* which looks like phone cable. Twisted-pair cable is sometimes called *UTP,* or *10baseT cable,* for reasons I try hard not to explain later (in the section "Unshielded twisted-pair cable").

The yellow stuff isn't used much for small networks, but I describe it anyway. The real choice you must make is between thinnet cable and twisted-pair cable.

Stop me before I tell you about Token Ring!

Just in case you do get into an argument about Ethernet with a Token Ring fanatic, let me tell you where he or she is coming from. Ethernet can get bogged down if the network gets really busy and messages start colliding like crazy. Token Ring uses a more orderly approach to sending packets through the network. Instead of sending a message whenever it wants to, a computer on a Token Ring network must wait its turn. In a Token Ring network, a special packet called the token is constantly passed through the network from computer to computer. A computer can send a packet of data only when it has the token. In this way, Token Ring ensures that collisions won't happen.

Sometimes, a computer with a defective network interface card accidentally swallows the token. If the token disappears for too long, the network assumes that the token has been swallowed, and the network burps to generate a new token.

Two versions of Token Ring are in use. The older version runs at 4Mbps. The newer version runs at 16Mbps, plus it allows two tokens to exist at once, which makes the network even faster.

Oh, in case you're wondering, ARCnet uses a similar token-passing scheme.

Who cares what CSMA/CD stands for?

Besides specifying the mechanical and electrical characteristics of network cables, Ethernet specifies the techniques used to control the flow of information over the network cables. The technique that Ethernet uses is called *CSMA/CD*, which stands for "carrier sense multiple access with collision detection." This phrase is a mouthful, but if you take it apart piece by piece, you get an idea of how Ethernet works (as if you want to know).

Carrier sense means that whenever a computer wants to send a message on the network cable, it first listens to the cable to see whether anyone else is already sending a message. If it doesn't hear any other messages on the cable, the computer assumes that it's free to send one.

Multiple access means that nothing prevents two or more computers from trying to send a message at the same time. Sure, each computer listens before sending. But suppose that two

computers listen, hear nothing, and then proceed to send their messages? Picture what happens when you and someone else arrive at a four-way stop sign at the same time. You wave the other driver on, he or she waves you on, you wave, he or she waves, you all wave, and then you both end up going at the same time.

Collision detection means that after a computer sends a message on the network, it listens carefully to see whether the message crashed into another message. Kind of like listening for the screeching of brakes at the four-way stop. If the computer hears the screeching of brakes, it waits for a random period of time and tries to send the message again. Because the delay is random, two messages that collide are sent again after different delay periods, so a second collision is unlikely.

Now, wasn't that a waste of time?

The yellow stuff

The original Ethernet networks were wired with thick, heavy cable called *thick coaxial cable,* or *yellow cable,* because of its color. Thick coaxial cable isn't used much anymore, especially for small networks, because it's expensive, heavy, and not very flexible. (I mean that literally: Making yellow cable bend around tight corners is difficult.)

Here are some of the advantages and disadvantages of thick yellow cable:

- The yellow stuff is less susceptible to interference from mongo-magnets and motors and what-not, so it's still used sometimes in factories, warehouses, nuclear test sites, Frankenstein laboratories, and so on.

- You can string yellow cable along greater distances than other types of Ethernet cable. A single run of yellow cable (called a *segment*) can be as long as 500 meters.

✔ The way that yellow cable is attached to individual computers is weird. Usually, a long length of yellow cable is run along a path that takes it near each computer on the network. Each computer must be connected to the yellow cable via a device called a *transceiver.* The transceiver usually includes a device called a *vampire tap,* a clamp-like thingamabob that taps into the yellow cable without cutting and splicing it. The transceiver is connected to the network interface card by means of an *AUI cable.* (AUI stands for *attached unit interface,* not that the information matters.)

✔ I think you can see why the yellow stuff isn't used much anymore.

✔ That's really too bad. The yellow stuff would coordinate so well with this book.

Thinnet

A more practical type of cable for Ethernet networks is thin coaxial cable, usually called *thinnet.* Thinnet is less expensive than yellow cable — not only because the cable itself is less expensive, but also because separate transceivers aren't required to attach computers to the cable. (Thinnet does use transceivers, but the transceiver is built into the adapter card.) Figure 10-1 shows a typical thinnet cable.

Figure 10-1:
A thinnet
cable.

Here are some salient points about thin coaxial cable:

✔ Thinnet is about ⅕ inch in diameter, so it's much lighter and more flexible than the yellow stuff. You can easily wrap it around corners, drape it over doorways, around potted plants, and so on.

✔ You attach thinnet to the network interface card by using a goofy twist-on connector called a *BNC connector.* You can purchase pre-assembled cables with BNC connectors already attached in lengths of 25 or 50 feet, or you can buy bulk cable on a big spool and attach the connectors yourself by using a special tool. (I suggest buying pre-assembled cables. Attaching connectors to bulk cable can be tricky.)

✔ Yellow cable is usually wired with a single length of cable with vampire taps placed wherever a computer needs to access the cable. In contrast, thinnet is run with a separate length of cable between each computer. At each computer, a T connector is used to connect two cables to the network interface card. Figure 10-2 shows a typical thinnet arrangement. One length of thinnet connects Ward's computer to June's, a second length of cable connects June's computer to Wally's, and a third length of cable connects Wally's computer to Beaver's.

Figure 10-2:
A network wired with thinnet cable.

June's computer

Wally's computer

Thinnet cables

Ward's computer

Beaver's computer

✔ A special plug called a *terminator* is required at each end of a series of thinnet cables. In Figure 10-2, terminators are required at Ward's computer and at Beaver's computer. The terminator prevents data from spilling out the end of the cable and staining the carpet.

✔ The cables strung end-to-end from one terminator to the other are collectively called a *segment*. The maximum length of a thinnet segment is about 200 yards (actually, 185 meters). You can connect as many as 30 computers on one segment. To span a distance greater than 185 meters or to connect more than 30 computers, you must use two or more segments with a funky device called a *repeater* to connect each segment.

Unshielded twisted-pair cable

A popular alternative to thinnet cable is *unshielded twisted-pair cable,* or *UTP.* UTP cable is even cheaper than thin coaxial cable, and best of all, many modern buildings are already wired with twisted-pair cable because this type of wiring is often used with modern phone systems. Figure 10-3 shows a twisted-pair cable.

Figure 10-3:
Unshielded
twisted-pair
cable.

When you use UTP cable to construct an Ethernet network, you connect the computers in a star arrangement, as Figure 10-4 illustrates. In the center of this star is a device called a *hub*. Depending on the model, Ethernet hubs enable you to connect from 4 to 24 computers using twisted-pair cable.

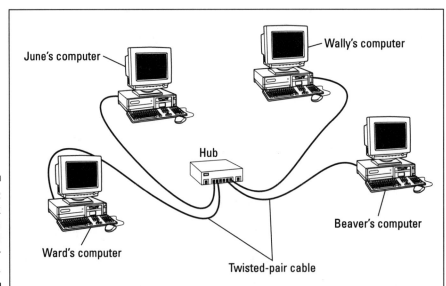

Figure 10-4:
A network
cabled with
unshielded
twisted-pair
cable.

An advantage of UTP's star arrangement is that if one cable goes bad, only the computer attached to that cable is affected; the rest of the network continues to chug along. With thinnet, a bad cable affects the entire network, not just the computer that the bad cable is connected to.

Here are a few other details that you should know about twisted-pair cabling:

- UTP cable consists of pairs of thin wire twisted around each other; several such pairs are gathered up inside an outer insulating jacket. Ethernet uses two pairs of wires, or four wires all together. The number of pairs in a UTP cable varies, but it is often more than two.

- UTP cable comes in five grades: Category 1 through Category 5. The higher the Category number, the greater the amount of protection that the cable provides from outside electrical interference. Category 3 cable is adequate for 10Mbps networks, but for 100Mbps networks (100BaseT), you must use Category 5 cable.

  Although higher Category cables are more expensive than lower Category cables, the real cost of installing Ethernet cabling is the labor required to actually pull the cables through the walls. As a result, I recommend that you always spend the extra money to buy Category 5 cable.

- If you want to sound like you know what you're talking about, say "Cat 5" instead of "Category 5."

- Although Category 5 cable is fine for 100Mbps networks, the newer 1000Mbps networks require an even better cable. Category 5e cable (the *e* stands for *enhanced*) is a slightly improved type of cable that will work for Fast Ethernet networks. And new standards for Category 6 and even Category 7 cables are expected soon.

- UTP cable connectors look like modular phone connectors but are a bit larger. UTP connectors are officially called *RJ-45 connectors*.

- Like thinnet cable, UTP cable is also sold in prefabricated lengths. However, RJ-45 connectors are much easier to attach to bulk UTP cable than BNC cables are to attach to bulk coaxial cable. As a result, I suggest that you buy bulk cable and connectors unless your network consists of just two or three computers. A basic crimp tool to attach the RJ-45 connectors costs about $50.

- The maximum allowable cable length between the hub and the computer is 100 meters (about 328 feet).

Hubs and the Network

The biggest difference between using thinnet cable and twisted-pair cable is that when you use twisted-pair cable, you also must use a separate device called a *hub*. Until recently, hubs were expensive enough that most do-it-yourself networkers who were building small networks opted for thinnet cable to avoid the expense and hassle of using hubs.

Nowadays, the cost of hubs has dropped so much that the advantages of twisted-pair cabling outweigh the hassle and cost of using hubs. With twisted-pair cabling, you can more easily add new computers to the network, move computers, find and correct cable problems, and service the computers that you need to remove from the network temporarily.

If you do decide to use twisted-pair cabling, you need to know some of the ins and outs of using hubs:

- Because you must run a cable from each computer to the hub, find a central location for the hub to which you can easily route the cables.

- The hub requires electrical power, so make sure that an electrical outlet is handy.

- When you purchase the hub, purchase one with at least twice as many connections as you need. Don't buy a four-port hub if you want to network four computers; when (not *if*) you add the fifth computer, you have to buy another hub.

- An alternative to a hub is a device called a *switch*. A switch is like a hub on steroids: It provides the same function as a hub, but at a much faster speed. The drawback of switches is that they are more expensive than hubs. (The term *hub* is often used generically to refer to either a true hub or a switch.)

- You can connect hubs to one another as shown in Figure 10-5; this is called *daisy-chaining*. When you daisy-chain hubs, you connect a cable to a standard port on one of the hubs and the daisy-chain port on the other hub. Be sure to read the instructions that come with the hub to make sure that you daisy-chain them properly.

- You can daisy-chain no more than three hubs or switches together. If you have more computers than three hubs can accommodate, don't panic. For a small additional cost, you can purchase hubs that have a BNC connection on the back. Then, you can string the hubs together using thinnet cable. The three-hub limit doesn't apply when you use thinnet cable to connect the hubs. You can also get stackable hubs or switches that have high-speed direct connections that enable two or more hubs or switches to be counted as a single hub or switch.

- When you shop for network hubs, you may notice that the expensive ones have network-management features that support something called *SNMP*. These hubs are called *managed hubs*. Unless your network is very large and you know what SNMP is, don't bother with the more expensive managed hubs. You'd be paying for a feature that you may never use.

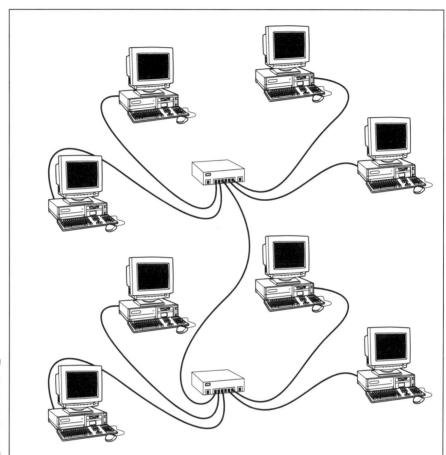

Figure 10-5:
You can
daisy-chain
hubs
together.

Network Interface Cards

Now that you know far more about network cable than you really need to, I want to point out a few things about network interface cards that you should consider before you buy:

✔ The network interface cards that you use must have a connector that matches the type of cable that you use. If you plan on wiring your network with thinnet cable, make sure that the network cards have a BNC connector. For twisted-pair wiring, make sure that the cards have an RJ-45 connector.

✔ Some network cards provide two or three connectors. I see them in every combination: BNC and AUI, RJ-45 and AUI, BNC and RJ-45, and all three. Selecting a card that has both BNC and RJ-45 connectors isn't a bad idea. That way, you can switch from thinnet cable to twisted-pair cable or vice versa without buying new network cards. You can get both types of connectors for a cost of only $5 to $10 more per card. Don't worry about the AUI connector, though. You'll probably never need it.

✔ You can get 10Mbps cards, 100Mbps cards, or 10/100Mbps cards, which automatically determine whether your network is running at 10Mbps or 100Mbps and switch accordingly. I suggest that you always purchase 10/100Mbps auto-sensing cards. They are a few dollars more, but well worth the additional cost. Even if you don't need a 100Mbps network now, you may eventually.

✔ Long ago and far away, Novell manufactured a network interface card known as the *NE2000*. The NE2000 card is no longer made, but NE2000 remains a standard of compatibility for network interface cards. If a card is NE2000-compatible, you can use it with just about any network. If you buy a card that is not NE2000-compatible, make sure that the card is compatible with the network operating system that you intend to use.

✔ When you purchase a network card, make sure that you get one that's compatible with your computer. Most computers can accommodate cards designed for the standard 16-bit ISA bus. Newer Pentium-based computers can also accommodate cards with 32-bit PCI bus. For a Pentium computer, PCI cards are well worth the extra few bucks. Not only are PCI cards faster than ISA cards, they are also easier to configure.

✔ Make sure that the computer in which you're going to use the card has an available slot of the same type as the card that you purchase. For example, suppose your computer has four ISA bus slots and three PCI bus slots, but all three of the PCI slots are already in use, while two of the ISA slots are available. In this case, get an ISA card.

✔ Make sure that the card is compatible with Plug and Play. This feature enables Windows to automatically configure the card so that you don't have to go through a bunch of tedious configuration gyrations just to get the card working.

✔ Network cards can be a bit tricky to set up — even Plug and Play cards. Each different card has its own nuances. You can simplify your life a bit if you use the same card for every computer in your network. Try not to mix and match network cards.

✔ If you see Ethernet cards advertised on late-night television for an unbelievably low price (like for $2.95, or free with Proof of Purchase seals from three cereal boxes), make sure that the cards are 16-bit cards. You won't be satisfied with the slow performance and configuration problems that are inherent with bargain-basement 8-bit cards unless your computer is also of the bargain-basement variety. If you have a 486 or Pentium computer, don't even think about using 8-bit cards.

Ten base what?

The IEEE, in its infinite wisdom, has decreed that the following names shall be used to designate the three types of cable used with 802.3 networks (in other words, with Ethernet):

✔ 10base5 is thick coaxial cable (the yellow stuff).

✔ 10base2 is thin coaxial cable (thinnet).

✔ 10baseT is unshielded twisted-pair cable (UTP).

In each moniker, the number *10* means that the cable operates at 10Mbps, and *base* means that the cable is used for baseband networks as opposed to broadband networks (don't ask). The number *5* in 10base5 is the maximum length of a yellow cable segment: 500 meters. The number *2* in 10base2 stands for 200 meters, which is about the 185-meter maximum segment length for thinnet cable. (For a group of engineers, the IEEE is odd; I didn't know that the word *about* can be part of an engineer's vocabulary.) And the letter *T* in 10baseT stands for *twisted*.

Of these three official monikers, 10baseT is the only one used frequently; 10base5 and 10base2 are usually just called *thick* and *thin*, respectively.

Also, Fast Ethernet running over 10baseT cabling uses the designation 100baseT.

Network Starter Kits

Often, the easiest way to buy the equipment that you need to build a network is to purchase a network starter kit. A typical network starter kit includes everything that you need to network two computers. To add additional computers, you purchase add-on kits that include everything that you need to add one computer to the network.

For example, suppose you want to network three computers in a small office. You could start with a two-computer network starter kit, which would include the following items:

✔ Two 10/100Mbps auto-switching PCI Ethernet cards

✔ One 5-port Ethernet 10/100Mbps auto-switching hub

✔ Two 25-foot-long 10baseT twisted-pair cables

✔ Software for the cards

✔ Instructions

This kit, which should set you back about $100, connects two of the three computers. To connect the third computer, purchase an add-on kit that includes a 10/100 auto-switching PCI Ethernet card, another 25-foot-long twisted-pair cable, software, and instructions — all for about $40.

Installing Network Cable

The hardest part about working with network cable is attaching the cable connectors. That's why the easiest way to wire a network is to buy prefabricated cables, with the connectors already attached. Thinnet cable is commonly sold in prefabricated lengths of 25, 50, or 100 feet. You can buy prefabricated twisted-pair cable, or you can attach the connectors yourself (it isn't hard to do).

Before I show you how to attach cable connectors, here are a few general tips for working with cable:

- ✓ Always use more cable than you need, especially if you're running cable through walls. Leave plenty of slack.

- ✓ When running cable, avoid sources of interference like fluorescent lights, big motors, and so on. The most common source of interference for cables run behind fake ceiling panels are fluorescent lights; be sure to give light fixtures a wide berth as you run your cable. Three feet should do it.

- ✓ If you must run cable across the floor where people walk, cover the cable so that no one trips over it. Inexpensive cable protectors are available from most hardware stores.

- ✓ When running cables through walls, label each cable at both ends. Most electrical supply stores carry pads of cable labels that are perfect for the job. These pads contain 50 sheets or so of precut labels with letters and numbers. They look much more professional than wrapping a loop of masking tape around the cable and writing on the tape with a marker.

  Or, if you want to scrimp, you can just buy a permanent marker and write directly on the cable.

- ✓ When several cables come together, tie them with plastic cable ties. Avoid masking tape if you can; the tape doesn't last, but the sticky glue stuff does. It's a mess a year later. Cable ties are available from electrical supply stores.

- ✓ Cable ties have all sorts of useful purposes. On my last backpacking trip, I used a pair of cable ties to attach an unsuspecting buddy's hat to a high tree limb. He wasn't impressed with my innovative use of the cable ties, but my other hiking companions were.

- ✓ When you run cable above acoustic ceiling panels, use cable ties, hooks, or clamps to secure the cable to the actual ceiling or to the metal frame that supports the ceiling tiles. Don't just lay the cable on top of the tiles.

Getting the tools that you need

Of course, to do a job right, you must have the right tools.

Start with a basic set of computer tools, which you can get for about $15 from any computer store or large office-supply store. These kits include the right screwdrivers and socket wrenches to open up your computers and insert adapter cards. (If you don't have a computer tool kit, make sure that you have several flat-head and Phillips screwdrivers of various sizes.)

If all your computers are in the same room, and you're going to run the cables along the floor, and you're using prefabricated cables, the computer tool kit should contain everything that you need.

If you're using bulk cable and plan on attaching your own connectors, you need the following tools in addition to the tools that come with the basic computer tool kit:

- ✔ **Wire cutters.** Big ones for thinnet cable; smaller ones are okay for 10baseT cable. If you're using yellow cable, you need the Jaws of Life.

- ✔ **A crimp tool that is appropriate for your cable type.** You need the crimp tool to attach the connectors to the cable.

- ✔ **Wire stripper.** You need this only if the crimp tool doesn't include a wire stripper. For thinnet cable, a special wire-stripper-doohickey is required because the cable's inner conductor, outer conductor, and outer insulation must be cut at precise lengths.

If you plan on running cables through walls, you need these additional tools:

- ✔ **A hammer.**
- ✔ **A bell.**
- ✔ **A song to sing.** Just kidding about these last two.
- ✔ **A keyhole saw.** This is useful if you plan on cutting holes through walls to route your cable.
- ✔ **A flashlight.**
- ✔ **A ladder.**
- ✔ **Possibly a *fish tape*.** A fish tape is a coiled-up length of stiff metal tape. To use it, you feed the tape into one wall opening and fish it toward the other opening, where a partner is ready to grab it when the tape arrives. Next, your partner attaches the cable to the fish tape and yells something like "Let 'er rip!" or "Bombs away!" Then you reel in the fish tape and the cable along with it. (You can find fish tape in the electrical section of most well-stocked hardware stores.)

If you plan on routing cable through a concrete sub-floor, you need to rent a jackhammer and a backhoe and hire someone to hold a yellow flag while you work.

Attaching a BNC connector to thinnet cable

Properly connecting a BNC connector to thinnet cable is an acquired skill. You need two tools — a wire stripper that can cut through the various layers of the coaxial cable at just the right location, and a crimping tool that crimps the connector tightly to the cable after you get the connector into position. BNC connectors have three separate pieces, as shown in Figure 10-6.

Connector body

Center pin

Ferrule

Figure 10-6: Attaching a BNC connector to thinnet cable.

Properly stripped cable

Here's the procedure, in case you ignore my advice and try to attach the connectors yourself:

1. **Slide the hollow tube portion of the connector (lovingly called the *ferrule*) over the cable.**

   Let it slide back a few feet to get it out of the way.

2. **Cut the end of the cable off cleanly.**

3. **Use the stripping tool to strip the cable.**

   Strip the outer jacket back ½ inch from the end of the cable, strip the braided shield back ¼ inch from the end, and strip the inner insulation back ³⁄₁₆ inch from the end.

4. **Insert the solid center conductor into the center pin.**

   Slide the center pin down until it seats against the inner insulation.

5. **Use the crimping tool to crimp the center pin.**

6. **Slide the connector body over the center pin and inner insulation but under the braided shield.**

   After you push the body back far enough, the center pin clicks into place.

7. **Now slide the ferrule forward until it touches the connector body.**

   Crimp it with the crimping tool.

Don't get sucked into the trap of trying to use easy "screw-on" connectors. They aren't very reliable.

Attaching an RJ-45 connector to UTP cable

RJ-45 connectors for UTP wiring are much easier to connect than thinnet connectors. The only trick is making sure that you attach each wire to the correct pin. Each pair of wires in a UTP cable has complementary colors. One pair consists of one white wire with an orange stripe and an orange wire with a white stripe, and the other pair has a white wire with a green stripe and a green wire with a white stripe.

Here are the proper pin connections:

Pin Number	*Proper Connection*
Pin 1	White/orange wire
Pin 2	Orange/white wire
Pin 3	White/green wire
Pin 6	Green/white wire

One type of 100Mbps network, known as 100baseT4, requires that you use cable with four pairs of wires rather than two pairs and that all eight wires be connected. If you're wiring a 100baseT4 network, connect the wires like this:

Pin Number	*Proper Connection*
Pin 1	White/orange wire
Pin 2	Orange/white wire
Pin 3	White/green wire
Pin 4	White/blue wire
Pin 5	Blue/white wire
Pin 6	Green/white wire
Pin 7	White/brown wire
Pin 8	Brown/white wire

Figure 10-7 shows an RJ-45 plug properly connected.

Figure 10-7:
Attaching
an RJ-45
connector
to UTP
cable.

Pin connections:
Pin 1 - White/Orange
Pin 2 - Orange/White
Pin 3 - White/Green
Pin 6 - Green/White

Here's the procedure for attaching an RJ-45 connector:

1. **Cut the end of the cable to the desired length.**

   Make sure that you make a square cut — not a diagonal cut.

2. **Insert the cable into the stripper portion of the crimp tool so that the end of the cable is against the stop.**

   Squeeze the handles and slowly pull the cable out, keeping it square. This strips off the correct length of outer insulation without puncturing the insulation on the inner wires.

3. **Arrange the wires so that they lay flat in the following sequence from left to right: white/orange, orange/white, white/green, green/white.**

   Pull the green/white wire a bit to the right and then insert the cable into the back of the plug so that each wire slides into the channel for the correct pin.

4. **Make sure that the wires are in the correct pin channels; especially make sure that the green/white cable is in the channel for pin 6.**

5. **Insert the plug and wire into the crimping portion of the tool and then squeeze the handles to crimp the plug.**

   Remove the plug from the tool and double-check the connection.

Here are a few other points to remember when dealing with RJ-45 connectors and twisted-pair cable:

   ✔ The pins on the RJ-45 connectors are not numbered, but you can tell which is Pin 1 by holding the connector so that the metal conductors are facing up, as shown in Figure 10-7. Pin 1 is on the left.

✔ Some people wire 10baseT cable differently — using the green and white pair for Pins 1 and 2 and the orange and white pair for Pins 3 and 6. This doesn't affect the operation of the network (the network is color-blind), *as long as the connectors on both ends of the cable are wired the same!*

✔ Yes, I know that any normal person would have set up the RJ-45 connectors using Pins 1 through 4, and not Pins 1, 2, 3, and 6. But remember, computer people aren't normal in any particularly relevant sense, so why would you expect the fourth wire to connect to the fourth pin? That's pretty naive, don't you think?

✔ If you're installing cable for a Fast Ethernet system, you should be extra careful to follow the rules of Category-5 cabling. That means, among other things, make sure that you use Category-5 components throughout. The cable and all the connectors must be up to Category-5 specs. When you attach the connectors, do not untwist more than ½ inch of cable. And do not try to stretch the cable runs beyond the 100-meter maximum. When in doubt, have cable for a 100Mbps Ethernet system professionally installed.

Professional Touches

If most of the stuff that I discuss in this chapter makes sense to you, and if you want to impress your friends, consider adding the following extra touches to your network installation. These extra touches make the job look professionally done. (If you find this chapter to be hopelessly confusing, you should probably concentrate on just getting your network up and running. Worry about making it look pretty later.)

Figure 10-8 shows some of the following professional touches:

✔ Use 10baseT wiring — that's what most network pros are doing these days.

✔ Run the wiring through the ceiling and walls instead of along the floor, and mount a wall jack near each computer. Then plug each computer into the wall jack by using a short (10 foot or so) patch cable. Be sure to use top-quality Category-5 jacks and make sure that each pair of wires inside the cable is twisted right up to the point where the wires attach to the jack. In other words, don't untwist the wires any more than absolutely necessary to make them easier to work with.

✔ When you run the wiring through the walls and ceiling, take special care to avoid power cords, fluorescent lamps, and other electrical devices that may interfere with the signals traveling inside the network cable. And don't kink the cable: Curve it gently around corners. Inside false ceilings, hang the cable from the metal ceiling supports using cable ties, hooks, or cable clamps.

✔ To really do it right, run 10baseT cable to every possible computer location in your office, even if you don't yet have a computer there. That way, when you do decide to move a computer to this location, the hard wiring (up in the ceiling and through the wall) is already done. All you have to do then is attach the computer to the wall jack with a patch cord.

✔ Designate a corner of a closet or storeroom to be your wiring closet. Bundle all the cables together and attach them to a patch panel, which is nothing more than a series of RJ-45 jacks arranged neatly in a row.

✔ Connect the appropriate jacks in the patch panel to your network hub with short patch cables. The whole thing looks a bit like a rat's nest, but you can easily reconfigure the network at a moment's notice. If someone changes locations, all you have to do is adjust the patch cables in the wiring closet accordingly.

✔ Be careful about making your network look too good. People may assume that you're a network geek and start offering you Cheetos to solve their problems.

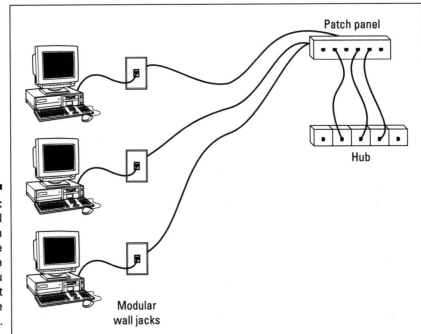

Figure 10-8:
Professional
touches can
create the
appearance
that you
know what
you're
doing.

Patch panel

Hub

Modular
wall jacks

Chapter 11

Configuring Your Network Computers

. . . .

In This Chapter

▶ Installing a network card

▶ Installing a server operating system

▶ Configuring a Windows computer to access the network

▶ Checking out your installation

. . . .

*A*fter the cable is all strung, the fun part begins: You actually get to connect your computers to your network and configure them so that your network runs properly. Get ready to roll up your sleeves and dig into the bowels of your computers. Make sure that you scrub thoroughly first.

Installing a Network Interface Card

You have to install a network interface card into each computer before you can connect the computers to the network cables. Installing a network card is a manageable task, but you have to be willing to roll up your sleeves.

If you've installed one adapter card, you've installed them all. In other words, installing a network card is just like installing a modem, a new video controller card, a sound card, or any other type of card. If you've ever installed one of these cards, you can probably install a network card blindfolded.

If you haven't installed a card, here's a step-by-step procedure:

1. **Shut down Windows and then turn the computer off and unplug it.**

   Never work in your computer's insides with the power on or the power cord plugged in!

2. Remove the cover from your computer.

Figure 11-1 shows the screws that you must typically remove to open the cover. Put the screws someplace where they won't wander off.

Figure 11-1:
Removing
your
computer's
cover.

3. Find an unused expansion slot inside the computer.

The expansion slots are lined up in a neat row near the back of the computer; you can't miss 'em. Most newer computers have at least two or three slots known as *PCI slots.*

Many computers, especially those that are a year or more old, also have several slots known as *ISA slots.* You can distinguish ISA slots from PCI slots by noting the size of the slots. PCI slots are smaller than ISA slots, so you can't accidentally insert a PCI card in an ISA slot or vice versa.

Some computers also have other types of slots — mainly VESA and EISA slots. Standard ISA or PCI networking cards won't fit into these types of slots, so don't try to force them.

4. When you find the right type of slot that doesn't have a card in it, remove the metal slot protector from the back of the computer's chassis.

A small retaining screw holds the slot protector in place. Remove the screw, pull the slot protector out, and put the slot protector in a box with all your other old slot protectors. Don't lose the screw. (After a while, you collect a whole bunch of slot protectors. Keep them as souvenirs.)

5. Insert the network card into the slot.

Line up the connectors on the bottom of the card with the connectors in the expansion slot, and then press the card straight down. Sometimes you have to press uncomfortably hard to get the card to slide into the slot.

6. **Secure the network card with the screw that you removed in Step 4.**

7. **Put the computer's case back together.**

   Watch out for the loose cables inside the computer; you don't want to pinch them with the case as you slide it back on. Secure the case with the screws that you removed in Step 2.

8. **Turn the computer back on.**

   If you're using a Plug and Play card with Windows 95/98, Windows Me, or Windows 2000, the card is automatically configured after you start the computer again. Otherwise, you may need to run an additional software installation program. See the installation instructions that come with the network interface card for details.

Installing a Server Operating System

After you install the network cards and cable, all that remains is to install the network software. The procedures for doing this task vary considerably, depending on the network that you use, so you need to consult your network software's manual for the details. Here, I describe some general things to keep in mind when you install software on a server computer.

Installing NetWare

If you're using NetWare, installing the server software is the most difficult part of setting up the network. Read the manual carefully, place it ceremoniously on your highest bookshelf, and pick up a copy of *Networking With NetWare For Dummies,* 4th Edition, by Ed Tittel, James E. Gaskin, and Earl Follis (IDG Books Worldwide, Inc.).

The tricky part about installing NetWare is that you must first completely remove any operating system that is already installed on your computer. Then, you use the DOS 7 floppy disk that comes with NetWare to boot your computer and create a 50MB DOS partition on the server's hard drive. You can then install NetWare from the distribution CD-ROM. After the installation program starts, you can simply follow the instructions that appear on the screen to complete the installation. (Installing NetWare is easier if the computer has a bootable CD-ROM drive.)

During the NetWare installation, the installation program asks you for a lot of detailed information about how you want the NetWare server to be set up. For example, if you are installing NetWare 5.1, you are asked to supply the following information:

✔ The version of NDS that you want to use (Version 7 or Version 8). Choose NDS 7 only if you are installing the server in an existing network and you have not already upgraded the network to NDS 8.

✔ The Server ID number. The installation program creates a default server ID for you, but you can provide your own number if you want to use some type of numbering scheme to identify your servers.

✔ The amount of hard drive space to allocate to the NetWare partition and the SYS volume.

✔ The name to use for the server.

✔ The name and size of any additional volumes that you want to create in the NetWare partition.

✔ The networking protocols that you want to enable. You can enable IP, IPX, or both. *IP* is the protocol used for the Internet, and \ is the original NetWare protocol. For most networks, you should enable both IP and IPX.

In most cases, you can simply choose the default options to create a functional server.

Installing Windows 2000 Server

Installing Windows 2000 Server is relatively straightforward. However, you should make a few decisions before you start the Setup process — in particular:

✔ The partitions arrangement for the server's disk. You can set the entire disk up as a single partition, or you can subdivide the disk into several smaller partitions that are easier to manage.

✔ The file system to use for each Windows 2000 volume. Windows 2000 Server supports three file systems: NTSF, FAT, and FAT32. In most cases, you should create NTSF volumes.

✔ The name of the domain that the server belongs to and whether the server is a domain controller.

✔ The server's computer name.

✔ The password for the administrator account.

After you start the Setup program, you simply follow the instructions that appear on the screen and provide any information that the Setup program requests. In most cases, the Setup program gives you default choices that allow you to create a functioning server.

Configuring Windows 9x/Me for file and printer sharing

If your server computer runs Windows 95, 98, or Millennium Edition, you must adjust the Windows settings to allow for file and printer sharing. For information about doing this, refer to Chapter 4.

Configuring Client Computers

Before your network setup is complete, you must configure the network's client computers. In particular, you have to configure each client's network interface card so that it works properly, and you have to install the right protocols so that the clients can communicate with other computers on the network.

Fortunately, configuring client computers for the network is child's play with Windows 95, 98, or Millennium Edition. For starters, Windows automatically recognizes your network interface card when you start up your computer. All that remains to connect to the network in Windows is to make sure that Windows installed the network protocols and client software properly. To do so, follow these steps:

1. **Choose the Start⇨Settings⇨Control Panel command to summon the Control Panel. Then double-click the Network icon.**

   The Network dialog box appears, as shown in Figure 11-2.

Figure 11-2:
The
Network
control
panel.

2. **Make sure that the network protocol that you're using appears in the list of network resources.**

   If you're creating a Windows-based network, make sure that you have the NETBEUI protocol listed. For a NetWare network, make sure that the IPX/SPX-compatible Protocol is listed. To enable access to the Internet or an intranet server, also make sure that TCP/IP is listed.

3. **If a protocol that you need isn't listed, click the Add button to add the protocol that you need.**

   A dialog box appears asking if you want to add a network client, adapter, protocol, or service, as shown in Figure 11-3. Click Protocol and then click Add. A list of available protocols appears. Select the one that you want to add and then click OK. (You may be asked to insert a disk or the Windows CD-ROM.)

Figure 11-3:
Adding a
network
component.

4. **Make sure that the network client that you want to use appears in the list of network resources.**

   For a Windows-based network, make sure that Client for Microsoft Networks is listed. For a NetWare network, make sure that Client for NetWare Networks appears. If your network uses both types of servers, you can choose both clients.

   If you have NetWare servers, use the NetWare client software that comes with NetWare rather than the client supplied by Microsoft with Windows.

5. **If the client that you need isn't listed, click the Add button to add the client that you need.**

   The dialog box in Figure 11-3 appears again. This time, click Client and then click Add. Select the network client that you want to add and then click OK.

6. **Click the client you just added and then click Properties.**

   This summons a properties dialog box, whose appearance varies slightly depending on which client you selected.

7. **Fill in the logon information and then click OK.**

   For the Microsoft Networks client, you can specify the name of the Windows NT or 2000 domain you want to log on to. For NetWare clients, you can type the name of the preferred server and a drive letter for the network drive.

8. **Click OK to dismiss the Network dialog box.**

   You're done! Your computer reboots itself to enable the new network features that you just installed.

Testing Your Network Installation

Your network isn't finished until you test it to make sure that it works. Hold your breath as you fire up your computers, starting with the server and then proceeding to the clients. Watch for error messages as each computer starts up. Then log on to the network to see whether it works. If it doesn't, the following paragraphs should help you find the problem:

- ✔ If you have a problem, the first culprit to suspect is your network cable. Check all your connections, especially any connections you crimped yourself. If you're using thinnet, make sure that the terminators are attached properly. If you're using UTP, make sure that the hub is plugged in and turned on.

- ✔ If you're using UTP, you can find a bad cable by checking the light on the back of each network card and each hub connection. The light should be glowing steadily. If it's not glowing at all or if it's glowing intermittently, replace the cable or reattach the connector.

- ✔ Make sure that your network card's resource settings are set correctly by choosing System from the Control Panel (Start⇨Settings⇨Control Panel) and clicking the Device Manager tab. If the card is configured incorrectly, an exclamation mark will appear next to the icon for the network card.

- ✔ Call up the Network Control Panel program and carefully review all the network settings. Make sure that you have bound the necessary protocols — NetBEUI, IPX/SPX, or TCP/IP — to your network card.

- ✔ If the network doesn't work, you may benefit from running the Windows built-in Networking Troubleshooter, as shown in Figure 11-4. To access the Networking Troubleshooter, click the Start button, and then choose the Help command. When the Help window appears, click Troubleshooting, and then locate the troubleshooter that you want to run.

Figure 11-4:
The
Networking
Trouble-
shooter.

Part III

Network Management For Dummies

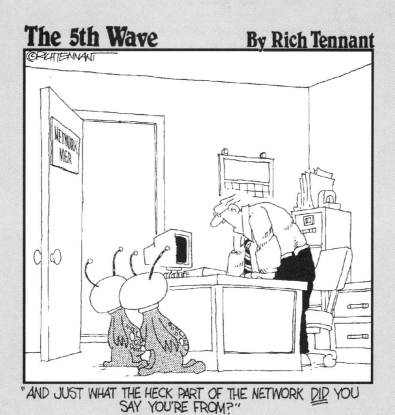

The 5th Wave   By Rich Tennant

"AND JUST WHAT THE HECK PART OF THE NETWORK DID YOU SAY YOU'RE FROM?"

In this part . . .

You discover that there's more to networking than installing the hardware and software. After you get the network up and running, you have to keep it up and running. That's called network management.

The chapters in this section show you how to set up your network's security system, how to improve its performance, and how to protect your network from disaster. I include a bit of technical stuff here, but no one said life was easy.

Chapter 12

Help Wanted: A Network Manager's Job Description

Help wanted. Network manager to help small business get control of a network run amok. Must have sound organizational and management skills. Only moderate computer experience required. Part-time only.

Does this sound like an ad that your company should run? Every network needs a network manager, whether the network has 2 computers or 200. Of course, managing a 200-computer network is a full-time job, whereas managing a 2-computer network isn't. At least, it shouldn't be.

This chapter introduces you to the boring job of network management. Oops . . . you're probably reading this chapter because you've been elected to be the network manager, so I'd better rephrase that: This chapter introduces you to the wonderful, exciting world of network management! Oh boy! This is going to be fun!

Identifying the Network Manager: A Closet Computer Geek

Most small companies can't afford and don't need a full-time computer geek. So the network manager is usually just a part-time computer geek. The ideal network manager is a *closet computer geek:* someone who has a secret interest in computers but doesn't like to admit it.

The job of managing a network requires some computer skills, but it isn't entirely a technical job. Much of the work that is done by the network manager is routine housework. Basically, the network administrator dusts, vacuums, and mops the network periodically to keep it from becoming a mess.

Here are some additional ideas about picking a network administrator:

- The network manager needs to be an organized person. Conduct a surprise office inspection and place the person with the neatest desk in charge of the network. (Don't warn them in advance, or everyone may mess up their desks intentionally the night before the inspection.)

- Allow enough time for network management. For a small network (say, no more than a dozen computers), an hour or two each week is enough. More time is needed up-front as the network manager settles into the job and finds out about the ins and outs of the network. But after an initial settling-in period, network management for a small office network doesn't take more than an hour or two per week. (Of course, larger networks take more time to manage.)

- Make sure that everyone knows who the network manager is and that the network manager has the authority to make decisions about the network, such as what access rights each user has, what files can and cannot be stored on the server, how often backups are done, and so on.

- In most cases, the person who installs the network is also the network manager. That's appropriate because no one understands the network better than the person who designs and installs it.

- The network manager needs an understudy — someone who knows almost as much about the network, is eager to make a mark, and smiles when the worst network jobs are "delegated."

- The network manager has some sort of official title, such as Network Boss, Network Czar, Vice President in Charge of Network Operations, or Dr. Network. A badge, a personalized pocket protector, or a set of Spock ears helps, too.

Going by the Book

One of the network manager's main jobs is to keep the network book up-to-date. In Chapter 7, I suggest that you keep all the important information about your network in a ¼-inch binder. Give this binder a clever name, such as *The Network Bible* or *My Network and Welcome to It.* Here are some things that it should include:

✔ An up-to-date diagram of the network. This diagram can be a detailed floor plan, showing the actual location of each computer, or something more abstract and Picasso-like. Any time that you change the network layout, update the diagram. And include a detailed description of the change, the date that the change was made, and the reason for the change.

Microsoft sells a program called *Visio* that is specially designed for creating network diagrams.

✔ A detailed inventory of your computer equipment. Here is a sample form that you can use to keep track of your computer equipment:

Computer Equipment Checklist

Computer location:

User:

Manufacturer:

Model number:

Serial number:

Date purchased:

CPU type and speed:

Memory:

Hard drive size:

Video type:

Printer type:

Other equipment:

Operating system version:

Application software & version:

Network card type:

Connector (BNC/RJ-45):

- ✔ A printout from Microsoft System Information for each computer. (For more information about Microsoft System Information, refer to Chapter 7.)
- ✔ A detailed list of network resources and drive assignments.
- ✔ Any other information that you think may be useful, such as details about how you must configure a particular application program to work with the network, and copies of every network component's original invoice — in case something breaks and you need to seek warranty service.
- ✔ Backup schedules.
- ✔ Do not put passwords in the binder!

 You may want to keep track of the information in your network binder using a spreadsheet or a database program. However, make sure you keep a printed copy of the information on hand.

Managing the Network

The most obvious duty of the network manager is to manage the network itself. The network's hardware — the cables, network adapter cards, hubs, and so on — needs oversight, as does the network operating system. On a big network, these responsibilities can become a full-time job. Large networks tend to be volatile: Users come and go, equipment fails, cables break, and life in general seems to be one crisis after another.

Smaller networks are much more stable. After you get your network up and running, you probably won't have to spend much time managing its hardware and software. An occasional problem may pop up, but with only a few computers on the network, problems should be few and far between.

Regardless of the network's size, all network administrators must attend to several common chores:

- ✔ The network manager should be involved in every decision to purchase new computers, printers, or other equipment. In particular, the network manager should be prepared to lobby for the most network-friendly equipment possible, such as new computers that already have network cards installed and configured and printers that are network-ready.
- ✔ The network manager must put on the pocket protector whenever a new computer is added to the network. The network manager's job includes considering what changes to make to the cabling configuration, what computer name and user ID to assign to the new user, what security rights to grant the user, and so on.

✔ Every once in a while, your trusty network vendor releases a new version of your network operating system. The network manager's job is to read about the new version and decide whether its new features are beneficial enough to warrant an upgrade. In most cases, the hardest part of upgrading to a new version of your network operating system is determining the *migration path* — that is, how to upgrade your entire network to the new version while disrupting the network or its users as little as possible. Upgrading to a new network operating system version is a bit of a chore, so you need to carefully consider the advantages that the new version can bring.

✔ One of the easiest traps that you can get sucked into is the quest for network speed. The network is never fast enough, and users always blame the hapless network manager. So the manager spends hours and hours tuning and tweaking the network to squeeze out that last 2 percent of performance. You don't want to get caught in this trap, but in case you do, Chapter 14 can help. It clues you in to the basics of tuning your network for best performance.

Doing the Routine Stuff That You Hate to Do

Much of the network manager's job is routine stuff — the equivalent of vacuuming, dusting, and mopping. Yes, it's boring, but it has to be done.

✔ The network manager needs to make sure that the network is properly backed up. If something goes wrong and the network isn't backed up, guess who gets the blame? On the other hand, if disaster strikes, yet you're able to recover everything from yesterday's backup with only a small amount of work lost, guess who gets the pat on the back, the fat bonus, and the vacation in the Bahamas? Chapter 15 describes the options for network backups. You'd better read it soon.

✔ Chapter 15 also describes another routine network chore — checking for computer viruses. If you don't know what a virus is, read Chapter 15 to find out.

✔ Users think that the network server is like the attic: They want to throw files up there and leave them there forever. The network manager gets the fun job of cleaning up the attic once in a while. Oh, joy. The best advice I can offer is to constantly complain about how messy it is up there and warn your users that spring-cleaning is coming up.

Managing Network Users

Managing network technology is the easiest part of network management. Computer technology can be confusing at first, but computers are not nearly as confusing as people. The real challenge of managing a network is managing the network's users.

The difference between managing technology and managing users is obvious: You can figure out computers, but you can never really figure out people. The people who use the network are much less predictable than the network itself. Here are some tips for dealing with users:

- Training is a key part of the network manager's job. Make sure that everyone who uses the network understands it and knows how to use it. If the network users don't understand the network, they may do all kinds of weird things to it without meaning to.

- Never treat your network users like they are idiots. If they don't understand the network, it's not their fault. Explain it to them. Offer a class. Buy them each a copy of this book and tell them to read the first six chapters. Hold their hands. But don't treat them like idiots.

- Make up a network cheat sheet that contains everything that the users need to know about using the network on one page. Make sure that everyone gets a copy.

- Be as responsive as possible when a network user complains of a network problem. If you don't fix the problem soon, the user may try to fix it. You probably don't want that.

Patching Things Up

One of the annoyances that every network manager faces is applying software patches to keep your operating system and other software up-to-date. A software *patch* is a minor update that fixes small glitches that crop up from time to time, such as minor security or performance issues. These glitches are not significant enough to merit a new version of the software, but they are important enough that they need to be fixed.

For all versions of Windows, you can use the Windows Update Web site to apply patches to keep your operating system and other Microsoft software up-to-date. You can access Windows Update by choosing Windows Update from the Start menu. Windows Update automatically scans your computer's software and creates a list of software patches and other components that you can download and install. You can also configure Windows Update to automatically notify you of updates so that you don't have to remember to check for new patches.

Novell periodically posts patches and updates to NetWare on its product support Web site (support.novell.com). You can subscribe to an e-mail notification service that automatically sends you e-mail to let you know of new patches and updates.

Getting the Tools of a Network Manager

Network managers need certain tools to get their jobs done. Managers of big, complicated, and expensive networks need big, complicated, and expensive tools. Managers of small networks need small tools.

Some of the tools that the manager needs are hardware tools like screwdrivers, cable crimpers, and hammers. But the tools that I'm talking about here are software tools.

- Many of the software tools that you need to manage a network come with the network itself. As the network manager, you should read through the manuals that come with your network software to see what management tools are available. For example, Windows includes a `net diag` command that you can use to make sure that all the computers on a network can communicate with one another. (You can run `net diag` from an MS-DOS prompt.) For TCP/IP networks, you can run the `winipcfg` command from an MS-DOS prompt to verify a computer's TCP/IP configuration.

- The Microsoft System Information program that comes with Windows is a useful utility for network managers.

- I suggest that you get one of those 100-in-1 utility programs, such as Symantec's Norton Utilities. Norton Utilities includes invaluable utilities for repairing damaged disk drives, rearranging the directory structure of your disk, gathering information about your computer and its equipment, and so on.

Never use a disk repair program that was not designed to work with the operating system version that your computer uses. Any time that you upgrade to a newer version of your operating system, you should also upgrade your disk repair programs to a version that supports the new operating system version.

- More software tools exist for NetWare and Windows NT/2000 networks than for peer-to-peer networks — not only because NetWare and Windows NT are more popular than peer-to-peer networks, but also because NetWare and Windows NT networks tend to be larger and more in need of software management tools than peer-to-peer networks.

Chapter 13

Who Are You? (Or, Big Brother's Guide to Network Security)

· ·

· ·

*B*efore you had a network, computer security was easy. You just locked your door when you left work for the day. You could rest easy, secure in the knowledge that the bad guys would have to break down the door to get to your computer.

The network changes all of that. Now, anyone with access to any computer on the network can break into the network and steal *your* files. Not only do you have to lock your door, but you also have to make sure that everyone else locks their doors, too.

Fortunately, just about every network operating system known to humankind has built-in provisions for network security. This situation makes it difficult for someone to steal your files even if they do break down the door. All modern network operating systems have security features that are more than adequate for all but the most paranoid users.

And when I say *more* than adequate, I mean it. Most networks have security features that would make even Maxwell Smart happy. Using all these security features is kind of like Smart insisting that the Chief lower the "Cone of Silence." The Cone of Silence worked so well that Max and the Chief couldn't hear each other! Don't make your system so secure that even the good guys can't get their work done.

If any of the computers on your network are connected to the Internet, then you have a whole new world of security issues to contend with. For more information about Internet security, refer to Chapter 18.

Do You Need Security?

Most small networks are in small businesses or departments where everyone knows and trusts everyone else. They don't lock up their desks when they take a coffee break, and although everyone knows where the petty cash box is, money never disappears.

Network security isn't necessary in an idyllic setting like this one, is it? You bet it is. Here's why any network should be set up with at least some minimal concern for security:

✔ Even in the friendliest office environment, some information is and should be confidential. If this information is stored on the network, you want to store it in a directory that's only available to authorized users.

✔ Not all security breaches are malicious. A network user may be routinely scanning through his or her files and discover a filename that isn't familiar. The user may then call up the file, only to discover that it contains confidential personnel information, juicy office gossip, or your resume. Curiosity, rather than malice, is often the source of security breaches.

✔ Sure, everyone at the office is trustworthy now. But what if someone becomes disgruntled, a screw pops loose, and he or she decides to trash the network files before jumping out the window? Or what if that same person decides to print a few $1,000 checks before packing off to Tahiti?

✔ Sometimes the mere opportunity for fraud or theft can be too much for some people to resist. Give people free access to the payroll files, and they may decide to vote themselves a raise when no one is looking.

✔ Finally, remember that not everyone on the network knows enough about how Windows and the network work to be trusted with full access to your network disks. One careless mouse click can wipe out an entire directory of network files. One of the best reasons for activating your network's security features is to protect the network from mistakes made by users who don't know what they're doing.

User Accounts

The first level of network security is the use of *user accounts* to allow only authorized users access to the network. Without an account, a computer user can't log in and therefore can't use the network.

Every user account is associated with a *user ID,* which the user must enter when logging in to the network. Each account also has other network information associated with it, such as the user's password, the user's full name, user rights that tell the network what the user can and cannot do on the network, and file system rights that determine which drives, folders, and files the user can access.

Besides simply identifying network users, user accounts provide additional controls as well:

- ✔ Both NetWare and Windows NT/2000 Server enable you to specify that certain users can log in only during certain times of the day. This feature enables you to restrict your users to normal working hours, so that they can't sneak in at 2 a.m. to do unauthorized work. The feature also discourages your users from working overtime because they can't access the network after hours, so use it judiciously.

- ✔ Both NetWare and Windows NT/2000 Server enable you to create *group accounts* that you can use to set up several accounts with identical access rights. When you use a group account, each user still has an individual account with a user ID and password. In addition, the user accounts indicate which group or groups the user belongs to. All user accounts that belong to a particular group "inherit" the group account's access rights.

- ✔ Group accounts are the key to managing your user accounts. Set up group accounts for each different type of network user that your network has. For example, you may create one type of group account for the accounting department and another for the sales department. Then you can easily configure the group accounts so that the accounting users can't mess with the sales users' files and vice versa.

- ✔ A user can belong to more than one group, in which case the user inherits the rights of each group. For example, suppose you have groups set up for Accounting, Sales, Marketing, and Finance. A user who needs to access both Accounting and Finance information can be made a member of both the Accounting and Finance groups. And a user who needs access to both Sales and Marketing information can be made a member of both the Sales and Marketing groups.

✔ Only real server operating systems such as NetWare and Windows NT/2000 Server have actual user accounts that prevent users who do not have accounts from accessing the network. Peer-to-peer networks that use Windows 95/98 or Millennium Edition for their servers do not use user accounts. Instead, they merely allow you to password-protect shared resources, such as hard drives and printers. Any user who knows the correct password can access a shared resource. That is why you should always use NetWare, Windows NT/2000, or a similar server operating system (such as Unix or Linux) if security is a concern.

Passwords

One of the most important aspects of network security is the use of passwords. User IDs are not usually considered secret. In fact, network users often need to know one another's user IDs. For example, if you use your network for e-mail, you have to know your colleagues' user IDs in order to address your e-mail properly.

Passwords, on the other hand, are top secret. Your network password is the one thing that keeps an impostor from logging on to the network using your user ID and therefore receiving the same access rights that you ordinarily have. *Guard your password with your life.*

Here are some tips for creating good passwords:

✔ Don't use obvious passwords, such as your last name, your kid's name, or your dog's name. Don't pick passwords based on your hobbies, either. A friend of mine is into boating, and his password is the name of his boat. Anyone who knows him can guess his password after a few tries. Five lashes for naming your password after your boat.

✔ Store your password in your head, not on paper. Especially bad: Writing your password down on a stick-on note and sticking it on your computer's monitor. Ten lashes for that. (If you must write your password down, write it on digestible paper that you can swallow after you've memorized the password.)

✔ Most network operating systems enable you to set an expiration time for passwords. For example, you can specify that passwords expire after 30 days. When a user's password expires, the user must change it. Your users may consider this process a hassle, but it helps limit the risk of someone swiping a password and then trying to break into your computer system later.

✔ You can also configure user accounts so that when they change passwords, they cannot specify a password that they've used recently. For example, you can specify that the new password cannot be identical to any of the user's past three passwords.

✔ Some network managers opt against passwords altogether because they feel that security is not an issue on their network. Or short of that, they choose obvious passwords, assign every user the same password, or print the passwords on giant posters and hang them throughout the building. In my opinion, ignoring basic password security is rarely a good idea, even in small networks. You should consider not using passwords only if your network is very small (say, two or three computers), if you do not keep sensitive data on a file server, or if the main reason for the network is to share access to a printer rather than sharing files. (Even if you don't use passwords, imposing basic security precautions like limiting certain users' access to certain network directories is still possible. Just remember that if passwords aren't used, nothing prevents a user from signing on using someone else's user ID.)

Generating Passwords For Dummies

How do you come up with passwords that no one can guess but that you can remember? Most security experts say that the best passwords don't correspond to any words in the English language but consist of a random sequence of letters, numbers, and special characters. But how in the heck are you supposed to memorize a password like `DKS4%DJ2`? Especially when you have to change it three weeks later to something like `3PQ&X(D8`.

Here's a compromise solution that enables you to create passwords that consist of two four-letter words back to back. Take your favorite book (if it's this one, you need to get a life) and turn to any page at random. Find the first four-letter word on the page. Suppose that word is `When`. Then repeat the process to find another four-letter word; say you pick the word `Most` the second time. Now combine the words to make your password: `WhenMost`. I think you agree that `WhenMost` is easier to remember than `3PQ&X(D8` and is probably just about as hard to guess. I probably wouldn't want the folks at the Los Alamos Nuclear Laboratory using this scheme, but it's good enough for most of us.

Here are some additional thoughts on concocting passwords from your favorite book:

✔ If the words end up being the same, pick another word. And pick different words if the combination seems too commonplace, such as `WestWind` or `FootBall`.

✔ For an interesting variation, pick one four-letter word and one three-letter word and randomly pick one of the keyboard's special characters (like *, &, or >) to separate the words. You end up with passwords like `Into#Cat`, `Ball$And`, or `Tree>Dip`.

- ✔ If you want to use longer passwords, just use longer words. For example, if your passwords can be ten characters long, use a five-letter word, a four-letter word, and a separator, as in `Right)Door`, `Horse!Gone`, or `Crime^Mark`. Or, combine three four-letter words, such as `WordGoodHard` or `WithThatYour`.

- ✔ To further confuse your friends and enemies, use medieval passwords by picking words from Chaucer's *Canterbury Tales*. Chaucer is a great source for passwords because he lived before the days of word processors with spell-checkers. He wrote *seyd* instead of *said, gret* instead of *great, welk* instead of *walked, litel* instead of *little*. And he used lots of seven-letter and eight-letter words suitable for passwords, such as *glotenye* (gluttony), *benygne* (benign), and *opynyoun* (opinion).

- ✔ If you use any of these password schemes and someone breaks into your network, don't blame me. You're the one who's too lazy to memorize `D#SC$H4@`.

User Rights

User accounts and passwords are only the front line of defense in the game of network security. After a user gains access to the network by typing a valid user ID and password, the second line of security defense comes into play — rights.

In the harsh realities of network life, all users are created equal, but some users are more equal than others. The Preamble to the Declaration of Network Independence contains the statement, "We hold these truths to be self-evident, that *some* users are endowed by the network administrator with certain inalienable rights. . . ."

Network rights that we'd like to see

The network rights allowed by most network operating systems are pretty boring. Here are a few rights I wish would be allowed:

- ✔ **Cheat:** Provides a special option that enables you to see what cards the other players are holding when you're playing Hearts.

- ✔ **Complain:** Automatically sends e-mail messages to other users that explain how busy, tired, or upset you are.

- ✔ **Set Pay:** Grants you special access to the payroll system so that you can give yourself a pay raise.

- ✔ **Sue:** In America, everyone has the right to sue. So this right should be automatically granted to all users.

The specific rights that you can assign to network users depend on which network operating system you use. Here is a partial list of the user rights that are possible with Windows NT/2000 Server:

- ✔ **Log on locally:** The user can log on to the server computer directly from the server's keyboard.

- ✔ **Change system time:** The user can change the time and date registered by the server.

- ✔ **Shut down the system:** The user can perform an orderly shutdown of the server.

- ✔ **Back up files and directories:** The user can perform a backup of files and directories on the server.

- ✔ **Restore files and directories:** The user can restore backed-up files.

- ✔ **Take ownership of files and other objects:** The user can take over files and other network resources that belong to other users.

NetWare has a similar set of user rights.

File System Rights (Who Gets What)

User rights control what a user can do on a network-wide basis. File system rights enable you to fine-tune your network security by controlling specific file operations for specific users. For example, you can set up file system rights to allow users into the accounting department to access files in the server's \ACCTG directory. File system rights can also enable some users to read certain files but not modify or delete them.

Each network operating system manages file system rights in a different way. Whatever the details, the effect is that you can give permission to each user to access certain files, folders, or drives in certain ways.

Any file system rights that you specify for a folder apply automatically to any of that folder's subfolders, unless you explicitly specify a different set of rights for the subfolder.

In Novell's NetWare, file system rights are referred to as *trustee rights*. NetWare has eight different trustee rights, listed in Table 13-1. For every file or directory on a server, you can assign any combination of these eight rights to any individual user or group.

Table 13-1		NetWare Trustee Rights
Trustee Right	*Abbreviation*	*What the User Can Do*
Read	R	The user can open and read the file.
Write	W	The user can open and write to the file.
Create	C	The user can create new files or directories.
Modify	M	The user can change the name or other properties of the file or directory.
File Scan	F	The user can list the contents of the directory.
Erase	E	The user can delete the file or directory.
Access Control	A	The user can set the permissions for the file or directory.
Supervisor	S	The user has all rights to the file.

Windows NT/2000 Server refers to file system rights as *permissions*. Windows NT/2000 Server has six basic permissions, listed in Table 13-2. As with NetWare trustee rights, you can assign any combination of Windows NT/2000 Server permissions to a user or group for a given file or folder.

Table 13-2		Windows NT/2000 Server Basic Permissions
Permission	*Abbreviation*	*What the User Can Do*
Read	R	The user can open and read the file.
Write	W	The user can open and write to the file.
Execute	X	The user can run the file.
Delete	D	The user can delete the file.
Change	P	The user can change the permissions for the file.
Take Ownership	O	The user can take ownership of the file.

Note the last permission listed in Table 13-2: Take Ownership. In Windows NT/2000 Server, the concept of file or folder ownership is important. Every file or folder on a Windows NT/2000 Server system has an owner. The *owner* is usually the user who creates the file or folder. However, ownership can be transferred from one user to another. So why the *Take Ownership* permission? This permission prevents someone from creating a bogus file and giving ownership of it to you without your permission. Windows NT/2000 Server does not allow you to give ownership of a file to another user. Instead, you can give another user the right to take ownership of the file. That user must then explicitly take ownership of the file.

You can use Windows NT/2000 Server permissions only for files or folders that are created on drives formatted as NTFS volumes. If you insist on using FAT or FAT32 for your Windows NT/2000 Server shared drives, you can't protect individual files or folders on the drives. This is one of the main reasons for using NTFS for your Windows NT/2000 Server drives.

It's Good to Be the Administrator

It stands to reason that at least one network user must have the authority to use the network without any of the restrictions imposed on other users. This user is called the *administrator*. The administrator is responsible for setting up the network's security system. To do that, the administrator must be exempt from all security restrictions.

Many networks automatically create an administrator user account when you install the network software. The user ID and password for this initial administrator are published in the network's documentation and are the same for all networks that use the same network operating system. One of the first things that you must do after getting your network up and running is to change the password for this standard administrator account. Otherwise, all your elaborate security precautions are a farce; anyone who knows the default administrator user ID and password can access your system with full administrator rights and privileges, bypassing the security restrictions that you so carefully set up.

✔ Most network administrators use a boring user ID for the supervisor account, such as `Admin`, `Manager`, or `Super`. Some network administrators like to pretend that they're creative by using a clever user ID for the supervisor account. Here are some suitable user IDs for your supervisor account:

Matrix	Yoda
Chosen1	QuiGon
Aladdin	Picard
Genie	Data

Titan	Borg
Zeus	Barney
Skipper	HAL
Gilligan	M5

✔ ***Don't forget the password for the supervisor account!*** If a network user forgets his or her password, you can log in as the supervisor and change that user's password. But if you forget the supervisor's password, you're stuck.

User Profiles

User profiles are a Windows feature that keeps track of an individual user's preferences for his or her Windows configuration. For a non-networked computer, profiles enable two or more users to use the same computer, each with his or her own desktop settings, such as wallpaper, colors, Start menu options, and so on.

The real benefit of user profiles becomes apparent when profiles are used on a network. A user's profile can be stored on a server computer and accessed whenever that user logs on to the network from any Windows computer on the network.

The following are some of the elements of Windows that are governed by settings in the user profile:

✔ Desktop settings from the Display Properties dialog box, including wallpaper, screen savers, and color schemes.

✔ Start menu programs and Windows toolbar options.

✔ Favorites, which provide easy access to the files and folders that the user accesses frequently.

✔ Network settings, including drive mappings, network printers, and recently visited network locations.

✔ Application settings, such as option settings for Microsoft Word.

✔ The My Documents folder.

Too Many Lists! (How to Manage Multiple Servers)

One of the problems that you encounter as your network grows is managing the user accounts and other directory information for multiple servers. In the early days of networking, each server kept its own directory of user accounts, access rights, computer names, and so on. That situation meant that if you set up five servers, you had to keep five separate directories up to date. Every time you added a new user to the system, you had to create five different user accounts — one for each server. What a bother.

NetWare 4.2 and 5.0 use NetWare Directory Services to avoid this problem. *NDS* is a single database of all network directory information. NDS enables you to create a single-user account for every user on the network — no matter how many servers are on the network, and no matter how many servers that user needs to access.

Windows NT Server uses a somewhat more complicated approach. NT enables you to create a *domain,* which is a group of network servers and client computers that fall under the umbrella of a single directory. Smaller networks consist of a single domain, but larger networks can be split into two or more domains to simplify the task of administration. That feature is why the login dialog box for a Windows NT network requires that you enter a domain name to access the network.

A company with offices in separate locations is likely to create a separate domain for each location. For example, the San Francisco and Los Angeles offices may have separate domains. Or different departments may have separate domains: The accounting and marketing departments may have their own domains.

Domains can be connected by *trust relationships.* For example, the marketing department domain can be set up so that it trusts the accounting department domain. That means that the marketing domain recognizes users in the accounting department domain.

As you can imagine, managing domains and trust relationships for a large network is the stuff of pocket protectors and propeller caps. If your network is large enough to require more than one domain, you need more help than this gentle introduction to network security can offer. I suggest that you consult *Windows NT Networking For Dummies,* by Ed Tittel, Mary Madden, and Earl Follis (IDG Books Worldwide, Inc.).

Every domain must have one server designated as the *Primary Domain Controller* (also known as the *PDC*) , which is responsible for managing the directory information for the domain. Large networks with several servers can also have one or more *Backup Domain Controllers,* which reduce the workload of the Primary Domain Controller and can take over in case the PDC server fails.

Windows 2000 partially alleviates the pain of managing large multi-domain networks with its new Active Directory. *Active Directory* is like the Novell NDS in that it provides a single directory database to cover the entire network, no matter how many different servers or users you have and regardless of whether your network is contained within a single room or spread across the entire planet.

Chapter 14

If I Could Save Time in a Bottleneck: Optimizing Your Network's Performance

In This Chapter

▶ Understanding network bottlenecks

▶ Tuning your network

▶ Tuning your server

▶ Making your network server faster

▶ Making your network clients faster

*T*he adage that there's no such thing as a free lunch really is true. When you network your computers, you reap the benefits of being able to share information and resources such as disk drives and printers. But you also have many costs. You have the cost of purchasing network cards, cable, and software, plus the cost of the time required to install the network, find out how to use it, and keep it running.

Another cost of networking exists that you may not have considered yet: the performance cost. No matter how hard you try, you can't hide the ugly truth that putting a computer on a network slows down the computer. Retrieving a word processing document from a network disk takes a bit longer than retrieving the same document from your local disk drive. Sorting that big database file takes a bit longer. And printing a 300-page report also takes a bit longer.

Notice that I use the word *bit* three times in the preceding paragraph. Lest my editor chide me for Overuse of a Three-Letter Word (OTLW), I better point out that I use the word three times to make a point. The network inevitably slows things down, but only a bit. If your network has slowed things down to a snail's pace — so that your users are routinely taking coffee breaks whenever they save a file — you have a performance problem that you can probably solve.

What Exactly Is a Bottleneck?

The term *bottleneck* does not in any way refer to the physique of your typical computer geek. (Well, I guess it *could*, in some cases.) Rather, computer geeks coined the phrase when they discovered that the tapered shape of a bottle of Jolt Cola limited the rate at which they could consume the beverage. "Hey," a computer geek said one day, "the narrowness of this bottleneck limits the rate at which I can consume the tasty caffeine-laden beverage contained within. This draws to mind an obvious analogy to the limiting effect that a single slow component of a computer system can have upon the performance of the system as a whole."

"Fascinating," replied all the other computer geeks who were fortunate enough to be present at that historic moment.

The phrase stuck and is used to this day to draw attention to the simple fact that a computer system is only as fast as its slowest component. It's the computer equivalent of the old truism that a chain is only as strong as its weakest link.

For a simple demonstration of this concept, consider what happens when you print a word processing document on a slow printer. Your word processing program reads the data from disk and sends it to the printer. Then you sit and wait while the printer prints the document.

Would buying a faster CPU or adding more memory make the document print faster? No. The CPU is already much faster than the printer, and your computer already has more than enough memory to print the document. The printer itself is the bottleneck, so the only way to print the document faster is to replace the slow printer with a faster one.

Here are some other random thoughts about bottlenecks:

- ✔ **A computer system always has a bottleneck.** For example, suppose you've decided that the bottleneck on your file server is a slow IDE disk drive, so you replace it with the fastest SCSI drive money can buy. Now, the disk drive is no longer the bottleneck: The drive can process information faster than the controller card the disk is connected to. That doesn't mean you have eliminated the bottleneck; it just means that the disk controller is now the bottleneck instead of the disk drive. No matter what you do, the computer will always have some component that limits the overall performance of the system.

✔ **One way to limit the effect of a bottleneck is to avoid waiting for the bottleneck.** For example, print spooling lets you avoid waiting for a slow printer. Spooling doesn't speed up the printer, but it does free you up to do other work while the printer chugs along. Similarly, disk caching lets you avoid waiting for a slow hard drive.

✔ **One of the reasons computer geeks are switching from Jolt Cola to Snapple is that Snapple bottles have wider necks.**

The Eight Most Common Network Bottlenecks

Here are the eight most common network bottlenecks, in no particular order:

✔ **The CPU in the file server:** If the file server is used extensively, it should have a powerful CPU — Pentium III is best. If you use NetWare or Windows NT Server, look into getting a server computer that can house two or more processors for even better performance. This is especially true for servers that do more than simply serve up files, such as databases or Web servers.

✔ **The amount and type of memory in the file server:** You can never have too much memory in the server. With the cost of memory so cheap these days, why not upgrade to 256MB or even 1GB? Also, make sure that you get the fastest type of RAM your computer's motherboard will support. Don't try to save a few dollars by using cheap, slow RAM.

✔ **The file server computer's bus:** Oops . . . this is kind of technical, so I put the details in a sidebar that you can skip. The nontechnical version is this: Make sure that your server computer has plenty of PCI slots and use only PCI network cards and disk controllers.

✔ **The network card:** Use 32-bit PCI network cards for the best network performance. Remember that the server computer uses the network a lot more than any of the clients.

✔ **The file server's disk drives:** Get the fastest drives that you can find. And, if possible, use SCSI drives. Sorry! I went technical on you again. Time for another sidebar.

✔ **The file server's disk controller card:** All disks must connect to the computer via a controller card, and sometimes the bottleneck isn't the disk itself but the controller card. A beefed-up controller card can do wonders for performance. PCI cards are best.

✔ **The server's configuration options:** All network operating systems have options that you can configure. Some of these options can make the difference between a pokey network and a zippy network. Unfortunately, no hard-and-fast rules exist for setting these options. Otherwise, you wouldn't have options.

✔ **The network itself:** If you have too many users, the network can become bogged down. Many ways exist to improve the performance of the network itself. One is to upgrade from 10Mbps to 100Mbps. Another is to use fast 100Mbps switches instead of ordinary hubs. Still another is to segment the network into two or more smaller networks with a cool little device called a *bridge*.

The hardest part about improving the performance of a network is determining what the bottlenecks are. With sophisticated test equipment and years of experience, network gurus can make pretty good educated guesses. Without the equipment and experience, you can still make pretty good uneducated guesses. I give you some pointers on how to discover your computer's bottlenecks and improve your computer's performance in the remaining sections in this chapter.

Warning! Reading this may be hazardous to your sanity

Every computer has a *bus,* which is basically a row of slots into which you can plug expansion cards, such as disk controllers, modems, video controllers, and network adapter cards. New computers today come with two types of buses:

✔ **ISA:** ISA stands for Industry Standard Architecture. ISA bus is the most common type of expansion bus. It was designed many years ago when IBM introduced its first computers based on the 80286 processor. The ISA bus sends data between the CPU and the expansion cards at 8 or 16 bits at a time, depending on whether you use it with 8- or 16-bit adapter cards. The ISA bus runs at 8MHz.

✔ **PCI:** Modern computers include a high-speed bus called a PCI bus, which overcomes the speed limitation inherent in the

ISA bus design. Most new computers have several PCI slots and just one or two ISA slots. Some new computers have PCI slots exclusively, without even one ISA slot.

The original PCI slots, which came out with the first batch of Pentium computers, have PCI buses that work in 32-bit mode and operate at up to 33MHz. Newer computers have faster 64-bit PCI slots operating at up to 100MHz.

If your network server uses disk drives or networking cards that are connected to the ISA bus, don't bother with any other efforts to improve network performance until you upgrade your server to use faster PCI disk controllers and network cards.

Just say no to technical stuff about drive interfaces

Disk drives come in several varieties, and not all of them are made equal. Here are the two basic types of drives used today:

✔ **IDE:** IDE, which stands for Integrated Drive Electronics (as if that matters), is the most common drive type used today. Don't embarrass yourself by trying to pronounce this term in any way other than spelling out the letters. The newest form of IDE, which allows larger drives and faster performance, is called by various names, including EIDE, ATA, ATA-2, Fast ATA, Ultra IDE, DMA, and probably others.

✔ **SCSI:** SCSI stands for Small Computer System Interface but is pronounced *Scuzzy*. SCSI drives have several advantages over IDE drives but are also a bit more expensive.

SCSI also wins the prize for Best Computer Acronym, hands down. Two newer, faster forms of SCSI are now available. Fast SCSI is twice as fast as basic SCSI, and fast-wide SCSI is twice as fast as fast SCSI, making it four times as fast as basic SCSI.

Performance zealots assure us that SCSI's network performance and reliability are vastly superior to IDE's. Unfortunately, SCSI drives are also more expensive than IDE, which is why IDE remains so popular. In computers, as in everything else, you get what you pay for. If you want top-notch file server performance, use only SCSI drives. And whether you use IDE or SCSI drives, make sure that you use PCI controller cards rather than older ISA controller cards.

Tuning Your Network the Compulsive Way

You have two ways to tune your network. The first is to think about it a bit, take a guess at what may improve performance, try it, and see whether the network seems to run faster. This approach is the way most people go about tuning the network.

Then you have the compulsive way, which is suitable for people who organize their sock drawers by color and their food cupboards alphabetically by food groups — or worse, alphabetically within food groups. The compulsive approach to tuning a network goes something like this:

1. **Establish a method for objectively testing the performance of some aspect of the network.**

   This method is called a *benchmark*. For example, if you want to improve the performance of network printing, use a stopwatch to time how long printing a fairly large document takes.

2. Change one variable of your network configuration and rerun the test.

For example, if you think that increasing the size of the disk cache can improve performance, change the cache size, restart the server, and run the benchmark test. Note whether the performance improves, stays the same, or becomes worse.

3. Repeat Step 2 for each variable you want to test.

Here are some salient points to keep in mind if you decide to tune your network the compulsive way:

✔ If possible, test each variable separately — in other words, reverse the changes you've made to other network variables before proceeding.

✔ Write down the results of each test so that you have an accurate record of the impact that each change has on your network's performance.

✔ Be sure to change only one aspect of the network each time you run the benchmark. If you make several changes, you won't know which one caused the change. Or one change may improve performance, but the other change may worsen performance so that the changes cancel each other out — kind of like offsetting penalties in a football game.

✔ If possible, make sure that no one else uses the network when you conduct the test; otherwise, the unpredictable activities of other network users can spoil the test.

✔ To establish your baseline performance, run your benchmark test two or three times to make sure that the results are repeatable. If the print job takes one minute the first time, three minutes the second time, and 22 seconds the third time, something is wrong with the test. A variation of just a few seconds is acceptable, though.

Tuning a Windows 95/98 or Millennium Edition Server

When you use Windows 95/98 or Me as a server, you have several options available that you can fiddle around with to improve the performance. Taking the time to set these options is worthwhile, because all network users notice the effect of a more efficient server computer.

Setting the File System performance option

Windows has a handy tuning feature that enables you to configure server options with a single click of the mouse. Here's how to tune a Windows server computer:

1. **Choose Start⇨Settings⇨Control Panel and then double-click the System icon.**

   The System Properties dialog box appears.

2. **Click the Performance tab.**

   The performance settings for your computer appear, as shown in Figure 14-1.

Figure 14-1:
Performance
options for a
Windows
server.

3. **Click the File System button.**

   The File System Properties dialog box, shown in Figure 14-2, appears.

4. **Set the drop-down list box, which is labeled Typical Role of This Computer, to Network Server.**

   Your computer is now tuned as a network server.

Figure 14-2:
Tuning the
file system
of a
Windows
server.

5. **Click OK to dismiss the File System Properties dialog box.**

   You return to the System Properties dialog box.

6. **Click OK to dismiss the System Properties dialog box.**

That's all there is to it.

Using the FAT32 file system

FAT32, which was first introduced with Windows 98, is an improved method of storing data on your computer's hard drive. Formatting your disk drive with FAT32 slightly increases the amount of data you can store on the disk. Plus, it enables your computer to retrieve data from the disk faster, resulting in improved network performance.

The hard drives on most newer computers are already formatted with FAT32. To find out if yours is, double-click the My Computer icon on your desktop. Then, right-click the icon for the C drive and choose Properties from the menu that appears. That summons the Properties dialog box for the drive, as shown in Figure 14-3. The File System line, right below the disk drive's label, tells you whether the drive is formatted with FAT32.

If your hard drive is not already formatted with FAT32, you can convert the drive to FAT32 by choosing Start⇨Programs⇨Accessories⇨System Tools⇨ FAT32 Converter. The conversion takes a long time — perhaps an hour or more. You can't use your computer during the conversion, so just before lunch may be a good time to start.

Figure 14-3:
The hard
drive
Properties
indicates
whether the
drive is
formatted
with FAT32.

Unfortunately, FAT32 imposes some limitations on you:

✔ If you convert a drive to FAT32, you can't use Microsoft's disk compression program DriveSpace to compress the data on the drive.

✔ After you convert a drive to FAT32, you have no easy way to convert it back to the old format.

✔ If you set up your computer using a feature called *dual boot,* which enables you to choose between two operating systems when you start your computer, the dual boot feature is disabled by FAT32. So you should not use FAT32 if you also need to use another operating system on the same computer.

In spite of these limitations, I recommend that you always use FAT32 for Windows 9*x* computers.

Tuning up Windows 9x

To help you tweak the performance of your Windows 9*x* computers, Windows 98 and Windows Me include a performance-tuning feature called Windows Tune-Up. Windows Tune-Up enables you to run several programs that optimize the performance of Windows, including ScanDisk (which corrects errors on your disk drive); Disk Defragmenter (which juggles your disk data so that it's arranged efficiently on the disk); and a new program called Disk Cleanup (which removes unnecessary files from your computer).

The best thing about Windows Tune-Up is that it enables you to set up a schedule so that the tune-up programs run automatically on a periodic basis. For example, you can use Windows Tune-Up to specify that Disk Defragmenter and ScanDisk run every night at midnight and that Disk Cleanup runs every Friday at noon. This feature can help ensure that you always maintain your Windows 9*x* server computer at peak efficiency.

You can find Windows Tune-Up buried in the Start menu, under Programs⇨ Accessories⇨System Tools.

Tuning a Windows NT/2000 Server

Tuning a Windows NT/2000 Server computer is more difficult than tuning a Windows 9*x* computer. A Windows NT/2000 Server includes dozens of options that can affect server performance. You can spend hours tweaking these options to squeeze optimum performance out of NT/2000. Plus, NT/2000 supports advanced hardware features such as multiple processors and RAID disk arrays, which can boost network performance.

The good news is that NT/2000 tends to be somewhat self-tuning. After NT/2000 runs for a few days, it soon adjusts itself to the pattern of usage it sees on your network and is purring like a kitten. You only need to trouble yourself with tuning Windows NT/2000 if something appears drastically wrong with the network's performance — for instance, if users complain that opening a two-page document on the network server takes ten minutes or that the print job they sent to the printer last Tuesday still hasn't printed.

To help monitor performance so that you can determine exactly where a performance problem lies, NT/2000 comes with a program called Performance Monitor. Performance Monitor gathers statistics about all kinds of activities on your server computer, such as disk I/O, program execution, network traffic, and so on. By analyzing these statistics, you can determine the source of a network performance problem. Depending on the problem, adjusting one of NT/2000's configuration settings may solve it, or you may need to purchase additional hardware to correct the problem.

Using Performance Monitor is simple. But interpreting the statistics it gathers isn't. Unless you're really into counting cache hits and average disk seek times, you probably want to steer clear of Performance Monitor if you possibly can.

Tuning a NetWare Server

Like Windows NT/2000 Server, NetWare is also a self-tuning system. Let it run for a few days to adjust to the usage patterns of your network, and it runs just fine. If you have a problem, you can always play with the server settings to try to improve performance.

Many NetWare configuration options are controlled with SET commands that you place in the AUTOEXEC.NCF file or the STARTUP.NCF file. For example, SET enables you to specify the amount of memory to use for file caching, the size of each cache buffer, the size of packet-receive buffers, and a whole bunch of other stuff that's way too low-level and detailed to go into in a proud book such as this one.

Chapter 15

Things That Go Bump in the Night: How to Protect Your Network Data

*I*f you're the hapless network manager, the safety of the data on your network is your responsibility. You get paid to lie awake at night worrying about your data. Will it be there tomorrow? If it's not, will *you* be able to get it back? And — most importantly — if you can't get it back, will *you* be there tomorrow?

This chapter covers the ins and outs of being a good, responsible, trustworthy network manager. They don't give out merit badges for this stuff, but they should.

Planning for Disaster

On April Fool's Day about 15 years ago, my colleagues and I discovered that some kook had broken into the office the night before and pounded our computer equipment to death with a crowbar. (I'm not making this up.)

Sitting on a shelf right next to the mangled piles of what used to be a Wang minicomputer system was an undisturbed disk pack that contained the only complete backup of all the information that was on the destroyed computer. The vandal didn't realize that one more swing of the crowbar would have escalated this major inconvenience into a complete catastrophe. Sure, we were up a creek until we could get the computer replaced. And in those days, you couldn't just walk into your local Computer Depot and buy a new computer off the shelf — this was a Wang minicomputer system that had to be specially ordered. But after we had the new computer, a simple restore from the backup disk brought us right back to where we were on March 31. Without that backup, getting back on track would have taken months.

I've been paranoid about disaster planning ever since. Before then, I thought that disaster planning meant doing good backups. That's a part of it, but I can never forget the day we came within one swing of the crowbar of losing everything. Vandals are probably much smarter now: They know to smash the backup disks as well as the computers themselves. There's more to being prepared for disasters than doing regular backups.

Don't think it can happen to you? Wildfires in New Mexico recently came close to destroying the Los Alamos labs. How many computers do you think were lost to Hurricane Andrew? Not to mention the floods along the Mississippi in 1993 or the San Francisco earthquake in 1989? (I doubt that many computers were lost in the 1906 earthquake.) And I assume you saw *Armageddon*.

Most disasters are of the less spectacular variety. Make at least a rudimentary plan for how you can get your computer network back up and running should a major or minor disaster strike.

Here are a few additional things you can lay awake at night worrying about when it comes to disaster planning:

- ✓ The cornerstone of any disaster/recovery plan is a program of regular backups. I devote much of this chapter to helping you get a backup program started. Keep in mind, though, that your backups are only one swing of the crowbar from being useless. Don't leave your backup disks or tapes sitting on the shelf next to your computer: Store them in a fireproof box or safe and store at least one set at another location.

- ✓ Your network binder is an irreplaceable source of information about your network. You should have more than one copy. I suggest that you take a copy home so that if the entire office burns to the ground, you still have a copy of your network documentation. Then you can decide quickly what equipment you need to purchase, and how you need to configure it to get your network back up and running again.

✔ After your computers are completely destroyed by fire, vandalism, or theft, how can you prove to your insurance adjuster that you really had all that equipment? A frequently overlooked part of planning for disaster is keeping a detailed record of what computer equipment you own. Keep copies of all invoices for computer equipment and software in a safe place. And consider making a videotape or photographic record of your equipment, too.

✔ Another aspect of disaster planning that's often overlooked is expertise. In many businesses, the one person who takes charge of all the computers is the only one who knows anything more than how to start Word and print a letter. What if that person becomes ill, decides to go work for the competition, or wins the lottery and retires to the Bahamas? Don't let any one person at the office form a computer dynasty that only he or she can run. As much as possible, spread the computer expertise around.

Backing Up Your Data

The main goal of backups is simple: Make sure that no matter what happens, you never lose more than one day's work. The stock market may crash, and Ross Perot may run for president again, but you never lose more than one day's work if you stay on top of your backups.

Now that we agree on the purpose of backups, we can get to the good stuff: how to do it.

Why you should buy a tape drive

If you plan on backing up the data on your network server's disk drives, you need something to back up the data to. You could copy the data onto diskettes, but a 20GB disk drive would need about 14,000 diskettes to do a full backup. That's a few more diskettes than most of us want to keep in the closet. Instead of diskettes, you want to back up your network data to tape. With an inexpensive tape drive, you can copy as much as 10GB of data onto a single tape.

The beauty of a tape drive is that you can start your backups and leave. You don't have to baby-sit your computer, feeding it disk after disk and reading a bad novel in between disk swaps. The labor savings can pay for the cost of the tape drive in the first week.

- ✔ The most popular style of tape backup for smallish networks is called *Travan drives*. Travan drives come in a variety of models with tape capacities ranging from 8GB to 20GB. You can purchase a 8GB drive for under $200 and a 20GB unit for about $300. (Travan drives used to be known as QIC drives.)

- ✔ For larger networks, you can get tape backup units that offer higher capacity and faster backup speed than Travan drives, for more money of course. DAT (Digital Audio Tape) units can back up as much as 40GB on a single tape, and DLT (Digital Linear Tape) drives can store up to 80GB on one tape. DAT and DLT drives can cost $1,000 or more, depending on the capacity.

- ✔ If you're really up the backup creek with hundreds of gigabytes to back up, you can get robotic tape backup units that automatically fetch and load tape cartridges from a library, so you can do complete backups without having to load tapes manually. Naturally, these units aren't cheap: The small ones, which have a library of 8 tapes and a total backup capacity of over 300GB, start at about $5,000.

- ✔ An alternative to tape drives for backups is removable disk drives — disk drives housed in cartridges that you can insert or remove like a giant floppy disk. The best known removable disk drives are made by Iomega. Iomega's Jaz Drive sells for about $350 and can back up 2GB of data on each cartridge.

- ✔ Another alternative to tape drives for backups is rewritable CD drives, known as *CD-RW* drives. A CD-RW drive can write about 600MB of data to each CD.

Backup programs

Both Windows 9x and Windows NT/2000 Server come with built-in backup programs. In addition, most tape drives come with backup programs that are often faster or more flexible than the standard Windows backup. And you can purchase sophisticated backup programs that are specially designed for large networks, which have multiple servers with data that must be backed up.

For a simple Windows 9x server in a peer-to-peer network, the built-in backup program that comes with Windows is adequate for backing up the server. Figure 15-1 shows the Windows 98 backup program in action.

Backup programs do more than just copy data from your hard drive to tape. Backup programs use special compression techniques to squeeze your data so that you can cram more data onto fewer tapes. Compression factors of 2:1 are common, so you can usually squeeze 4GB of data onto a tape that would hold only 2GB of data without compression. (Tape drive manufacturers tend to state the capacity of their drives using compressed data, assuming a 2:1 compression ratio. So a 20GB tape has an uncompressed capacity of 10GB.)

Figure 15-1:
Windows
Backup.

Backup programs also help you keep track of which data has been backed up and which hasn't, and they offer options such as incremental or differential backups that can streamline the backup process, as described in the next section.

You don't have to back up every file every day

If you have a tape drive and all your network data can fit on one tape, the best approach to backups is to back up all your data every day. Backing up all of the data on a server is referred to as a *full* backup.

If you have more data than can fit on one tape, consider using *incremental* backups instead. An incremental backup backs up only the files that you've modified since the last time you did a backup. Incremental backups are a lot faster than full backups because you probably only modify a few files each day. And if a full backup takes three tapes, you can probably fit an entire week's worth of incremental backups on a single tape.

Here are some additional tips on using incremental backups:

  ✔ The easiest way to use incremental backups is to do a full backup every Monday and then do an incremental backup on Tuesday, Wednesday, Thursday, and Friday. (This assumes, of course, that you can do a full backup overnight on Monday. If your full backup takes more than 12 hours, you might want to do it on Friday instead so that it can run over the weekend.)

Stop me before I get carried away

The archive bit is not an old Abbott & Costello routine ("All right, I wanna know who modified the archive bit." "What." "Who?" "No, what." "Wait a minute ... just tell me what's the name of the guy who modified the archive bit!" "Right.").

The archive bit is a little flag that's tucked into each file's directory entry, right next to the file name. Any time that a program modifies a file, Windows (or your server operating system) sets the file's archive bit to the ON position. Then after a backup program backs up the file, it sets the file's archive bit to the OFF position.

Because backup programs reset the archive bit after they back up a file, they can use the archive bit to select just the files that have been modified since the last backup. Clever, eh?

Differential backups work because they don't reset the archive bit. When you use differential backups, each differential backup backs up all the files that have been modified since the last full backup.

> ✔ When you use incremental backups, the complete backup consists of the full backup tapes and all the incremental backup tapes you've made since you did the full backup.

> ✔ A variation of the incremental backup idea is the *differential* backup. A differential backup backs up all the files that have been modified since the last time you did a *full* backup. When you use differential backups, the complete backup consists of the full backup disks plus the disks from your most recent differential backup.

Server versus client backups

When you back up network data, you have two basic approaches to running the backup software: You can run the backup software on the file server itself, or you can run the backups from one of the network's clients. If you run the backups from the file server, you'll tie up the server while the backup is running. Your users will complain that their access to the server has slowed to a snail's pace. On the other hand, if you run the backup over the network from a client computer, you'll flood the network with gigabytes of data being backed up. Your users will complain that the entire network has slowed to a snail's pace.

Network performance is one of the main reasons you should try to run your backups during off hours, when other users are not accessing the network. Another reason is so that you can perform a more thorough backup. If you run your backup while other users are accessing files, the backup program will skip over any files that are being accessed by users at the time the backup runs. As a result, your backup won't include those files. Ironically, the files most likely to get left out of the backup are often the files that need backing up the most because they're the files that are being used and probably modified.

Here are some extra thoughts on client and server backups:

- ✔ You may think that backing up directly from the server would be more efficient than backing up from a client because data doesn't have to travel over the network. Actually, this assumption isn't usually the case, because most networks are faster than most tape drives. The network probably won't slow down backups unless you back up during the busiest time of the day, when hordes of network users are storming the network gates.

- ✔ To improve network backup speed and to minimize the effect that network backups have on the rest of the network, consider using a 100Mbps switch rather than a normal hub to connect the servers and the backup client. That way, network traffic between the server and the backup client won't bog down the rest of the network.

- ✔ Setting up a special user ID for the user who does backups is best. This user ID requires access to all the files on the server. If you're worried about security, take special precautions to guard the backup user's user ID and password. Anyone who knows it — and its password — can log in and bypass any security restrictions that you've placed on that user's normal user ID.

   You can counter potential security problems by restricting the backup user ID to a certain client and a certain time of the day. If you're really clever (and paranoid), you can probably set up the backup user's account so that the only program it can run is the backup program.

   Windows NT/2000 Server provides a special user group that you can use to create backup users.

How many sets of backups should you keep?

Don't try to cut costs by purchasing one backup tape and reusing it every day. What happens if you accidentally delete an important file on Tuesday and don't discover your mistake until Thursday? Because the file didn't exist on Wednesday, it won't be on Wednesday's backup tape. If you have only one tape that's reused every day, you're outta luck.

The safest scheme is to use a new backup tape every day and keep all your old tapes in a vault. Pretty soon, though, your tape vault can start looking like the warehouse where they stored the Ark of the Covenant at the end of *Raiders of the Lost Ark.*

As a compromise between these two extremes, most users purchase several tapes and rotate them. That way, you always have several backup tapes to fall back on in case the file you need isn't on the most recent backup tape. This technique is called *tape rotation,* and several variations are in common use:

- ✔ The simplest approach is to purchase three tapes and label them A, B, and C. You use the tapes on a daily basis in sequence: A the first day, B the second day, C the third day, then A the fourth day, B the fifth day, C the sixth day, and so on. On any given day, you have three *generations* of backups: today's, yesterday's, and the day-before-yesterday's. Computer geeks like to call these the *grandfather, father,* and *son* tapes.

- ✔ Another simple approach is to purchase five tapes and use one each day of the week.

- ✔ A variation of this scheme is to buy eight tapes. Take four of them and write *Monday* on one label, *Tuesday* on another, *Wednesday* on the third, and *Thursday* on the fourth label. On the other four tapes, write *Friday 1, Friday 2, Friday 3,* and *Friday 4.* Now, tack a calendar up on the wall near the computer and number all the Fridays in the year: 1, 2, 3, 4, 1, 2, 3, 4, and so on.

  On Monday through Thursday, you use the appropriate daily backup tape. When you do backups on Friday, you consult the calendar to decide which Friday tape to use. With this scheme, you always have four weeks' worth of Friday backup tapes, plus individual backup tapes for the past five days.

- ✔ If bookkeeping data lives on the network, making a backup copy of all your files (or at least all your accounting files) immediately before closing the books each month and retaining those backups for each month of the year is a good idea. Does that mean you should purchase 12 additional tapes? Not necessarily. If you back up just your accounting files, you probably can fit all 12 months on a single tape. Just make sure that you back up with the "append to tape" option rather than the "erase tape" option so that the previous contents of the tape aren't destroyed. And treat this accounting backup as completely separate from your normal daily backup routine.

You should also keep at least one recent full backup at another location. That way, if your office should fall victim to an errant Scud missile or a rogue asteroid, you can re-create your data from the backup copy you stored offsite.

A word about tape reliability

From experience, I've found that although tape drives are very reliable, once in a while they run amok. Problem is, they don't always tell you they're not working. A tape drive — especially the less expensive Travan type drives — can spin along for hours, pretending to back up your data, when in reality, your data isn't being written reliably to the tape. In other words, a tape drive can trick you into thinking that your backups are working just fine, but when disaster strikes and you need your backup tapes, you may just discover that the tapes are worthless.

Don't panic! You have a simple way to assure yourself that your tape drive is working. Just activate the "compare after backup" feature of your backup software. Then, as soon as your backup program finishes backing up your data, it rewinds the tape, reads each backed-up file, and compares it with the original version on disk. If all files compare, you know your backups are trustworthy.

Here are some additional thoughts about the reliability of tapes:

- ✔ The compare function doubles the time required to do a backup, but that doesn't matter if your entire backup fits on one tape. You can just run the backup after hours. Whether the backup and repair operation takes one hour or ten doesn't matter, as long as it's finished by the time you arrive at work the next morning.

- ✔ If your backups require more than one tape, you may not want to run the compare-after-backup option every day. But be sure to run it periodically to check that your tape drive is working.

- ✔ If your backup program reports errors, throw away the tape and use a new tape.

Changing the Oil Every 3,000 Miles

Like cars, disk drives need periodic maintenance. Fortunately, Windows 9*x*, as well as server operating systems such as Windows NT/2000 Server and NetWare, come with programs that can do some of the necessary maintenance for you.

ScanDisk

Bad news: Windows sometimes has trouble keeping track of all the files you heap onto your computer's disk drives. In particular, if your dog steps on your computer's power cord while you're working on a file, Windows may lose track of exactly where the file is located on the disk. The same thing can happen if you simply turn your computer off without first choosing Shut Down from the Start menu and waiting for Windows to tell you it's okay to turn off your computer.

Good news: Windows comes with a program called ScanDisk, which can correct the type of file damage that occurs when your computer is turned off at the wrong moment. In fact, ScanDisk does such a good job of correcting this type of problem that Windows runs it automatically when you turn your computer back on after turning it off without first using the Start⇨Shut Down command.

ScanDisk does more than repair files damaged by premature shutdown. ScanDisk can also check the reliability of your computer's disk drives by trying to write something onto every sector of your disk and then reading it back to see whether it took. (Don't worry — ScanDisk does this without upsetting any of the existing data on your disk.) Figure 15-2 shows the Windows 98 version of ScanDisk.

Figure 15-2:
ScanDisk.

ScanDisk can do a thorough check of your disk's recording surface to make sure that it can reliably read and write data. The check takes a while, but it's worth the wait.

If ScanDisk detects a problem, it displays a message that describes the problem and offers to fix it for you. Read the instructions on the screen and select the "More Info" function if you don't understand what's going on.

Windows NT includes its own version of ScanDisk built into the Disk Administrator program. To activate it, choose Start⇨Programs⇨Administrative Tools⇨Disk Administrator.

Disk defragmenting

Another routine type of service you should perform on your computer periodically is to defragment its disk drives. Defragmenting a drive rearranges all the data that's stored on the drive so that the data can be accessed efficiently. Because normal use causes the data on most drives to become scattered about, or fragmented, defragment your drives on a regular basis.

Windows includes a program that defragments your hard drives, named appropriately Disk Defragmenter. You can find it on the Start menu under Programs⇨Accessories⇨System Tools.

Guarding against Dreaded Computer Viruses

Viruses are one of the most misunderstood computer phenomena around these days. What is a virus? How does it work? How does it spread from computer to computer? I'm glad you asked.

What is a virus?

Make no mistake, viruses are real. Now that most of us are connected to the Internet, viruses have really taken off. Every computer user is susceptible to attacks by computer viruses, and using a network increases your vulnerability because it exposes all network users to the risk of being infected by a virus that lands on any one network user's computer.

Viruses don't just spontaneously appear out of nowhere. Viruses are computer programs that are created by malicious programmers who've lost a few screws and should be locked up.

What makes a virus a virus is its capability to make copies of itself that can be spread to other computers. These copies, in turn, make still more copies that spread to still more computers, and so on, ad nauseam.

Then, the virus patiently waits until something triggers it — perhaps when you type a particular command, press a certain key, or when a certain date arrives, depending on when the person who created the virus wants the virus to go off. What the virus does when it strikes also depends on what the virus creator wants the virus to do. Some viruses harmlessly display a "gotcha" message; others maliciously wipe out all the data on your hard drive. Ouch.

A few years back, viruses moved from one computer to another by latching themselves onto floppy disks. Whenever you borrowed a floppy disk from a buddy, you ran the risk of infecting your own computer with a virus that might have stowed away on the disk.

Nowadays, virus programmers have discovered that e-mail is a much more efficient method to spread their viruses. Typically, a virus masquerades as a useful or interesting e-mail attachment, such as instructions on how to make $1,000,000 in your spare time, pictures of naked celebrities, or a Valentine's Day greeting from your long lost sweetheart. When a curious but unsuspecting user double-clicks the attachment, the virus springs to life, copying itself onto the user's computer and, in some cases, sending out copies of itself to all of the names in the user's address book.

Once the virus has worked its way onto a networked computer, the virus can then figure out how to spread itself to other computers on the network.

Here are some more tidbits about protecting your network from virus attacks:

- The term *virus* is often used to refer not only to true virus programs (which are able to replicate themselves) but also to any other type of program that's designed to harm your computer. These programs include so-called *Trojan horse* programs that usually look like games but are in reality hard-disk formatters.

- Computer virus experts have identified several thousand "strains" of viruses. Many of them have colorful names, such as the I Love You, the Stoned Virus, and the Michelangelo Virus.

- Antivirus programs can recognize known viruses and remove them from your system, and they can spot the telltale signs of unknown viruses. Unfortunately, the idiots who write viruses aren't idiots (in the intellectual sense), so they're constantly developing new techniques to evade detection by antivirus programs. New viruses are frequently discovered, and the antivirus programs are periodically updated to detect and remove them.

Beware of autorun viruses

A few years ago, a new kind of virus appeared on the virus scene. Once, you could safely assume that viruses were only transmitted via program files. In other words, you couldn't catch a virus from a document file such as a word processing document. Unfortunately, this assumption is no longer absolutely true. Most modern word processing and spreadsheet programs (including Word, WordPerfect, WordPro, Excel, and Lotus 1-2-3) have a feature called *autorun macros,* which enable you to attach small programs called *macros* to document files. These macros then automatically run whenever the document is opened.

Unfortunately, unscrupulous people have figured out how to exploit this seemingly innocent feature to infect document files with viruses. So catching a virus from a document file is now possible.

The best protection against this new virus threat is to make sure that you have the most recent version of a good antivirus program such as McAfee's VirusScan. The latest versions of these programs should be able to detect document-borne viruses.

Antivirus programs

The best way to protect your network from virus infection is to use an antivirus program. These programs have a catalog of several thousand known viruses that they can detect and remove. In addition, they can spot the types of changes viruses typically make to your computer's files, decreasing the likelihood that some previously unknown virus will go undetected.

At one time, Microsoft got into the antivirus program business, bestowing its last and best version of MS-DOS with an antivirus program called MSAV. Unfortunately, neither Windows 9*x* nor Windows NT/2000 Server comes with antivirus protection, so you have to purchase a program on your own. The two best-known antivirus programs for Windows are Norton Antivirus by Symantec and McAfee's VirusScan.

The good folks who make antivirus programs maintain Internet sites that have updates that enable their programs to capture newly discovered viruses. Consult the documentation (ugh!) that came with your antivirus program to find out how you can obtain these updates.

Safe computing

Besides using an antivirus program, you have a few additional precautions that you can take to ensure virus-free computing. If you haven't talked to your kids about these safe-computing practices, you had better do so soon.

- ✔ Regularly back up your data. If you are hit by a virus, you may need the backup to recover your data. Make sure that you restore from a backup that was created before you were infected by the virus! If you are hit by a virus, run your antivirus program to check your backup tapes and delete any infected files on the tapes.

- ✔ If you buy software from a store and discover that the seal has been broken on the disk package, take the software back. Don't try to install it on your computer. You don't hear about tainted software as often as you hear about tainted beef, but if you buy software that's been opened, it may well be laced with a virus infection.

- ✔ Use your antivirus software to scan your disk for virus infection after your computer has been to a repair shop or worked on by a consultant. These guys don't intend harm, but they occasionally spread viruses accidentally, simply because they work on so many strange computers.

- ✔ Do not open e-mail attachments from people you don't know or attachments you were not expecting. And don't let your users enable the HTML feature in their e-mail programs. It's all too easy to embed a virus in an HTML e-mail message. Such viruses can be activated simply by reading the message that contains them.

- ✔ Use your antivirus software to scan any floppy disk that doesn't belong to you before you access any of its files.

Chapter 16

How to Stay on Top of Your Network and Keep the Users off Your Back

*N*etwork managers really have a rotten deal. Users come to you whenever anything goes wrong, regardless of whether the problem has anything to do with the network. They knock on your door if they can't log in, if they've lost a file, or if they can't remember how to use the microwave. They probably even ask you to show them how to program their VCRs.

This chapter brushes over a few basic things you can do to simplify your life as a network manager.

Training Your Users

After you first get your network up and running, invite all the network users to Network Obedience School, so that you can teach them how to behave on the network. Show them the basics of accessing the network, make sure that they understand about sharing files, and explain the rules to them.

A great way to prepare your users for this session is to ask them to read the first six chapters of this book. Remember, I wrote those chapters with the network user in mind, so they explain the basic facts of network life. If your users read those chapters first, they are in a much better position to ask good questions during obedience school.

Here are some more ways to make the training process painless for you and your users:

✔ **Write up a summary of what your users need to know about the network, on one page if possible.** Include everyone's user ID, the names of the servers, network drive assignments and printers, and the procedure for logging in to the network. Make sure that everyone has a copy of this Network Cheat Sheet.

✔ **Emphasize the etiquette of network life.** Make sure that everyone understands that all the free space on the network drive isn't his or her own personal space. Explain the importance of treating other people's files with respect. Suggest that users check with their fellow users before sending a three-hour print job to the network printer.

✔ **Don't bluff your way through your role as network manager.** If you're not a computer genius, don't pretend to be one just because you know a little more than everyone else. Be up front with your users. Tell them that everyone is in this together, and you're going to do your best to try to solve any problems that may come up.

✔ **If you ask your users to read the first six chapters of this book, place special emphasis on Chapter 6, especially the part about bribes.** Subtly suggest which ones are your favorites.

Organizing a Library

One of the biggest bummers about being the network manager is that every network user expects you to be an expert at every computer program he or she uses. That's a manageable enough task when you have only two network users and the only program they use is Microsoft Word. But if you have a gaggle of users who use a bevy of programs, being an expert at all of them is next to impossible.

The only way around this dilemma is to set up a well-stocked computer library that has all the information you may need to solve problems that come up. When a user bugs you with some previously undiscovered bug, you can say with confidence, "I'll get back to you on that one."

Your library should include the following:

- ✔ **A copy of your network binder:** All the information you need about the configuration of your network should be in this binder. (Don't put the original copy of the network binder in the library. Keep the original under lock and key in your office.)

- ✔ **A copy of the manuals for every program used on the network:** Most users ignore the manuals, so they won't mind if you "borrow" them for the library. If a user won't part with a manual, at least make a note of the manual's location so that you know where to find it.

- ✔ **A copy of the *Windows Resource Kit* for every version of Windows in use on your network:** You can get the *Windows Resource Kit* at any bookstore that has a well-stocked section of computer books.

- ✔ **A copy of *Windows 98 Secrets,* 2nd Edition, by Brian Livingston and Davis Straub (IDG Books Worldwide, Inc.):** This book has an excellent section on networking.

- ✔ **A copy of the network software manual or manuals.**

- ✔ **At least 20 copies of this book:** (Hey, I have bills to pay.) Seriously, your library should contain books appropriate to your level of expertise. Of course, *For Dummies* books are available on just about every major computer subject. Devoting an entire shelf to these yellow-and-black books isn't a bad idea.

Keeping Up with the Computer Industry

The computer business changes fast, and your users probably expect you to be abreast of all the latest trends and developments. "Hey, Ward," they ask, "what do you think about the new version of SkyWriter? Should we upgrade, or should we stick with Version 23?"

"Hey, Ward, we want to build an Intranet Web site. What's the best Web page editor for under $200?"

"Hey, Ward, my kid wants me to buy a sound card. Which one is better, the SoundSmacker Pro or the BlabberMouth 9000?"

The only way to give halfway intelligent answers to questions like these is to read about the industry. Visit your local newsstand and pick out a few computer magazines that appeal to you.

✔ Subscribe to at least one general-interest computer magazine and one magazine specifically written for network users. That way, you can keep abreast of general trends plus the specific stuff that applies just to networks.

✔ Look for magazines that have a mix of good how-to articles and reviews of new products.

✔ Don't overlook the value of the advertisements in many of the larger computer magazines. Some people (including me) subscribe to certain magazines to read the ads as much as to read the articles.

✔ Keep in mind that most computer magazines are very technical. Try to find magazines written to your level. You may discover that after a year or two, you outgrow one magazine and are ready to replace it with one that's more technical.

The Guru Needs a Guru, Too

No matter how much you know about computers, plenty of people know more than you do. This rule seems to apply at every rung of the ladder of computer experience. I'm sure that a top rung exists somewhere, occupied by the world's best computer guru. But I'm not sitting on that rung, and neither are you. (Not even Bill Gates is sitting on that rung. In fact, Bill Gates got to where he is today by hiring people on higher rungs.)

As the local computer guru, one of your most valuable assets can be a knowledgeable friend who's a notch or two above you on the geek scale. That way, when you run into a real stumper, you have a friend you can call for advice. Here are some tips for handling your own guru:

✔ In dealing with your own guru, don't forget the Computer Geek's Golden Rule: "Do unto your guru as you would have your own users do unto you." Don't pester your guru with simple stuff that you just haven't spent the time to think through. But if you have thought it through and can't come up with a solution, give your guru a call. Most computer experts welcome the opportunity to tackle an unusual computer problem. It's a genetic defect.

✔ If you don't already know someone who knows more about computers than you do, consider joining your local PC users' group. The group may even have a subgroup that specializes in your networking software or may be devoted entirely to local folks who use the same networking software you do. Odds are, you're sure to make a friend or two at a users' group meeting. And you can probably convince your boss to pay any fees required to join the group.

✔ If you can't find a real-life guru, try to find an online guru. Check out the various computing newsgroups on the Internet. And subscribe to online newsletters which are automatically delivered to you via e-mail. (You can find a good list of online newsletters by searching Yahoo's computer category for *Newsletter*.)

✔ Remember that you can use the bribes listed in Chapter 6 on your own guru. The whole point of these bribes is to make your guru feel loved and appreciated.

Helpful Bluffs and Excuses

As network manager, you sometimes just won't be able to solve a problem, at least not immediately. You can do two things in this situation. The first is to explain that the problem is particularly difficult and that you'll have a solution as soon as possible. The second is to lie. Here are some of my favorite excuses and phony explanations:

✔ Blame it on the version of whatever software you're using.

✔ Blame it on cheap, imported memory chips.

✔ Blame it on Democrats. Or Republicans. Whatever.

✔ Blame it on Janet Reno.

✔ Hope that the problem wasn't caused by stray static electricity. Those types of problems are very difficult to track down. Tell your users that not properly discharging themselves before using their computers can cause all kinds of problems.

✔ You need more memory.

✔ You need a bigger disk.

✔ You need a Pentium III to do that.

✔ Blame the problem on Y2K. If your users point out that Y2K was last year, calmly explain to them that, although the world's mindless masses may have believed that, all educated people know that 2000 is the last year of the 20th century, not the first year of the 21st century. Which, of course, calls for another huge New Year's Eve party.

✔ You can't do that in Windows 2000.

✔ You can only do that in Windows 2000.

✔ You're not using Windows 2000, are you?

✔ Could be a virus.

✔ Or sunspots.

✔ All work and no beer make Homer something something something. . . .

Part IV
Webifying Your Network

The 5th Wave   By Rich Tennant

"IT'S JUST UNTIL WE GET BACK UP ON THE INTERNET."

In this part . . .

You discover how to meld your network with the Internet. In Chapter 17, you find out just what the Internet is and why you should connect to it. In Chapter 18, you figure out how to safely and efficiently connect your network users to the Internet. In Chapter 19, you find out how to create your own presence on the Internet by using your network to host your very own Web site. In Chapter 20, you discover how to create an intranet, which is sort of like a Local Area Internet. With an intranet, you can set up a Web server that only users on your own network can access.

Chapter 17

Welcome to the Internet

• •

• •

*T*he Internet is a hot topic among computer users. Thousands of new users are jumping on the Internet every day, and the explosion shows no signs of slowing down. Should you link your computer network to the Internet? This chapter helps you to decide.

What Is the Internet?

As the Goliath of all computer networks, the Internet links millions of computer users throughout the world. Strictly speaking, the Internet is a network of networks. It consists of tens of thousands of separate computer networks that are all interlinked so that a user on any network can reach out and touch a user on any other network. This network of networks connects more than 72 million computers to each other.

The Internet consists of several distinct types of networks:

- ✔ Government agencies, such as the Library of Congress and the White House
- ✔ Military sites (Did you ever see *War Games?*)
- ✔ Educational institutions, such as universities and colleges (and their libraries)
- ✔ Businesses, such as IBM and Microsoft
- ✔ Internet service providers (ISPs), which enable individuals to access the Internet
- ✔ Commercial online services, such as CompuServe and America Online

---

Just how big is the Internet?

Because no particular organization owns or controls the Internet, no one really knows just how big the Internet actually is. Several organizations do attempt to periodically determine the size of the Internet. The science is far from exact, but these organizations are able to come up with pretty reasonable estimates.

One of the best known Internet surveys is the Internet Domain Survey, conducted twice a year by a company called Network Wizards. In January 2000, Network Wizards found that more than 72 million computers were connected to the Internet. When compared with the January 1999 survey, the 2000 survey shows that the Internet has grown by 28 percent over the past year. In that one-year period, more than 16 million computers were added to the Internet.

That's about one every two seconds. Surveys, such as those of Network Wizards, count only those computers that have registered a *host name,* such as www.mycomputer.com. Thus, the Network Wizards survey doesn't even include the millions of home computers that access the Internet without having their own host names.

Truth is, no one really knows how many people use the Internet. The only indisputable point is that the Internet is big — and getting bigger every day.

If you find these figures interesting, you can visit the Network Wizards Web site at www.nw.com to check the results of the latest Internet Domain Survey.

What Does the Internet Have to Offer?

In addition to its massive size, the Internet also boasts a great number of different services for its users. The following sections describe the various services available on the Internet.

World Wide Web

The *World Wide Web,* or *WWW* as it's alliteratively called, is the main method of accessing information on the Internet. Think of it as a graphical interface to Internet information with an important twist: The Web is filled with special hypertext links that enable you to jump from one Internet locale to another.

Information on the World Wide Web is organized into documents called *pages.* A single Web page can be as short as one word, or it can contain hundreds of lines of text. Most pages contain no more information than you can comfortably squeeze onto an 8½ x 11-inch printed page.

Each page on the Web can contain text, graphics, sounds, videos, and — most important — links to other Web pages with related information. For example, a page that contains information about frogs may contain links to other pages with information about princes, Muppets, or hallucinogenic substances.

A *Web site* is a collection of pages related to a particular subject and kept on one or more computers known as *Web servers.* Every Web site has a *home page,* which is the starting point for accessing the pages that are available at the Web site. The home page has *links* that let you access the Web site's other pages in an organized fashion.

Besides links to other pages at the same Web site, a Web page can also have links to pages that live on different Web sites. Thus, clicking a link may take you to an entirely different Web site that's located halfway around the world from the one you were accessing, without jet lag, airsickness, or even a noticeable hesitation!

To access the Web, you need a special program called a Web browser. A *Web browser* knows how to display the special formats and codes used to send information over the World Wide Web. The Web browser reads these special codes over the Internet and translates them into fancy displays and beautiful pictures for your screen. The browser also enables you to follow links from one Web page to another simply by clicking the link.

The two most popular Web browsers are Netscape Navigator and Microsoft Internet Explorer. I say more about Web browsers in Chapter 18.

Internet e-mail

E-mail is the main reason most people use the Internet. Internet e-mail is similar to e-mail on your local area network (LAN), except that you aren't limited to exchanging e-mail with users of your own network. With Internet e-mail, you can send messages to and receive messages from anyone anywhere on the Internet.

Mailing lists

A *mailing list* is a list of the e-mail addresses of a group of people who are interested in a particular subject, such as flat-tax proposals, *Star Trek* movies, or origami. The mailing list itself has an e-mail address. When you send e-mail to the mailing-list address, your message is automatically distributed to everyone else on the list. To get on a mailing list, you subscribe to it by sending an e-mail message to the list's administrator. (The subscription address is almost always different from the mailing list's normal address, so be careful to send your subscription request to the correct address.)

Some mailing lists are moderated, which means that any messages you submit to the list must first pass the scrutiny of the list moderator before being sent out to the list. Moderated lists tend to stay more focused, but sometimes the censorship can squelch interesting lines of discussion.

You can find a good directory of Internet mailing lists at `www.liszt.com`.

Usenet newsgroups

Newsgroups are online discussion groups where users with common interests gather to share ideas. Newsgroups exist for just about every topic you can imagine, from gardening to car repair.

For technical reasons you don't need or want to know, Internet newsgroups are distributed over what is called *Usenet*. As a result, you sometimes see the terms Usenet and newsgroups used together.

Unlike instant messaging, which I discuss later in this section, Usenet newsgroups are not real-time discussions. Newsgroups are more like e-mail: You post a message and then check back a day or two later to see if anyone replied.

Instant messaging

Instant messaging is an online feature that lets you chat online — that is, you can exchange messages directly with other Internet users, kind of like a phone call with your computer. The most popular instant message services are ICQ (which is a clever acronym for "I Seek You"), America Online's AIM (which stands for *America Online Instant Messenger*) and Microsoft's MSN Messenger.

Another form of online chatting is *Internet Relay Chat*, or *IRC*. Unlike instant message services, such as AIM or MSN Messenger, IRC does not let you set up lists of friends to chat with. Instead, IRC hosts thousands of chat rooms, where anyone can join in on the discussion.

Boring Internet history you can skip

The Internet has a fascinating history, if such things interest you. You don't have to be interested in such things, of course, except that a superficial understanding of how the Internet began may help you understand and cope with the way this massive computer network exists today. So here goes the story.

The Internet traces its beginnings back to a small network called ARPANET, built by the Department of Defense in 1969 to link defense installations. ARPANET soon expanded to include not only defense installations, but universities as well. In the 1970s, ARPANET was split into two networks, one for military use (which was renamed MILNET) and the original ARPANET for nonmilitary use. The two networks were connected using a networking link called IP, the Internet Protocol, so called because it allowed communication between two networks.

The good folks who designed IP had the foresight to realize that soon more than two networks would want to be connected. In fact, they left room for tens of thousands of networks to join the game, which is a good thing, because not long afterward the Internet began to take off.

By the mid-1980s, ARPANET was beginning to reach the limits of what it could do. Enter the National Science Foundation (NSF), which set up a nationwide network designed to provide access to huge supercomputers, much like those monolithic computers used to discover new prime numbers and to calculate the orbits of distant galaxies. The supercomputers themselves were never put to much use, but the network that was put together to support the supercomputers, called NSFNET, did. It replaced ARPANET as the new backbone for the Internet.

Then, out of the blue, the whole world became interested in the Internet. Stories about it appeared in *Time* and *Newsweek.* The Net began to grow so fast that even NSFNET couldn't keep up, so private commercial networks got into the game. The size of the Internet has doubled every year for the past few years, and who knows how long this dizzying rate of growth may continue.

File Transfer Protocol

File Transfer Protocol, or *FTP,* as it's usually called, is the Internet's way of moving files around. Think of FTP as the Internet equivalent to a network file server. Thousands of computers make libraries of files available for downloading on the Internet. These computers are called FTP sites. You can use FTP to get files from Microsoft and other computer companies, government agencies, and universities. Most of these FTP sites enable anyone to access their treasures, but access to some is restricted to a lucky few.

Microsoft Office 97 and 2000 enable you to access FTP sites from any Office program by using the standard File Open and Save As dialog boxes. Thus, if you want to retrieve a word processing document that's been archived at an FTP site, you can do so directly from Word. Or, if you want to upload an Excel spreadsheet file to an FTP site, you can do so directly from Excel.

Telnet

Telnet is a way of connecting to another computer on the Internet and actually running programs on that computer as if your computer were a terminal attached to the other computer. Telnet is one of the many Internet services that is rapidly losing popularity as the World Wide Web (which I describe earlier in this chapter) becomes more popular. However, many Internet services — such as the ability to scan the card catalogs of many public libraries — are still available only via Telnet.

Understanding Internet Addresses

Just as every user of a LAN must have a user ID, everyone who uses the Internet must have an Internet address. Because the Internet has so many computers and so many users, a single user ID would not be sufficient. As a result, Internet addresses are constructed using a method called the *Domain Name System,* or *DNS.*

The term *domain,* when used in discussing Internet addresses, has nothing to do with Windows NT/2000 Server domains. Windows NT/2000 Server domains are used to segment large networks into smaller groups to simplify the task of managing user IDs and other network directory information. In contrast, Internet domains are simply a method of naming computers on the Internet.

The complete Internet address for a Web page is known as a URL, which stands for *Uniform Resource Locator.* A URL consists of three parts, written as follows:

```
protocol://host_address/resource_name
```

- ✔ For World Wide Web pages, the *protocol* portion of the URL is usually http (http stands for *Hypertext Transfer Protocol,* but you don't need to know that to use URLs). For secure Web sites, the protocol is https.

- ✔ The *host address* is the Internet address of the computer on which the Web page resides (for example, www.dummies.com).

✔ The final part, the *resource name,* is a name that the host computer assigns to a specific Web page or other file. In many cases, the resource name contains additional slashes that represent directories on the host system. Most of the time, you can omit the resource name completely if you simply want to display the home page for a company's Web site.

Here are some examples of complete URLs:

```
http://www.yahoo.com
```

```
http://www.cbs.com/network/tvshows/mini/lateshow
```

```
http://vol.com/~infidel/halloween/halloween.html
```

Notice that `http://` must prefix all Web page addresses. However, Internet Explorer, Navigator, and other Web browsers cleverly add the `http://` automatically, so you don't have to type it yourself.

Because the Web browser lets you omit the protocol part (`http://`), and because you can often omit the resource name, the only URL component you usually need to worry about is the host address. Host addresses themselves consist of three components separated from one another by periods, usually called *dots.*

✔ The first part of the Internet address is almost always www, to indicate that the address is for a page on the World Wide Web.

✔ The second part of the Internet address is usually a company or organization name, which is sometimes abbreviated if the full name is too long. Sometimes this second part actually consists of two or more parts in itself separated by periods. For example, in the address www.polis. iupui.edu, the second part is polis.iupui.

✔ The third and final part of an Internet address is a category that indicates the type of organization the name belongs to. The six most commonly used categories are summarized in Table 17-1. The category portion of an Internet address is also known as the *top-level domain.*

Besides the six top-level domains listed in Table 17-1, the top-level domain can also be a two-digit country code to indicate the country where the Web site resides, such as fr for France, ec for Ecuador, and la for Laos.

Table 17-1	Categories Used in Internet Addresses
Category	*Explanation*
edu	Education
mil	Military

(continued)

Table 17-1 *(continued)*

Category	Explanation
gov	Government
com	Commercial
net	Network
org	Organizations that don't fit one of the other categories — usually nonprofit organizations

Putting these three address parts together, you get addresses such as www.microsoft.com, www.nasa.gov, and www.ucla.edu.

Occasionally, some Web addresses use a prefix other than www. Addresses get complicated when large organizations want to subdivide their networks into two or more groups. For example, a university may break its network down by department. Thus, the address of the history department at a university may be history.gadolphin.edu, whereas the track team may be located at track.gadolphin.edu.

Internet e-mail addresses are a bit different than Web page addresses. An e-mail address follows this format:

```
username@organization.category
```

As you can see, the address consists of a user name followed by an at-sign (@) and the organization and category portion of the domain name for the computer system which provides the user's e-mail account. For example, the e-mail address for a user named Neil who has an e-mail account at nasa.gov would be neil@nasa.gov.

When pronouncing an Internet address, the @ symbol is pronounced *at,* and the periods are pronounced *dot.* Thus, the address neil@nasa.gov would be pronounced *Neil at NASA dot gov.*

Coping with TCP/IP

TCP/IP — which stands for Transmission Control Protocol/Internet Protocol — is the low-level networking protocol that the Internet uses to send data back and forth between computers. Fortunately, you don't need to know many details about TCP/IP to work with the Internet, other than knowing that you have to make sure that TCP/IP is configured properly on each network computer if you want it to be able to access the Internet.

In network terms, a *protocol* is a set of rules that computers use to communicate with one another over a network. Unfortunately, the Internet uses different protocols than most local area networks use. To use the Internet successfully from a LAN, you have to convince your LAN's protocols and the Internet's protocols to coexist on the same network without stepping on one another's toes. Don't worry . . . you can do it. All modern network operating systems get along just fine with Internet protocols.

Here are a few other TCP/IP tidbits you should be aware of:

- ✔ TCP/IP is an open protocol, which means that it isn't tied to any one particular hardware or software vendor. Just about any vendor's hardware or software can work with TCP/IP. Earlier versions of both NetWare and Windows NT Server preferred to use their own protocols (IPX/SPX for NetWare, NetBEUI for Windows NT). But nowadays, both NetWare and Windows NT and 2000 Server can work as well with TCP/IP as with IPX/SPX or NetBEUI.

- ✔ TCP/IP isn't a cabling standard. TCP/IP works with whatever network cabling you already have installed. Thus, you can run TCP/IP on your existing Ethernet network cables.

- ✔ TCP/IP doesn't conflict with NetWare or Windows networking protocols. Thus, you can run the IPX/SPX, NetBEUI, and TCP/IP protocols together, over the same cables, at the same time.

- ✔ TCP/IP is easy to configure. To add TCP/IP to your network, all you have to do is click the right buttons in the Network Control Panel.

What Is an Intranet?

Okay, enough said about the Internet for now. We know that the Internet has millions and millions of users, that the World Wide Web is the best thing to happen to computers since the invention of the Off switch, and that TCP/IP is the key protocol for the Internet.

Shortly after the Web became popular, companies began to discover that the Web protocols are useful not only for the Internet, with its worldwide reach, but also for a company's local area network. In other words, TCP/IP can be used on a LAN to create a private Internet, a localized version of the World Wide Web that only computers on the LAN can access. Local area Webs became known as *intranets,* because they resemble the Internet but work within a single network rather than across the global network.

TECHNICAL STUFF

What about IP addresses?

Friendly Internet addresses, such as microsoft.com and idgbooks.com, make surfing the Internet easy for us end users. But as you might imagine, computers don't deal directly with friendly addresses. Instead, TCP/IP uses special addresses called *IP addresses* to uniquely identify every computer in the world that's connected to the Internet.

An IP address is a 32-bit number that is usually written as a series of four decimal numbers separated by periods, like this: 130.32.15.3. Depending on the size of your network, the first two or three numbers in the address are assigned to your entire network. The rest of the address identifies an individual computer on your network.

If you connect your network to the Internet, every computer on your network that attempts to access the Internet needs its own IP address. Fortunately, you don't have to manually assign an IP address to each computer. Instead, a special server computer, which is called a *DHCP server*, can assign Internet addresses automatically. (Don't ask what *DHCP* stands for — you really don't need to know.) If you connect to the Internet via an Internet service provider (ISP), your ISP probably has its own DHCP Server that assigns IP addresses for you. If not, you can configure a Windows NT Server or NetWare server computer to operate as a DHCP server for your network. Or, you can manually assign an IP address to each of your computers.

Why go to all the trouble to add TCP/IP to an already complicated LAN? Because TCP/IP enables you to create Web applications that run on your LAN. Here are just a few examples of the types of applications that companies build on their intranets:

- **Company policy manuals.** Any employee can access an up-to-date version of a manual from a Web browser. Large companies save huge amounts of money by not printing manuals.

- **Company bulletin boards, company newsletters, and other forms of internal corporate communications.**

- **Benefits administration, such as medical insurance, retirement plans, and so on.**

- **Support services, such as the computer help desk.** An intranet is an ideal way to track problem reports through to their resolution.

- **Product information and catalogs.**

- **Executive Information Systems, such as sales trend analysis and production control.**

The list goes on and on. For more information about creating your own intranet, refer to Chapter 20.

Chapter 18

Connecting Your Network to the Internet

· ·

In This Chapter

▶ Connecting your computers to the Internet

▶ Selecting a Web browser

▶ Making your Internet connection secure

· ·

So you've decided to connect your network to the Internet. All you have to do is run to the local computer discount store, buy a modem, and plug it in, right? Wrong. Unfortunately, connecting to the Internet involves more than just installing a modem. For starters, you have to make sure that a modem is the right way to connect — other methods are faster but more expensive. Then, you have to select and configure the software you use to access the Internet. And finally, you have to lie awake at night worrying that hackers are breaking into your network via its Internet connection.

Connecting to the Internet

If you want to enable the users of your network to access the Internet, you have several options. The following sections describe the most commonly used methods of connecting network users to the Internet.

Connecting with modems

A *modem* is a device that enables your computer to connect to another computer via the telephone. Modems are the most common way to connect to the Internet. Modems are inexpensive — you can get cheap ones for as little as $30. The standard speed for modems is 56Kbps, which means that the modem can send about 56,000 bits of information per second over a standard phone connection.

To use a modem, you must also have a phone line with a phone jack located near the computer. The modem ties up the phone line whenever you're connected to the Internet, so you can't use the phone for a voice conversation and connect to the Internet at the same time.

The easiest way to connect your network users to the Internet with modems is to give each user who needs Internet access his or her own modem and a phone line for the modem to use. This system enables each user to access the Internet independently of the LAN. After you install the modems and phone lines, contact a local Internet service provider, and the folks there can help you set up your Internet accounts.

Setting up a separate modem and phone line for each user is probably the easiest way to set up your Internet access, but it is not the most efficient method. For information about sharing modems among several users, see the section "Sharing an Internet Connection" later in this chapter.

Connecting with cable or DSL

If your network users will use the Internet frequently, you may want to consider one of two relatively new methods of connecting to the Internet: cable and DSL. Cable Internet access works over the same cable that brings 40 billion TV channels into your home, whereas DSL is a digital phone service that works over a standard phone line. Both offer three major advantages over normal dial-up connections:

- ✔ **Cable and DSL are much faster than dial-up connections.** A cable connection can be anywhere from 10 to 200 times faster than a dial-up connection, depending on the service you get. And the speed of a DSL line is comparable to cable.

- ✔ **With cable and DSL, you are always connected to the Internet.** You don't have to connect and disconnect each time you want to go online. No more waiting for the modem to dial your service provider and listening to the annoying modem shriek as it attempts to establish a connection.

- ✔ **Cable and DSL do not tie up a phone line while you are online.** With cable, your Internet connection works over TV cables rather than phone cables. And with DSL, the phone company installs a separate phone line for the DSL service, so your regular phone line is not affected.

Unfortunately, there's no such thing as a free lunch, and the high-speed, always-on connections offered by cable and DSL do not come without a price. For starters, you can expect to pay a higher monthly access fee for cable or DSL. In most areas of the United States, cable runs about $50 per month for residential users; business users can expect to pay more, especially if more than one user will be connected to the Internet via the cable.

What about ISDN?

ISDN, which stands for *Integrated Services Digital Network,* is a digital phone service that was popular a few years ago as an alternative to dial-up connections. ISDN allows data to be sent about twice as fast as a conventional phone line — up to 128Kbps (kilobits per second) rather than 56Kbps. As an added plus, a single ISDN line can be split into two separate channels, so you can carry on a voice conversation while your computer is connected to the Internet.

Sounds great — the only catch is that it's expensive. An ISDN connection doesn't require a modem. Instead, you use a special ISDN adapter, which sets you back at least $250. In addition, you have to pay the phone company anywhere from $50 to $200 to install the ISDN line, and you pay a monthly fee ranging from $25 to $50 in the United States (depending on your area). On top of that, you may be billed by the minute for usage. For example, in my area, an ISDN line costs $24.95 per month, plus usage fees of about a penny a minute.

With the spread of low-cost cable modem access in many areas and the cost of DSL access coming down, ISDN is fast becoming a thing of the past. It was a good idea for its time, but its time has passed.

The cost for DSL service depends on the access speed you choose. In some areas, residential users can get a relatively slow DSL connection for as little as $30 per month. For higher access speeds or for business users, DSL can cost substantially more.

Cable and DSL access are not available everywhere. If you live in an area where cable or DSL is not available, you can still get high-speed Internet access via a satellite hookup. With satellite access, you still need a modem and a phone line to send data from your computer to the Internet. The satellite is used only to receive data from the Internet. Still, a satellite setup like this is much faster than a modem-only connection.

DSL stands for *Digital Subscriber Line,* but that won't be on the test.

Connecting with high-speed private lines: T1 and T3

If you're really serious about high-speed Internet connections, contact your local phone company (or companies) about installing a dedicated high-speed digital line. These lines can cost you plenty (on the order of hundreds of dollars per month), so they're best suited for large networks in which 20 or more users are accessing the Internet simultaneously.

A T1 line has more than ten times the capacity of an ISDN connection, with speeds up to 1.544Mbps. A T1 line can service as many as 24 users simultaneously. Each user has a 64Kbps connection to the Internet, roughly equivalent to the speed each user can achieve with a dedicated 56Kbps modem and phone line or an ISDN connection.

A T3 line is even faster than a T1 line. A T3 line transmits data at an amazing 44.184Mbps. Each T3 line can be divided into 28 T1 lines. Because each T1 line can handle 24 users at 64Kbps, a T3 line can handle 672 users (24 x 28 = 672). Of course, T3 lines are also considerably more expensive than T1 lines.

If you don't have enough users to justify the expense of an entire T1 or T3 line, you can lease just a portion of the line. With a *fractional T1 line,* you can get connections with speeds of 128Kbps to 768Kbps, and with a *fractional T3 line,* you can choose speeds ranging from 4.6Mbps to 32Mbps.

Setting up a T1 or T3 connection to the Internet is stuff best left to professionals. Getting this type of connection to work is far more complicated than setting up a basic LAN.

Sharing an Internet Connection

After you have chosen a method to connect to the Internet — dial-up modem, DSL, cable modem, or a high-speed T1 or T3 line — you can turn your attention to setting up the connection so that it can be shared by more than one user on your network.

One way to share an Internet connection among several network users is to use a Windows feature known as ICS, which stands for Internet Connection Sharing. ICS comes with the newer versions of Windows — Windows 2000, Windows Millennium Edition, and Windows 98 Second Edition. With ICS, only one computer, known as the *gateway computer*, has a direct connection to the Internet, such as a dial-up modem connection or a DSL connection. The other computers on your network connect to the Internet through the gateway computer.

Here are a some key points to keep in mind about Internet Connection Sharing:

  ✔ ICS uses a technique called *Network Address Translation*, or *NAT*, to fool the Internet into thinking that your entire network is really just one computer with a single IP address. Whenever one of the computers on your network requests information from the Internet, ICS replaces that computer's IP address with the gateway computer's IP address before sending the request out to the Internet. Then, when the requested information returns from the Internet, ICS figures out which computer on your network actually requested the information and sends the information to the correct computer. In this way, all interaction with the Internet is funneled through the gateway computer.

✔ ICS allows several network users to share an Internet connection simultaneously. As a result, multiple users can browse the Web, read their e-mail, or play online games all at the same time.

✔ Unfortunately, ICS can share only one Internet connection. If your network is large enough that a single Internet connection — even a high-speed cable or DSL connection — is not enough to satisfy your users' Internet demands, you have to use the more advanced communication features of Windows 2000 Server or NetWare instead of ICS.

✔ The gateway computer must be on before other computers can connect to the Internet through ICS.

An alternative to ICS is to use a special-purpose device that connects your network to the Internet via dial-up modems or a cable or DSL connection. For example, Linksys makes a product called the EtherFast Cable/DSL Router, which you can purchase for about $200. As its name suggests, the EtherFast Cable/DSL Router includes a router that creates a link between your LAN and a Cable or DSL modem. In addition, the EtherFast Cable/DSL Router provides a four-port 10/100Mbps Ethernet switch, which enables you to connect four computers (or more if you cascade additional hubs or switches).

The EtherFast Cable/DSL Router provides Network Address Translation so that anyone on the LAN can access the Internet through the cable or DSL connection and also acts as a firewall by preventing unauthorized users from accessing your LAN via the Internet connection. (For more information about firewalls, see Chapter 19.)

Figure 18-1 shows how a small network can use a cable/DSL router to share a cable Internet connection among six network users. As you can see, the cable modem, which is connected to the cable system via a coaxial cable, connects to the cable/DSL router via a twisted-pair Ethernet cable. Two of the six computers on the network are connected directly to the cable/DSL router's 10/100Mbps switch. The other four computers are connected to the cable/DLS router through an Ethernet hub.

Figure 18-1:
Using a
cable/DSL
router to
share a
high-speed
Internet
connection.

Choosing a Web Browser

When you connect your LAN to the Internet, you must provide software known as a *Web browser* for your network's users to use when accessing the network. Although you have many different Web browsers to choose from, most people use one of two popular programs: Netscape Navigator or Microsoft Internet Explorer.

The debate about which browser is better — Navigator or Internet Explorer — is one of the hottest holy wars being fought in computerdom these days. Proponents of each program have a nasty tendency to demonize the other, suggesting either that Navigator is a relic of the Stone Age or that Internet Explorer is nothing more than Microsoft chairman Bill Gates's most recent attempt at world domination.

The truth is that both Navigator and Internet Explorer are excellent programs. Both are so good, in fact, that recommending one over the other on any basis, other than personal preference, is difficult. I recommend that you use Internet Explorer, but I base my recommendation solely on the fact that I've written three books about Internet Explorer titled *Internet Explorer 4 For Windows For Dummies, Internet Explorer 5 For Windows For Dummies*, and

Internet Explorer 5.5 For Windows For Dummies (all published by IDG Books Worldwide, Inc., naturally). I would like to retire young. Choose whichever book matches the version of Internet Explorer that you're using.

Both Internet Explorer and Navigator come loaded with features that go beyond simple Web browsing. The complete Internet Explorer package includes a bunch of extra goodies, such as the following:

- **Outlook Express:** An e-mail program that can also handle Internet newsgroups

- **NetMeeting:** A conferencing program that enables you to conduct online meetings with other Internet users

- **MSN Messenger:** An online chatting program that lets you wile away the hours conversing with your online friends

Netscape distributes its Navigator program in a bundle of Internet products called Communicator. Besides Navigator, the Communicator package includes the following:

- **Netscape Messenger:** An e-mail and news reader program

- **Netscape Composer:** A tool for creating Web pages

- **Netscape Conference:** A feature, much like Microsoft's NetMeeting, that enables you to conduct online meetings with other users

The best news about Internet Explorer and Navigator is that both programs are free. You can go to `www.microsoft.com/ie` to download Internet Explorer from Microsoft's Web site, and you can go to `www.netscape.com` to download Communicator from Netscape's Web site.

Whichever browser you choose, you should standardize your entire network on one browser or the other. After all, when someone's Internet connection breaks, you're the one who's called in to fix it. If you standardize your Web browser, you become an expert in only one of them. If you don't standardize, you have to be an expert in both Navigator and Internet Explorer.

Worrying about Security Issues

After any computer on your network connects to the Internet, a whole host of security issues arise. One of the most important security issues to worry about is that, unbeknownst to you, your Internet connection can function as a two-way street. Not only does it enable you to step outside the bounds of your network to access the Internet, but your Internet connection can also allow others to step in and access your network.

Securing your network

If any computer on your network is going to connect to the Internet via a modem, using proper security measures on the entire network is absolutely imperative. Here are some suggestions:

- ✔ **Never allow a computer attached to the Internet via a modem to enable file sharing for TCP/IP on its modem.** Doing so practically invites Internet hackers to explore your network. See the next section, "Disabling TCP/IP file sharing on a modem connection," for more information.

- ✔ **Make sure that every user must enter a password to access the system.** If you're using Windows NT/2000 Server or NetWare, require users to change passwords periodically and don't allow short passwords (fewer than seven or eight characters).

- ✔ **Make sure that all shared disk drives have restrictions so that only specific users or groups can access them.**

- ✔ **For Windows NT Server, use only NTFS volumes so that you can provide adequate security.**

Disabling TCP/IP file sharing on a modem connection

For a modem connection from a single Windows computer to the Internet, Windows allows you to enable file and printer sharing for TCP/IP connections over your modem. If you use that modem to connect to the Internet, you are inviting disaster. To make sure that file sharing is not enabled for TCP/IP via the modem, follow these steps:

1. **Choose Start⇨Settings⇨Control Panel and then double-click the Network icon.**

   This action brings up the Network control panel application, as shown in Figure 18-2.

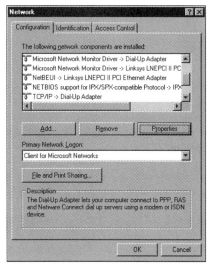

Figure 18-2:
The
Network
control
panel.

2. **Click TCP/IP⇨Dial-Up Adapter in the list of network components.**

   You may have to scroll down this list to find it.

3. **Click the Properties button.**

   A dialog box appears, instructing you that this isn't the correct way to change the TCP/IP settings. Ignore it.

4. **Click OK to summon the TCP/IP Properties dialog box and then click the Bindings tab.**

   The dialog box shown in Figure 18-3 appears.

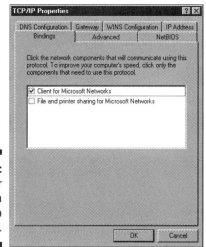

Figure 18-3:
Bindings for
TCP/IP on
the dial-up
adapter.

5. **Make sure that the File and Printer Sharing for Microsoft Networks option is *not* checked.**

    If this option is checked, click it to remove the check mark.

6. **Click OK to dismiss the TCP/IP Properties dialog box and then click OK again to dismiss the Network control panel.**

    Windows may pretend to look busy for a few moments and may even ask you to reboot your computer. If so, be patient.

For the best Internet security, you should install and use a proxy server or firewall, which I describe in Chapter 19.

Considering other Internet security issues

Besides intruders breaking into your network via your Internet connection, you have other security concerns to worry about when your network users have Internet access. Here are some of the more important ones:

- **Sending information over the Internet.** Without the right security measures, sensitive information that users send out over the Internet can be intercepted and stolen. Sensitive information, such as passwords and credit card numbers, should always be transmitted over the Internet in an encrypted form.

- **Downloading programs over the Internet.** Programs that your users download to their computers may contain viruses that can infect your entire network. Virus protection is in order.

- **Viewing Web pages that do more than meets the eye.** Empowered by advanced programming tools, such as Java and ActiveX, and scripting languages, such as JavaScript and VBScript, a Web page can do more than display information: The page itself can act like a computer program. An unscrupulous Web programmer can set up a Web page that displays a smiley face while it secretly erases files on a user's hard disk or plants a virus that infects your network.

- **Opening unfriendly e-mail attachments.** One of the most common ways for viruses to spread themselves these days is via e-mail attachments. Be sure to provide adequate virus scanning for your mail server and instruct your users to never open attachments they are not expecting.

To guard against these threats, make sure that your Internet users use the built-in security features of their Web browsers. Fortunately, both Internet Explorer and Navigator have adequate security features to keep the bad guys at bay.

Chapter 19

Hosting Your Own Web Site

- -

In This Chapter

▶ Adding a Web server to your LAN

▶ Protecting your LAN from unauthorized access

▶ Choosing tools to build your Web pages

▶ Considering Java and all that jive

- -

Sooner or later, you will discover that all your competitors have created their own home pages on the World Wide Web, and you will want to do likewise. Take a deep breath. Setting up your LAN so that your users can access the Internet is difficult enough. Creating your own Internet site is another matter altogether. I'm going to start by saying outright that this isn't something you should attempt on your own. Seek professional help.

If you choose to ignore my sage advice, read on. (Don't worry; I'm accustomed to being ignored. I have three teenaged daughters.)

The Web is one of the fastest changing fields in all of computerdom. As soon as you master one Web development tool, another one comes along to render the one you just learned obsolete. And every few months some hot new technology comes along that promises to revolutionize the way the Web works. Good luck and hang on!

Serving Up Your Web Page

You have two basic approaches to setting up a server to host your Web page on the Internet. The first and simplest approach is to contact the folks at a local Internet service provider and find out how much setting up shop on their computer costs. Most ISPs allow their users to store a few megabytes of data on the ISP's computers, so you can easily set up a simple home page if you don't want it to be too fancy. However, a couple of megabytes isn't nearly enough disk space to include complicated graphics, sounds, and video clips — things that make a Web page worth viewing. You probably want to pay for additional space. For the right price, your ISP will probably set up an entire server computer for you.

The second way to create your own home page is to set up your own Web server computer. The Web server computer is connected to the Internet via a high-speed connection, such as a DSL or a T1 or T3 line. The Internet server computer may run Windows NT or 2000 Server, NetWare, or a version of UNIX (including Linux). Most Internet servers run UNIX, although Windows NT/2000 is growing in popularity. In addition, you need special Internet server software.

Life gets more complicated if you want to connect the Internet server computer to your LAN. In that case, you must take special precautions to ensure that strangers can't use your Internet server as a back door into your LAN. Hackers love to break into computer systems this way, either to trash files, steal information, or just prove they can do it.

Selecting a Web server

To set up a Web site, you need to dedicate a separate computer to act as a Web server. All the information that's available via your Web site resides on this computer's disk, so plenty of disk storage is a must for your Web server. Plenty of RAM is a must also — consider 256MB to be the minimum. And get the biggest and fastest SCSI hard drives you can afford.

Selecting a Web-friendly operating system

For a Web-friendly network operating system, you have two basic choices: Windows NT/ 2000 Server or UNIX. Because the Internet got its start in the UNIX world, more Web sites run UNIX than Windows NT. However, Windows NT is gaining ground, especially in intranets. If you're familiar with Windows but have never touched a UNIX computer, Windows NT Server is the way to go.

Oh, I know that Novell has recently endowed NetWare with Internet server tools. However, the vast majority of Web sites are hosted on Windows NT Server or UNIX. Stick with one of these options unless you're a NetWare zealot and want to be a renegade.

Selecting Web server software

In addition to a server operating system, you also need Web server software. The following sections briefly describe the three most popular Web server software choices.

Apache
By some estimates, two thirds or more of the Web servers on the Internet run Apache as their Web server software. Apache is available for several operating

systems, including Windows NT/2000 and Mac OS Server, but most people who use Apache run the UNIX version.

Apache is popular for several reasons:

- **Apache is free.** You can download it from www.apache.org.

- **Apache is very reliable.** Apache is not the fastest Web server software available, but it is among the most bug-free.

- **Apache runs on just about any version of UNIX, including Linux.** In fact, just about all distributions of Linux come with Apache.

- **Apache is the direct descendant of the NCSA HTTPd server, which was the very first Web server.** Many of Apache's most ardent followers are Web old-timers, who started Web sites back when the Internet had only a few million users.

Microsoft Internet Information Server

A distant second in popularity behind Apache is Microsoft's Internet Information Server (IIS). IIS is a built-in part of Windows NT and Windows 2000 Server. Because IIS runs well with Windows NT/2000, IIS is the best Web server to use if you don't know or don't want to learn UNIX.

Sun/Netscape Web servers

In an effort to compete with Microsoft, Sun, the people who make high-power UNIX workstations and Java, have formed an alliance with Netscape to produce a Web server, known as iPlanet Web Server, that competes with Apache and Microsoft's IIS. Unlike Apache and IIS, however, iPlanet Web Server gives you a choice of operating systems: You can run it on UNIX or Windows NT.

You can choose from two versions of iPlanet Web Server. The most powerful is known as iPlanet Web Server, Enterprise Edition, which includes advanced features that are designed for large companies. Smaller companies can probably get by with the scaled-back version, known as iPlanet Web Server, FastTrack Edition.

The bad news is that iPlanet Web Server isn't free. You must pay a license fee of $295–$1,495, depending on which edition you choose.

Registering Your Own Domain Name

An important part of setting up a Web site is obtaining your own domain name. You can choose any name you want for your domain name, provided that the name satisfies the basic rules for Internet domain names and no one else has already claimed the name. (For more information about domain names, refer to Chapter 17.)

Fortunately, getting your own domain name is easy and not very expensive. You can register a domain name for $35 per year. For a small additional charge, most domain name registration companies will also provide you with a one-page Web site you can use until you get your Web server up and running and may also throw in an e-mail account or two.

For a list of companies that can register a domain name for you, search for "Domain Registration" on an Internet search service such as Yahoo! or msn.com. One of the most popular domain registration companies is Network Solutions (`www.networksolutions.com`).

The bad news is that with so many companies and individuals already on the Web, odds are that the domain name you want has already been taken. Domain registration companies such as Network Solutions offer free search services that will tell you if the name you want is available. You may have to try several searches before you find a domain name that is available.

Protecting Your LAN from the Internet

A *firewall* is a security-conscious router that sits between the outside world and your network, in an effort to prevent *them* from getting to *us*. The firewall acts as a security guard between the Internet and your LAN. All network traffic into and out of the LAN must pass through the firewall, which prevents unauthorized users from accessing the LAN.

Some type of firewall is a must if you host a Web site on a server computer that's connected to your LAN. Without a firewall, anyone who visits your Web site can potentially break into your LAN and steal your top-secret files, read your private e-mail, or worse yet, reformat your hard drive.

Firewalls can also work the other way, preventing your network users from accessing Internet sites that you designate as off-limits.

There are several ways to set up a firewall. Probably the easiest is to purchase a hardware firewall, which is basically a router with built-in firewall features. Most hardware firewalls include a Web-based management program that enables you to connect to the firewall from any computer on your network using a Web browser. You can then customize the firewall settings to suit your needs.

Alternatively, you can set up a Windows NT/2000, NetWare, or UNIX/Linux server computer to function as a router and firewall. In fact, you'll find some tips for creating a firewall using Linux in Chapter 26.

Choosing Tools for Creating Web Pages

Back when the Web was young, the easiest way to crank out Web pages was to fire up your trusty text editor and start typing. Your text had to include complicated formatting commands, called *HTML tags,* which resembled a rudimentary programming language and therefore required a graduate degree in computer science to comprehend.

Those days are gone. Now, point-and-click tools are available to help you create Web pages without worrying about the details of HTML tags. Here are the four basic categories of development tools for creating the pages that make up a Web site:

✓ **Web site development tools:** For most Web developers, the best type of program to use is one dedicated to the task of creating sophisticated Web sites. Such programs have excellent HTML page editors, plus tools that help you coordinate all the pages of a complete site. One of the most popular Web site development tools is Microsoft's FrontPage, which you can see in Figure 19-1. (For hard-core Web developers, Microsoft offers an even more sophisticated Web site develop tool called Visual InterDev.)

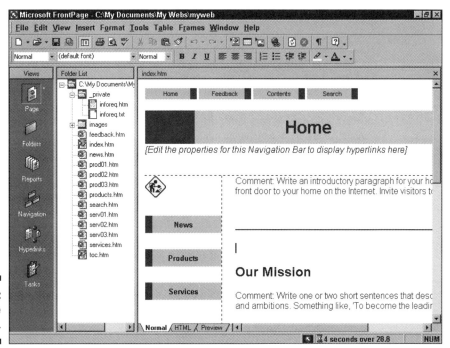

Figure 19-1:
FrontPage
2000.

✔ **Simple Web page editors:** These programs enable individuals or small businesses to create simple Web pages. Internet Explorer comes with a free program of this type called FrontPage Express (it's a scaled-back version of FrontPage), and Netscape Communicator comes with a similar program called Composer. Although these programs are easy to use, their HTML capabilities are limited.

✔ **Hard-core development tools:** Serious Web developers should look into a comprehensive Java development tool, such as Symantec's Visual Café and Microsoft's Visual J++ or Microsoft's Visual InterDev.

✔ **Web-enhanced office suites:** All three major office suites — Microsoft Office, Lotus SmartSuite, and Corel Office — are now Internet enabled. That means, for example, that you can create a document in Microsoft Word and save it in HTML format, making the document suitable for publishing on the Web. These applications are ideal when your Intranet exists primarily as a means of making corporate publications (policy manuals, for example) available.

Dealing with CGI

The earliest forms of HTML allowed only static information to appear on Web pages. Users could request the display of certain pages, but information flowed only in one direction: from the server to the client.

Then along came an HTML feature called *forms,* which enables Web developers to put simple data entry fields on their Web pages. Form fields were limited to simple text boxes, radio buttons, check boxes, and just two types of command buttons: one to send data to the server, the other to clear data entered on the form. This limited repertoire of controls allowed only simple interactions, but forms took off. The best Web sites used forms to create simple interactive applications.

Probably the best-known examples of Web sites that use forms are the search sites like Yahoo! and AltaVista. In a search site, you type a keyword into a text box and then click a command button. The search site then displays a list of Web sites that are related to the keyword you entered.

To use HTML forms, you have to contend with a feature called *CGI,* which stands for *Common Gateway Interface.* Here's how a form-based interaction using CGI works:

1. The client (that is, the Web browser) requests a page that contains a form. The server sends the requested page to the Web browser, which displays the page along with its form fields.

2. The user types information into the form fields and then clicks the Submit button. The Web browser gathers the information entered by the user and sends it back to the server.

3. The server receives the information sent from the Web browser, realizes that the information is data from a form, and runs a program that's specially designed to handle the form's data.

    This program is called a *CGI program.* You have to create the CGI program yourself, which means you have to understand the CGI scripting language if you want to use forms in your Web site.

4. The CGI program examines the data and does something worthwhile with it.

    In most cases, the CGI program retrieves information from a database.

5. The CGI program generates an HTML document that contains the results of the processing done in Step 4.

    For example, if the CGI program performed a database query, the HTML document contains the results of the query.

6. The server sends the HTML document generated by the CGI program to the Web browser.

7. The client displays the HTML document.

The key thing to note about CGI is that the CGI program itself always runs on the server. So, although CGI enables you to create interactive applications on the Web, it isn't very flexible or efficient.

Keep in mind that using CGI on your Web server opens up a can of security worms that you must deal with. For example, you must make sure that users cannot modify your CGI scripts or create their own CGI scripts to run on your server.

Wake Up and Smell the Java

For some reason, the movers and shakers of the Web world think that naming new Internet products after various types of coffee is cool. The whole thing started when Sun Microsystems released a revolutionary programming language for Web pages called *Java.* Everyone soon jumped on the bandwagon. Now you have JavaScript, Visual Café, Latte, Mocha, Hot Java (as if you want your Java cold), Star Buck, and JavaBeans. It all sounds like a scene from *L.A. Story.* ("I'll have a double decaf JavaBean Latte with a twist.")

So what exactly is Java? Java is a programming language that's used to create programs that run on an Internet user's computer rather than on the server computer. Java Web programs are called *applets* because they're not standalone programs. An applet must run within a Java-enabled Web browser, such as Navigator or Internet Explorer. (Java can also be used to create programs that run on the Web server rather than on the Internet user's computer.)

Java solves many of the problems inherent in the form-based CGI approach to building interactive Web applications. For starters, form-based applications can use only a limited range of controls: text boxes, radio buttons, check boxes, and Submit and Reset buttons. In contrast, you can build a Java applet to display any type of custom control that you want on a Web page. With Java, you can build interactive Web applications that sport fancy slider boxes, spin buttons, draggable objects, and any other type of control that you can imagine.

But even better than the ability to use fancy controls is the simple fact that Java programs run within the Internet user's Web browser. In contrast, CGI programs run on the Web server computer. As a result, Java programs run more efficiently than CGI programs.

Scripts

Java is good, but its main drawback is that it's a complicated programming language that requires special tools to use. Enter scripts, which are simple programs that you can place directly into HTML documents without the need for any special type of programming tool. Scripts run much slower than Java applets but are much easier to create and use.

You have two competing scripting languages to choose from:

- **JavaScript:** This language was developed by Netscape and is the main scripting language for Navigator. Don't be fooled by the clever name: JavaScript bears little resemblance to Java. In fact, when Netscape first started developing JavaScript, it was called LiveScript. Netscape changed the name to JavaScript in an attempt to capitalize on Java's popularity, even though JavaScript is not related in any way to Java.

- **VBScript:** This is Microsoft's scripting language for Internet Explorer. VBScript is based on Microsoft's popular Visual Basic programming language and is a tad bit easier to learn than JavaScript.

Note that Microsoft also ships Internet Explorer with its own version of JavaScript, called JScript. So with Internet Explorer, you have two scripting languages to choose from: JScript and VBScript. With Navigator, JavaScript is the only choice.

JavaBeans and ActiveX

Warning: The following information requires full pocket protectors and beanie caps to understand.

One of the latest developments in Web page design is the ability to create *objects* using programming languages such as Java or Visual Basic, embed those objects in a Web page, and allow the Web page and the object to communicate with one another via a script written in JavaScript or VBScript.

For example, you may create a stock ticker object that displays stock market information on a Web page. The Web page may include buttons or other controls that set options for the stock ticker, such as which stocks to track or how often to refresh the display. When the user activates one of these controls, the Web page runs a script, which in turn communicates with the stock ticker object to tell it which stocks to track or how often to refresh its display.

Two competing styles of Web objects exist: Microsoft and non-Microsoft. The Microsoft style is called *ActiveX;* the non-Microsoft style is called *JavaBeans.* The main difference between the two is that Microsoft controls ActiveX and practically every other computer company thinks you should use JavaBeans instead, just to get back at Bill Gates for being such a meanie.

Active Server Pages

One more recent development in the world of programmable Web pages is Microsoft's Active Server Pages (ASP). ASP lets you create Web pages that include VBScript scripts that run at the Web server, before the page is sent to the Internet user's computer. This development allows the script to customize the page before it is delivered. With ASP, you no longer have to use the clunky CGI method of customizing Web pages at the server before sending them over the Internet.

For Apache users, a similar feature called Java Server Pages (JSP) is also available. Like ASP, JSP lets you create scripts that run on the server rather than on the Web browser. But JSP scripts are written in JavaScript rather than VBScript.

Chapter 20

Creating an Intranet

. . . .

. . . .

*N*o, I'm not mispronouncing the word *Internet. Intranet* is a term that's gained popularity in recent years. It's similar to the Internet, but with a twist: Instead of connecting your computer to millions of other computers around the world, an intranet connects your computer to other computers in your company or organization. How is an intranet different from your ordinary, run-of-the-mill network? Read on — that's what this chapter is all about.

What Is an Intranet?

Everyone knows that the Internet, and especially the World Wide Web, has become a phenomenon. Millions of computer users worldwide surf the Web, and thousands join the bandwagon every day.

Recently, ingenious network managers at large companies figured out that although the Web is interesting for distributing public information to the world, the Web is just as useful for distributing private information within a company. Thus, the idea of intranets was born. An intranet is a network that's built using the same tools and protocols that are used by the global Internet but applied to an organization's internal network.

You can think of an intranet as a small, private version of the World Wide Web. An intranet runs on your local area network (LAN) rather than on the global Internet. As a result, only users who are connected to your LAN can access your intranet. You can access the intranet via a Web browser, such as Netscape Navigator or Microsoft Internet Explorer. However, users don't need a dial-up connection or Internet service provider because the information on the intranet is stored on server computers that are connected to your LAN rather than on servers that must be accessed via the Internet. (As a side benefit, accessing a Web page on an intranet is much faster than accessing a page on the Internet. That's because LAN connections, which use Fast Ethernet cards and hubs, are usually much faster than Internet connections, which often use slow dial-up connections and modems.)

The intranet is analogous to a closed-circuit television system, and only those within the organization that owns the system can view the channels. In contrast, the Internet is more like cable television in that anyone who's willing to pay $20 or so per month can watch.

Here are two interesting but contradictory points of view about the significance of intranets:

- ✔ According to some computer industry pundits, intranets are actually more popular than the Internet. For example, Netscape, one of the biggest and best-known Internet browser companies, actually makes more money selling software used for intranets than for the Internet.

- ✔ On the other hand, some industry pundits think the intranet phenomenon is merely a fad that some other promising new technology, such as pet rocks or hula hoops, will replace in a few years. Only time will tell.

What Do You Use an Intranet For?

Intranets can distribute just about any type of information within a company. You have two basic types of intranet applications:

- ✔ **Publishing applications:** Information is posted in the form of pages that you can view from any computer with access to the intranet. This type of intranet application is commonly used for company newsletters, policy manuals, online training, price lists, and so on.

- ✔ **Transaction applications:** Information is gathered from intranet users. Examples include filing online expense reports, reporting problems to the help-desk, enrolling in employee-benefit programs, and so on.

The key difference between these two types of intranet applications is that in a publishing application, the flow of information is one way: from the intranet to the user. The user requests some information, and the intranet system delivers it. In a transaction application, information flows in both directions — not only does the user request information from the intranet system, but also the intranet system itself requests information from the user.

Publishing applications are simple to set up. In fact, you may be able to set one up yourself without a lot of outside help from highly paid computer consultants. Transaction applications are much more complicated, however. Expect to spend big bucks on computer consulting to get an intranet transaction application set up.

What You Need to Set Up an Intranet

An intranet is fairly simple to set up. Here's a list of the various requirements:

- ✔ **A LAN.** An intranet doesn't require its own cabling; it can operate on an existing Ethernet LAN using twisted-pair or coax wiring.

- ✔ **A server computer that's dedicated to the intranet.** Make sure that this computer has plenty of RAM (at least 256MB) and gigabytes (at least 20GB) of disk space. Of course, the more users your network has and the more information you intend to place on the server, the more RAM and disk storage you need.

- ✔ **Windows NT/2000 Server or a UNIX operating system.** Web server software requires one or the other. Sure, you can do it with Netware, but only a small portion of intranets are built using NetWare. That vast majority use UNIX or Windows NT/2000.

- ✔ **Web server software for the server computer.** You can find more information about Web server software in Chapter 19.

- ✔ **Programs to help you create Web pages.** If you're the type who dreams in binary, you can create Web pages by typing HTML codes directly into text files. In that case, the only program you need is Notepad. Alternatively, you can use a Web-authoring program, such as Microsoft FrontPage. For more information, refer to Chapter 19.

- ✔ **Client computers with at least the minimum system requirements.** Make sure that each client computer that accesses the intranet has a Pentium or better processor, at least 32MB of RAM, and a connection to the LAN.

- ✔ **A Web browser such as Navigator or Internet Explorer on each client computer.**

Creating a Small Intranet with Personal Web Server

It is possible to host an intranet for a small network using a Windows 98 server or Windows NT Workstation by using a free Microsoft program called Personal Web Server (PWS). PWS is included with Windows 98 Second Edition. However, PWS is not usually installed on Windows 98 SE or Windows Me systems, so you have to install it yourself. To install PWS, choose Start⇨Programs⇨Accessories⇨Internet Tool⇨Personal Web Server; then follow the instructions that appear on the screen.

Personal Web Server is a significantly scaled-back version of Internet Information Server (IIS), which requires Windows NT or 2000. PWS is an ideal way to set up an intranet on a small LAN that has just a few users and as a way to learn how Web servers work. However, once your intranet grows beyond a few users, you'll want to devote a separate server computer running IIS or Apache to the intranet.

Starting Personal Web Server

To start Personal Web Server, choose Start⇨Programs⇨Accessories⇨ Internet Programs⇨Internet Explorer⇨Personal Web Server⇨Personal Web Manager from the Windows Start menu. Personal Web Manager enables you to control how Personal Web Server operates. Figure 20-1 shows the main Personal Web Manager dialog box.

Figure 20-1:
Personal
Web Server
comes
to life.

Notice in Figure 20-1 that Personal Web Manager indicates the status of the Web server; in this case, the message shows that PWS is inactive. To activate Web publishing and make your Web site available to others on your network, click the Start button. The PWS Manager dialog box changes, as shown in Figure 20-2.

Figure 20-2:
Web
publishing
is on!

You can disable the server by clicking the Stop button. When you do, the Personal Web Manager dialog box changes back to the way it was before you activated Web publishing.

 After Personal Web Server starts, the Personal Web Server icon shown in the margin appears in the Windows taskbar. You can double-click this icon at any time to summon the Personal Web Manager.

Personal Web Server comes with a set of Web pages that serve as Help files to give you an overview of how PWS works and how to manage it. To access these help files, start up Personal Web Manager and then choose Help⇨Personal Web Server Topics.

Publishing a Web page to Personal Web Server

Publishing your HTML files to Personal Web Server so that you or other network users can view them is easy. PWS uses a folder named `C:\Inetpub\wwwroot` as the root directory for your Web pages. To post an HTML file to Personal Web Server, all you have to do is save the file in the `C:\Inetpub\wwwroot` folder.

 Alternatively, you can use Personal Web Server's built-in Publishing Wizard to publish Web files to your PWS folder. To do so, start Personal Web Manager and click the Publish icon (shown in the margin). This action brings up the Publishing Wizard, as shown in Figure 20-3. Fill in the blanks to publish your HTML files to your PWS folder.

Figure 20-3:
The
Publishing
Wizard.

If you haven't already created Web pages that you want to publish and if you don't have a sophisticated Web-development program such as Microsoft FrontPage, you can use Personal Web Server's built-in Home Page Wizard to create a simple Web site. For more information, see the section "Using the Home Page Wizard," later in this chapter.

Accessing a Web page on Personal Web Server

To access a page stored in Personal Web Server, you need to know the Internet address for your Personal Web Server root directory. To find out what that address is, start Personal Web Manager. The Internet address of your PWS site appears in the Personal Web Manager dialog box. For example, as Figure 20-2 shows, the address for the PWS site is http://Athlon8.

The default Web page for Personal Web Server is default.html. Thus, if you create a file named default.html in C:\Inetpub\wwwroot, you can display that page by entering your Personal Web Server address in the Internet Explorer Address box. For example, if your Web server address is Athlon8, just type **Athlon8** in the Address box to display your home page.

To display a different HTML file, type the filename after the Internet address, separated by a slash. For example, to display a page named softball.html, you type **Athlon8/softball.html**.

The Internet address used by Personal Web Server is based on your Windows computer name, which you create when you first install Windows on your computer. If you want to change this name, open Control Panel and double-click the Network icon, which reveals the Network dialog box. Click the Identification tab, and then type a new computer name in the Computer Name field. After you click OK, your computer restarts and then you can use the new name for your Personal Web Server Internet address.

Using the Home Page Wizard

 Personal Web Server includes a Home Page Wizard that helps you create a Web site without requiring that you work directly with HTML. To use the Home Page Wizard, start Personal Web Manager and click the Web Site icon (shown in the margin). A Wizard appears and asks you a few questions about what features you want to include on your home page. Then, the Wizard generates the page for you. Figure 20-4 shows an example of a home page created by the Home Page Wizard.

Figure 20-4:
A simple home page created with the Home Page Wizard.

After you create a home page, clicking the Web Site icon enables you to manage your home page by using the options shown in Figure 20-5. Click Edit Your Home Page to make changes to your home page, click View Your Guest Book to see a list of users who have visited your Web site and signed your guest book, or click Open Your Drop Box to see private messages users have left for you.

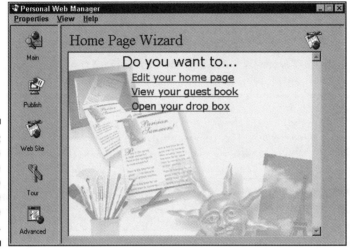

Figure 20-5:
Using the
Home Page
Wizard to
manage
your home
page.

Part V

More Ways to Network

"As a candidate for network administrator, how well versed are you in remote connectivity protocols?"

In this part . . .

After you have the basics down, this part helps you do some of the more advanced stuff, which includes setting up a network at your home, creating a dial-up connection so that you can access your network while you're at home or on the road, using the network features of Microsoft Office, building a network that includes older MS-DOS and Windows computers as well as Macintosh computers, and setting up a server that runs the Linux operating system.

Chapter 21

Networking Your Home

• •

In This Chapter

▶ Different ways to network your home

▶ Using the Windows Millennium Edition Home Networking Wizard

▶ Manually setting up a home network

▶ Addressing some home network concerns

• •

*T*hese days, more and more people have more than one computer in the home. Some families have several generations of hand-me-down computers: an old clunker 386, a workable 486, a Pentium (or maybe even two), and perhaps a notebook computer that one of the kids got through a school program.

In this chapter, I show you how to network the computers in your home so that you can share a printer, disk drive, CD-ROM drive, and an Internet connection. Nothing fancy here, just the bare necessities you need to get a network up and running.

To keep things simple, this chapter assumes that all the computers you want to network are already running Windows 9x/Me. If you want to add Macintosh computers to your network, refer to Chapter 25. If you have an older computer that can't run Windows 9x/Me, see Chapter 24.

For more complete information about creating a network in your home, refer to *Networking Home PCs For Dummies,* by Kathy Ivens (IDG Books Worldwide, Inc.).

Choosing How You Want to Network Your Home

Although nearly all business and office networks use Ethernet to connect their computers, several simpler alternatives are available for home networks. The following sections describe four ways to network the computers in your home.

Phone line networks

Phone line networks let you network your computers using your home's existing phone lines. Phone line networks are slower than Ethernet networks, sending data over the phone lines at about 1Mbps (as opposed to Ethernet's 10 or 100Mbps). But 1Mbps is fast enough to share a printer or to share small files. The only real limitation is that each computer must be located near a phone jack.

You might think that using your home phone wiring to network your computers would tie up your phone lines, but that's not the case. Phone line networks do not interfere with normal phone use, so you can talk on the phone and exchange information over your phone line network at the same time.

Each computer on the phone line network needs a phone line adapter. Phone line adapters come in two basic varieties:

  ✔ **Internal adapters:** PCI or ISA cards, which you must install inside your computer, much like an Ethernet adapter card. Make sure your computer has a free PCI or ISA slot before purchasing an internal adapter.

  ✔ **External adapters:** Little boxes that sit next to your computer that you plug into an available port on your computer. The most popular external adapters plug into a USB port, but you can also get adapters that plug into a parallel printer port, and you can even get adapters that plug into Ethernet ports, for computers that have built-in Ethernet adapters (such as Macintosh computers).

After you install an Internet adapter or plug an external adapter into the appropriate port, you just plug the adapter into the nearest phone jack and you're ready to start networking.

Several industry-leading companies have formed an organization called the Home Phone Line Networking Alliance, or HomePNA, to create standards for phone line networking. In December of 1999, HomePNA published a new phone line standard that allows phone line networks to operate at 10Mbps rather than 1Mbps, which makes phone line networks almost as fast as basic 10BaseT Ethernet networks.

In theory, the HomePNA standard means that you should be able to mix and match phone line network adapters from different companies on a single network. I wouldn't try it, though. Phone line adapters tend to work best with their own kind, so use the same brand adapters for all your computers.

Power line networks

Another way to connect your home computers without having to string wire through your house is to use networks that work over your home's electrical power system. In most homes, there's a power outlet on just about every wall, so power line networks are more flexible than phone line networks in terms of where you can locate your computers.

Unfortunately, running a network over power lines presents several built-in technical problems, the most significant of which is that power lines are notoriously filled with electrical noise and disturbances that interfere with network communications. For this reason, the power line networks that are available today are slow — on the order of a few hundred Kbps.

Faster power line networks are expected to be available in 2001, with speeds as fast as 14Mbps. But until then, I suggest you steer clear of power line networks.

Wireless networks

The most flexible of all home networking technologies is wireless, which sends network data through the air using radio signals. With a wireless network, you don't have to string any wire anywhere in your house, and you don't have to locate your computers near an existing phone or power outlet. In fact, you can roam around the house with a laptop computer and connect to the network anywhere — even out by the pool!

Wireless networking is slower than Ethernet networking but about the same speed as first-generation phone line networks. Most wireless networks work at about 1Mbps.

Wireless is also the most expensive way to network your home computers. You can buy Ethernet adapter cards for as little as $20, and phone line network adapters for about $60, but a wireless network will cost you about $100 per computer.

Ethernet

Although phone line and wireless networks are easier to set up than an Ethernet network, Ethernet is still the fastest and most flexible choice for networking your home. If you decide to use Ethernet to build your home network, you will need the following Ethernet components:

✔ **A 10/100baseT Ethernet network card for each computer.** You have no need to spend big money on the networking cards. If you can find them for $20 each, buy them.

   Make sure that the cards say "Plug and Play" on the box. If they don't, you have to fuss around with configuring the cards' IRQ settings and port addresses. With Plug and Play cards, all the configuration settings are made automatically, so you don't have to worry about such details.

   Also, make sure that you get a card that fits one of the available expansion slots inside your computer. You need to know what type of available expansion slots your computer has. Most newer computers have two types of slots: ISA and PCI. If you have an older computer, you may have a different type of slot, most likely VESA or EISA in addition to the standard ISA slots. Check the manual that came with your computer to find out for sure.

✔ **A 10/100baseT hub with enough ports for all of your computers.** You can get four- or five-port hubs for about $50.

✔ **A twisted-pair cable with RJ-45 connectors on both ends for each computer.** A 25-foot cable costs about $10.

   Do *not* buy phone cable. The twisted-pair cable used for 10baseT networks looks like phone cable, but it isn't the same.

You can probably find an inexpensive starter kit that includes everything you need to network two computers together: two twisted-pair network cards, a hub, and two cables. If you have more than two computers, you can buy an add-on kit for each additional computer.

Using the Windows Millennium Edition Home Networking Wizard

Microsoft's latest version of Windows, Millennium Edition, has a special Home Network Wizard that is designed to simplify the task of setting up a home network. Before you run the Home Networking Wizard, you should first install a network adapter card in each computer, then connect the computers together using the correct type of cable for the network adapter cards you are using.

You should also make a few decisions before you run the wizard. In particular:

✔ You'll need to come up with a unique name for each computer on the network. You can use the name of the person who uses the computer the most, or the room where the computer is located, or you can make up random names like Herbie or Gertrude.

✔ Are you going to share an Internet connection among two or more computers on the network? If so, identify the computer that has the Internet connection you want to share (that is, the computer with the modem) and the computers that you want to access the Internet via the shared connection.

✔ Do you want to share files? If so, make a note of which computers have files you want the other computers to be able to access. (In most cases, you'll want to share files on all the computers on the network.)

✔ Do you want to share a printer? If so, make a note of each computer that has a printer you want to share.

When you're ready to run the wizard, just follow these steps:

1. **Double-click the My Network Places icon on your desktop; then double-click the Home Networking Wizard icon in the My Network Places folder.**

   Or, if you prefer, you can start the Home Networking Wizard by choosing Start⇨Programs⇨Accessories⇨Communications⇨Home Networking Wizard. Either way, the Home Networking Wizard comes to life, as shown in Figure 21-1.

Figure 21-1:
The Home
Networking
Wizard.

2. **Click Next.**

   The Home Networking Wizard asks if your computer is connected to the Internet, as shown in Figure 21-2.

3. **Select the Internet option you want to use for the computer.**

   To use the Internet on the computer, select Yes, This Computer Uses the Following. Then, select A Connection to Another Computer . . . if you want this computer to access the Internet via a modem that is connected to one of your other computers. Or select A Direct Connection to My ISP . . . if this is the computer that has the direct Internet connection that you want to access from other computers on your network.

   If you do not want to use the Internet from this computer, select No, This Computer Does Not Use the Internet.

4. **Click Next.**

   The wizard asks for a name for the computer, as shown in Figure 21-3.

5. **Type the name you want to use for the computer in the Computer Name field.**

   You can use any name you want, but the name of the person who will use the computer or the location of the computer is best.

   For dramatic effect, take the computer's mouse outside on a starry night, hold it up toward the sky with both hands, and shout the computer's name three times.

Figure 21-2:
Do you use
the Internet
on this
computer?

Home Networking Wizard

Internet Connection
A computer can access the Internet directly or use the shared connection of another computer.

Do you use the Internet on this computer?

○ Yes, this computer uses the following:

  ○ A connection to another computer on my home network that provides direct access to my Internet service provider (ISP).

  ○ A direct connection to my ISP using the following device:

    [Linksys Lnepci II Ethernet PCI Adapter]

○ No, this computer does not use the Internet.

< Back   Next >   Cancel

Figure 21-3:
What do you
want to
name this
computer?

6. **If you want to change the workgroup name, click Use This Workgroup Name and type the name of the workgroup you want to use in the text box.**

   There's usually no reason to change the workgroup name from the default (MSHOME), so you'll probably want to just skip this step.

7. **Click Next.**

   The Home Networking Wizard asks if you want to share files or printers, as shown in Figure 21-4.

Figure 21-4:
Do you want
to share
files or
printers?

8. **If you want other computers to be able to access this computer's My Documents folder, select the My _Documents Folder and All Folders in It check box.**

If you want, you can password-protect the My Documents folder by clicking the Password button and typing a password. Then, anyone who tries to access the My Documents folder on this computer will have to know the password.

If you want to share other folders besides the My Documents folder, you have to share them manually, after the wizard is finished. For information about how to share folders, see the section "Sharing a Folder" later in this chapter.

9. **If this computer has a printer you want to share, make sure there is a check mark in the box next to the printer.**

If you do not want to share the printer, deselect the printer before proceeding to the next wizard screen.

10. **Click _Next.**

The wizard offers to create a Home Networking Setup disk, as shown in Figure 21-5. You'll want to create this disk if you want to include computers that do not run Windows Me in your network.

Figure 21-5: Ready to create a Home Networking Setup disk.

If you did not provide a password when you shared your My Documents folder in Step 8, the wizard displays a warning saying that you should protect your files with a password. Click OK to return to the wizard; then click Next again if you still don't want to use a password. The warning message will appear only once.

11. **If all of the computers on your network run Windows Millennium Edition, select N̲o, Do Not Create a Home Networking Setup Disk; then click N̲ext and move ahead to Step 13. Otherwise, click N̲ext to create the disk.**

    The wizard instructs you to insert a blank formatted diskette in your diskette drive.

12. **Insert a blank formatted disk in your diskette drive and click N̲ext.**

    The Home Network Wizard writes a bunch of files to the disk. When it finishes, the wizard displays its final screen, shown in Figure 21-6.

Figure 21-6: The Home Networking Wizard is ready to set up your network.

13. **Remove the disk (if you created one) and click Finish.**

    The wizard then restarts your computer. This will take a few moments, but when your computer comes back to life, the congratulations screen shown in Figure 21-7 appears.

Figure 21-7: Congratulations! Aren't you proud?

14. **Click <u>O</u>K to dismiss the wizard; then run the wizard on the other computers in your network.**

    For other Windows Millennium Edition computers, just repeat the entire procedure step-by-step.

    For Windows 95 or Windows 98 computers, insert the disk you created in Step 12 into the computer's diskette drive. Then choose Start⇨<u>R</u>un, type **a:setup**, and press OK to start the Home Networking Wizard.

If you want to change any of the settings you made when you ran the wizard, just run the wizard again. The wizard will ask whether you want to edit your network settings or create another Home Network Setup disk. If you choose to edit your network settings, the wizard will walk you through the same set of dialog boxes it displayed when you first ran the wizard, allowing you to make any changes you want.

Setting Up a Network without the Wizard

If you don't have Windows Millennium Edition, don't despair. You can still set up a home network just as good as the one the Home Networking Wizard can create. You just have to trudge your way through the network settings yourself.

First, configure your computer for networking by double-clicking the Network icon in the Control Panel to summon the Network dialog box, shown in Figure 21-8.

Figure 21-8:
The
Network
control
panel.

Then check to make sure that the following items appear in the list of installed network components:

☑ Client for Microsoft Networks.

☑ Your network card, which may appear as "NE2000 Compatible" or may be specific to the brand of network card you purchased.

☑ NetBEUI __ NE2000 Compatible. (If your network card is other than "NE2000 Compatible," the name of your network card appears here instead.)

☑ File and printer sharing for Microsoft Networks.

If any of these items are missing, click the Add button to add them. (If other items appear in the list, leave them alone.)

Now click the Identification tab in the Network dialog box. This brings up the computer identification settings shown in Figure 21-9. Type a different name and description for each computer but make sure that all your computers use the same Workgroup name.

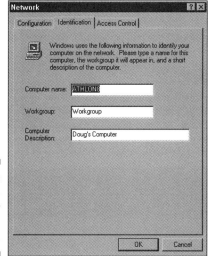

Figure 21-9:
The computer identification settings.

Finally, share your folders and printers by following the instructions in the "Sharing a Folder" and "Sharing a Printer" sections that appear later in this chapter.

Sharing a Folder

The Home Networking Wizard can share your My Documents folder so that other network users can access the files you store there. If you want to share another folder on your hard disk, or if you didn't use the Home Networking Wizard to set up your network and you want to share a folder, you have to manually share your folders. Fortunately, sharing a folder is easy. Just follow these steps:

1. **Double-click My Computer.**

   The My Computer window appears.

2. **Click the folder that you want to share.**

   You may have to navigate your way around your disk drives to find the folder.

3. **Choose the File⇨Sharing command.**

   The Sharing properties dialog box appears, as shown in Figure 21-10. (The figure shows how the dialog box appears after you make the settings in Steps 4 and 5.)

4. **Click Shared As.**

   If you want, you can change the Share Name and Comment fields.

Figure 21-10:
Sharing a
folder.

5. **Click Full for the Access Type.**

   This action enables you to do anything you want to the shared drive from the other computer — including creating, deleting, or renaming files or folders.

6. **Click OK.**

The Properties dialog box disappears.

To access another computer's shared disk drive, double-click the Network Neighborhood (My Network Places in Windows Me) icon. All of the computers in the workgroup you created are listed. Double-click any computer to see a list of shared folders for that computer.

Sharing a Printer

If you have a printer that you want to share on the network and you didn't use the Home Networking Wizard to share it, you can share the printer manually by following these steps:

1. **On the computer with the printer that you want to share, choose Start➪Settings➪Printers.**

The Printers folder appears, listing all the printers available on your computer.

2. **Click the printer that you want to share and then choose the File➪Sharing command.**

The Sharing tab of the Properties dialog box for the printer appears.

3. **Select the Share As radio button.**

This action enables the sharing options, so the Properties dialog box resembles Figure 21-11.

Figure 21-11:
Sharing a
printer.

4. **Type a name for the printer if you want.**

5. **Click OK.**

6. **On the other computer, choose Start⇨Settings⇨Printers.**

   The Printers folder appears.

7. **Double-click the Add Printer icon.**

   The Add Printer Wizard springs to life.

8. **Follow the Add Printer Wizard steps to add the printer you shared in Steps 1 through 5.**

   The Add Printer Wizard asks if you're installing a local or network printer and enables you to browse the network to locate the printer you want to access. You also have to indicate to the wizard the make and model of the printer that you're adding. If the exact make and model of the printer doesn't appear in the list provided by the wizard, you have to insert the disk that came with the printer to complete the installation.

9. **You're done!**

   You can now print to the network printer by choosing the network printer from the normal File⇨Print command in any Windows program.

Sharing an Internet Connection

If you use the Windows Me Home Networking Wizard to set up your home network, Internet Connection Sharing will already be configured for you so your network computers can easily access the Internet through a single Internet connection.

If you don't have Windows Millennium Edition or if you don't want to use the wizard, you can configure Internet Connection Sharing yourself. To configure Internet Connection Sharing, choose Start⇨Settings⇨Control Panel to open the control panel folder; then double-click the Internet Options icon. Click the Connections tab; then click the Sharing button that appears in the LAN Settings section of the dialog box.

For more information about sharing an Internet connection, refer to Chapter 18.

Managing Your Home Network

After you network the computers in your home, you — or whoever has the most computer savvy in your household — must become the home network manager. Unfortunately, all the concerns that arise when using a network in a business situation apply to home networks as well. In particular, the following list highlights some of the things to stay on top of with your home network:

- ✔ **Make sure that everyone knows how to access the network and use the shared drives and printers.** Hold a family meeting to go over the do's and don'ts of the network.

- ✔ **Think about whether or not you really want to grant full access to everyone's documents over the network.** What if your teenager gets mad at you because you won't let him borrow the car, so he decides to delete a bunch of your important files from the privacy of his bedroom? Maybe you should think about security, giving each user a user ID and password and password-protecting folders that contain private information.

- ✔ **Make sure that everyone knows that backing up is his or her own responsibility.** Don't let your kid blame you when he or she loses a 30-page term paper because of the "stupid network." The epitome of parenting for the new millennium may be to add backing up the network to the kids' list of Saturday chores, right after mowing the lawn and cleaning the bathrooms.

- ✔ **Keep an eye on disk space.** With the whole family using the network, you may be amazed at how quickly the gigabytes fill up.

Chapter 22

Dialing In to Your Network

. . . .

. . . .

*W*ith portable computers and home computers becoming more and more popular, many computer users take work home with them to work on in the evening or over the weekend and bring back to the office the following weekday. This arrangement works reasonably well, except that exchanging information between a portable or home computer and your office computer is far from easy.

One way to exchange files is to copy them from one computer to a diskette and then copy the files from the diskette to the other computer. However, this approach has its drawbacks. What if the files you want to exchange won't fit on a single floppy disk? And what if, in the rush to get out of the house the following morning, you forget to put the disk in your pocket or bag? (You can get around the size limitation of floppy disks by using Zip disks, which have a capacity of 100MB each. But you still have the problem of forgetting the disks or losing them in the subway on the way to work.)

If you use a laptop computer, you can add a network interface card to the laptop computer and then connect the laptop computer to your office network and exchange files with your office computer. But Ethernet cards for laptop computers are not cheap, and you have to enable file sharing on the laptop computer, your office computer, or both.

Alternatively, you can use a program, such as LapLink, which allows you to connect your portable computer to your office computer using a cable connected to both computers' serial, parallel, or USB ports. After you connect the computers, you can then transfer files over the cable. This process is much more efficient than copying the files using diskettes but still has drawbacks. What if you get home and discover that you forgot to copy one important file?

If you must work from home, the best way to access your work at the office is to create a dial-up connection that uses modems to connect your home computer directly to your office network. Using this setup, you can access from your home computer any shared disk drives available on the office network, just as if your home computer were a part of the office network.

This chapter shows you how to create a remote connection using a feature of Windows called Dial-Up Networking. This feature provides a simple but limited modem link between a remote computer and a networked computer. I also point out some advantages of using a more sophisticated approach to remote access, such as Windows NT/2000 Remote Access Service or NetWare Connect.

Security is a major concern whenever you enable dial-up networking. If you can dial in to your office computer and access your files, so can anybody else. Passwords offer some measure of protection, but serious computer hackers can get past simple password protection as easy as experienced car thieves can hotwire a car. For that reason, I suggest you do not use Windows 98 or Millennium Edition as a dial-up server if security is a concern.

Throughout this chapter, I assume that you're using remote access to call in to your work computer from a home computer. Of course, this isn't the only way to use dial-up connections. You can do it the other way around by calling up your home computer from the office. Or you can call your office or home computer from a hotel room using a laptop computer. The point is that I refer to the computer that you use to call in to another computer as the *home computer,* and I refer to the other computer — the one that you're calling in to — as the *office computer.*

Understanding Dial-Up Networking

All versions of Windows since Windows 95 include a feature called *Dial-Up Networking,* which enables you to connect to a network using modems and a phone line. With Dial-Up Networking, you can easily set up a dial-up connection between your home computer and your office computer so you can access your office computer's disk drives and printers while you're at home. In addition, any network resources that are available to your office computer will also become available to your home computer.

Because computer geeks love confusing us with three-letter acronyms, they have designated *DUN* as the official three letter acronym for Dial-Up Networking. I promise not to use the term *DUN* again in this chapter.

To use DUN — oops, I mean Dial-Up Networking — to connect from home to office, both your home and office computers must have a modem, and they must both be connected to a phone line.

In Dial-Up Networking terminology, the computer that you dial in to — that is, your office computer — is referred to as a *dial-up server*. Likewise, the computer you dial in from — your home computer — is called a *dial-up client*. Note that the dial-up server computer doesn't have to be a dedicated server computer. The computer in your office can function as a dial-up server, provided that it has a modem connected to a phone line.

Because Dial-Up Networking uses modems and phone lines rather than Ethernet cards to connect your home computer to your office computer, the connection will be slow. The slow speed of the Dial-Up Networking connection won't bother you too much if you just want to access a couple of small Excel files or send a short document to your printer, but if you try to copy a 20MB file over a dial-up, you'll have enough time to watch a couple of Kevin Costner movies while you're waiting.

Installing the Dial-Up Server Feature

Dial-Up Networking has been a standard part of Windows since Windows 95, but the capability to configure a dial-up server is not. You must install this feature separately before you can designate your office computer as a dial-up server.

The ability to create a dial-up server is built in to Windows 2000 Professional, so you don't have to install it separately. If your office computer uses Windows 2000 Professional, you can skip the rest of this section.

Windows 98 and Millennium Edition comes with the necessary dial-up server programs on the Windows CD. To install the programs, follow these steps:

1. **Choose Start⇨Settings⇨Control Panel.**

   The Control Panel comes to life.

2. **Double-click Add/Remove Programs.**

   The Add/Remove Programs Properties dialog box appears.

3. **Click the Windows Setup tab.**

   The Windows Setup options appear, as shown in Figure 22-1.

Figure 22-1:
The
Windows
Setup
options
in the
Add/Remove
Programs
Properties
dialog box.

4. **Click Communications and then click the Details button.**

   This brings up the Communications dialog box, shown in Figure 22-2.

Figure 22-2:
The
Communi-
cations
dialog box
lets you
select
optional
networking
features.

5. **Select the Dial-Up Server check box by clicking it.**

   A check mark appears in the check box. (If the check mark does not appear, click again until the check mark appears.)

6. **Click OK to return to the Windows Setup options.**

7. **Click OK again to install the Dial-Up Server feature.**

   The Add/Remove Programs Properties dialog box disappears, and Windows installs the Dial-Up Server feature.

   If Windows asks you to insert the Windows CD-ROM, do it.

8. **That's all!**

You're ready to use Dial-Up Networking.

If the computer at your office runs Windows 95, you must first add a program called Microsoft Plus! or upgrade to Windows 98. You can purchase Microsoft Plus! for about $50, but because Microsoft Plus! for Windows 95 might be hard to find and the cost of upgrading to Windows 98 isn't much more, I recommend upgrading instead.

Before you can use a dial-up connection, you must configure both your home and office computers for Dial-Up Networking. First, you must configure your office computer to work as a dial-up server. Then you must configure your home computer to function as a dial-up client. After you configure both computers, you can use the dial-up client computer at home to call in to the dial-up server computer at work. I describe how to configure the dial-up server and client in the following sections.

Configuring a Windows 98/Me Dial-Up Server

After you install Dial-Up Networking in Windows 98 or Millennium Edition (Me), you can configure your office computer so that it can function as a dial-up server by following these steps:

1. **Double-click the My Computer icon on your desktop and then double-click the Dial-Up Networking icon.**

   The Dial-Up Networking window appears, as shown in Figure 22-3.

Note that if you previously used Dial-Up Networking to create a connection to an Internet service provider or some other dial-up network, other icons besides the Make New Connection icon appear in the Dial-Up Networking window. However, if you have not yet created any dial-up connections, Windows may decide to start the Make a New Connection Wizard for you when you open the Dial-Up Networking window. If the Make a New Connection Wizard appears, just click Cancel to close the wizard.

Figure 22-3:
The Dial-Up
Networking
window.

2. Choose the Connections➪Dial-Up Server command.

If you can't find the Connections menu, widen the Dial-Up Networking window by dragging its right border to the right until the Connections menu appears.

The Dial-Up Server dialog box appears, as shown in Figure 22-4.

Figure 22-4:
The Dial-Up
Server
dialog box.

3. Select Allow Caller Access.

Doing so allows other computers to call in to the office computer. After you select Allow Caller Access, the Change Password button is enabled.

4. Click the Change Password button.

A dialog box appears asking you to enter a password.

5. Type a password and then click OK.

Choose a password to use when you call in to your office computer. Write it down somewhere so that you won't forget it.

Creating a password when you set up a dial-up server is very important. If you don't create a password, anyone who knows the phone number can call up your computer and access not only your computer but also your entire network.

6. **Click OK.**

The computer is now set up as a dial-up server. All that remains is to share any disk drives or printers you want to be able to access from home.

7. **To share a folder so that you can access it from home, double-click My Computer. Then click the drive you want to share and choose File⇨Sharing. Click Share As and then click OK.**

For security reasons, you should share just the folder you need to access from home rather than your entire hard drive. And be sure to use a password to prevent unauthorized users from accessing your files.

8. **To share a printer, double-click the Printers icon in the My Computer window, select the printer in the My Computer window, choose File⇨Sharing, click Share As, and then click OK.**

You're all set.

Here are a few additional points to ponder when you use a dial-up server:

✔ After you click OK in Step 6, the Dial-Up Server icon (shown in the margin) appears in your taskbar. This icon indicates that the computer is monitoring the phone line, waiting to pick up an incoming call to establish a dial-up connection.

✔ To disable the dial-up server, double-click the Dial-Up Server icon in the taskbar. This summons the Dial-Up Server dialog box. Select No Caller Access and then click OK. The Dial-Up Server dialog box disappears, and the Dial-Up Server icon vanishes from the taskbar. To reinstate the Dial-Up Server, you have to repeat the entire procedure to configure the dial-up server.

✔ Don't, under any circumstances, set up a Dial-Up Server without a password! Yes, I know I already warned you about this, but it's worth a second warning.

✔ If you shut down your computer while it's in Dial-Up Server mode, the Dial-Up Server is automatically restarted after you restart your computer.

✔ If the Dial-Up Networking window doesn't have a Connections⇨Dial-Up Server command, you must first install dial-up server support. See the section "Installing the dial-up server feature," earlier in this chapter. (For Windows 95, you must purchase either Microsoft Plus! or upgrade to Windows 98 or Millennium Edition to get the dial-up server feature.)

✔ If you're a network administrator, the thought of users creating Dial-Up Servers to gain remote access to your network may give you the willies. If so, you can ban the Dial-Up Server function by using a Windows program called the System Policy Editor.

Configuring a Windows 2000 Dial-Up Server

Windows 2000 Professional has much better dial-up server security features than Windows 98 or Millennium Edition. For starters, Windows 2000 Pro lets you designate which user accounts can access your computer by dialing in. You can even set up a separate user account to use just for dial-up access. In addition, Windows 2000 Pro lets you use call-back security, which is one way to secure a dial-up connection. (For more information about call-back security, see the section "Don't Call Us — We'll Call You," later in this chapter.)

To set up a dial-up server in Windows 2000 Pro, call up the Network and Dial-Up Connections folder (which you find in My Computer) and double-click the Make a New Connection icon to start the Network Connection Wizard. After the opening screen, the Network Connection Wizard displays the screen shown in Figure 22-5, which lets you select the type of network connection you want to create. Choose Accept Incoming Connections and then click Next.

Figure 22-5:
Creating a
network
connection
in Windows
2000
Professional.

To create a dial-up server, the Network Connection Wizard displays a series of dialog boxes asking for the following information:

✔ **The device you want to allow incoming connections on.** In most cases, a modem and a LAN connection will be listed. Choose the modem to allow dial-up connections.

✔ **Whether to allow Virtual Private Networking.** For a simple dial-up connection, choose No.

✔ **Which users to allow access.** All of the user accounts authorized to use your computer will be listed. Choose the user account you want to use for the dial-up connection.

Creating a separate user account that you can use for dial-up access is a good idea. Then, you can give this account access just to the folders and printers you need to access from home.

✔ **The network protocols you want to use for the dial-up connection.** The default is to use TCP/IP, Microsoft File and Printer Sharing, and Client for Microsoft Networks. Change these settings only if you have a reason and you know what you're doing.

✔ **A name for your connection.**

Configuring Your Home Computer for Dial-Up Networking

To configure your home computer to act as a dial-up client, you must create a new dial-up connection that is set up to dial in to you office computer. You can follow these steps, which are the same for Windows 98 or Windows Me:

1. **Double-click the My Computer icon on your desktop and then double-click the Dial-Up Networking icon.**

   The Dial-Up Networking window appears (refer to Figure 22-3).

2. **Double-click the Make New Connection icon.**

   The Make New Connection Wizard comes to life, as shown in Figure 22-6.

Figure 22-6:
The Make New Connection Wizard.

   3. **Type a name for the connection to your office computer.**

   Use a simple name, such as *Office*.

   4. **Click Next.**

   The wizard displays another dialog box that asks for your office computer's phone number.

   5. **Type the phone number for the phone line that's connected to your office computer's modem and then click Next.**

   The wizard displays a confirmation dialog box saying that it's ready to create the connection.

   6. **Click Finish.**

   The wizard creates the new connection, which appears as an icon in the Dial-Up Networking window.

Here are a few tidbits to consider when setting up your home computer for Dial-Up Networking:

   ✔ The Make New Connection Wizard may ask for additional information if it discovers that you have not yet configured your modem for Windows. If this happens, just follow the bouncing ball and answer whatever questions it asks as best you can. If you become confused, just act like you know what you're doing, and the wizard won't notice. In almost all cases, the wizard can automatically detect and configure your modem properly, so all you have to do is sit and watch.

   ✔ If you can't find Dial-Up Networking anywhere on your computer, you may not have installed it. Find your Windows CD and then double-click the Add/Remove Programs icon in the Control Panel. Click the Windows Setup tab in the Add/Remove Programs dialog box and then double-click the Communications icon and make sure that Dial-Up Networking is selected. Click OK and then insert your Windows CD in your CD-ROM drive to install Dial-Up Networking.

   ✔ If you plan on calling your office computer often, drag the office computer connection icon from the Dial-Up Networking window onto your desktop. Then you won't have to wade through My Computer every time you want to connect.

Making the Connection

After you configure your office and home computers for Dial-Up Networking, you undoubtedly want to call your office computer and put Dial-Up Networking to work. Here's how:

1. **When you leave work to go home, make sure you leave the dial-up server computer turned on.**

   You can't dial in to the dial-up server from home if you turn the dial-up server computer off.

2. **On your home computer, choose the Start⇨Programs⇨Accessories⇨ Dial-Up Networking and then double-click the icon for the office computer's connection.**

   Or if you dragged a copy of the icon to your desktop, just double-click the icon on your desktop. Either way, the Connect To dialog box appears, as shown in Figure 22-7.

Figure 22-7: The Connect To dialog box.

3. **Make sure that the phone number, user name, and password are correct. Then click Connect.**

   Windows calls in to your office computer and establishes a connection. This process may take a minute or so, so be patient. You see various messages on the screen while the connection is being made, such as `Dialing`, `Verifying User Name and Password`, `Waiting for Godot`, `Twiddling Thumbs`, and so on. Eventually, the message says `Connected`, at which point you're officially connected to your office computer.

Using Network Resources with a Dial-Up Connection

After you're connected to the dial-up server, you can access the dial-up server's disk drives and printers. However, you can't use the Network Neighborhood icon to access your office computer's resources. Windows automatically disables Network Neighborhood for dial-up connections because the dial-up connection is so slow compared to a normal Ethernet connection. Instead, follow these steps to access your office computer's resources when connected over the phone:

1. **Choose the Start⇨Run command.**

2. **Type two backward slashes followed by the name of your office computer.**

   For example, type **Office**.

3. **Click OK.**

   Your home computer takes a while to access your office computer over the phone. Eventually, though, a window, such as the one shown in Figure 22-8, appears. You can access your office computer's shared disk drives and printers from this window.

Figure 22-8: Accessing another computer's resources using Dial-Up Networking.

To disconnect from the office computer, double-click the modem icon that appears in the taskbar and then click Disconnect. Or if you prefer, right-click the modem icon and choose Disconnect from the pop-up menu that appears.

You can also access files on your the dial-up server's disk drive by using the standard Open and Save As dialog boxes. To see how, refer to the section about accessing network files in Chapter 23.

Don't Call Us — We'll Call You

One of the advantages of using Windows 2000 for your dial-up server is that you can use the callback feature. Callback is both a security feature and a cost-cutting feature. It works like this:

1. From your remote computer, you dial in to the dial-up server computer.

2. The dial-up server verifies your user name and password.

3. The dial-up server hangs up on you.

4. The dial-up server then calls you back.

5. Your computer answers the phone and verifies the connection.

6. You can then use the network.

When used as a security feature, the dial-up server calls you back using a pre-arranged number. That way, you can only dial in to the network from a fixed location, such as your home. For a hacker to break in to your network using a callback connection, he or she would have to break into your home and call in using your phone line.

The callback feature can also be used as a simple cost-cutting measure for users who need to connect to the office computer while they are on the road. For example, suppose you are in your hotel room in St. Louis and you need to connect to your office computer in Detroit. With a callback connection, you can place a short long distance call from the hotel room to the dial-up server computer in the Detroit office. Before it hangs up on you, the dial-up server asks you what number to call you back at. Then, the dial-up server hangs up and calls you right back, your computer answers and reconnects, and you can use the network while the call is billed to the dial-up servers' phone rather than to your hotel room's phone.

Callback for a Windows 2000 Professional dial-up server is set on a user-by-user basis, because each user can have a different phone number to call back. To configure callback, follow these steps:

1. **Double-click My Computer; then click the Network and Dial-up Connections link.**

   The Network and Dial-up Connections folder appears.

2. **Right-click the Incoming Connections icon; then choose Properties from the pop-up menu that appears.**

   This brings up the Incoming Connections Properties dialog box.

3. **Click the Users tab.**

   A list of user accounts appears in the dialog box, as shown in Figure 22-9.

Figure 22-9:
The Users
tab.

4. **Click the user account you will use to call in to the dial-up server and then click Properties.**

   The User Properties dialog box appears. This dialog box has two tabs: General and Callback. The General tab is shown first.

5. **Click the Callback tab.**

   The callback options appear, as shown in Figure 22-10.

6. **Set the callback option you want to use.**

   The choices are

   - **Do Not Allow Callback**, which disables the callback feature for this user. (This is the default setting.)

   - **Allow the Caller to Set the Callback Number**, which means that the dial-up server will ask you to enter a number before hanging up, then call you back at the number you provide.

   - **Always Use the Following Callback Number**, which means that the dial-up server will call you back at a fixed number.

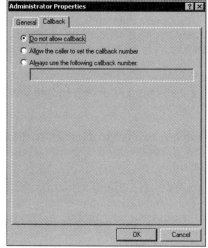

Figure 22-10:
Setting the callback options for a dial-up user.

7. **If you choose Al̲w̲ays Use the Following Callback Number, type the number you want the server to call back in the text box.**

   For example, if you will be dialing in to the dial-up server from your home, type the number your home computer's modem is connected to.

8. **Click OK.**

   You are returned to the Incoming Connections Properties dialog box.

9. **Repeat Steps 4 through 8 for any other users you want to configure callback options for.**

   In most cases, you'll configure just one user for the dial-up server. However, if you are setting up the dial-up server so that several users can access it, repeat Steps 4 through 8 for each user.

10. **Click OK to dismiss the Incoming Connections Properties dialog box.**

You're done! Now, when you call in to the dial-up server, the server will hang up on you and call you back.

Using Remote Access Service

Both Windows NT and 2000 Server include built-in support for remote access, with a feature called *Remote Access Service*, also known as *RAS*. With RAS, you equip a server computer with one or more modems (standard modems or ISDN modems) and dedicate it as a remote access server. Remote users can then dial in to the network and, once connected, use the network as if they were connected with an Ethernet cable. Of course, the connection is much slower because it operates over phone lines rather than real Ethernet cable.

Remote Access Service has several advantages over a simple Windows dial-up server:

- ✔ RAS can work with more than one modem to allow more than one user to connect simultaneously. With special modem pooling equipment, RAS can service hundreds of dial-up users.

- ✔ RAS has better security features than a simple Windows dial-up server. With RAS, you can encrypt data that is transmitted over the phone line, and you can use more reliable authentication methods to verify that dial-up users are really who they say they are.

- ✔ RAS can use Caller ID to verify that a user is calling from a predetermined number. This provides the same protection as callback to a fixed number but is more convenient.

- ✔ RAS can limit dial-in access to specified times and days.

- ✔ RAS also supports Virtual Private Network (VPN) connections, which enable a user to connect to your network via the Internet rather than by dialing directly into your network.

Novell offers a similar remote access program called NetWare Connect.

Hardware-Based Remote Access

An alternative to devoting a server computer for remote access is to use specialized remote access hardware, which connects directly to your network and allows users to dial in. That way, you don't have to contend with setting up and maintaining a Windows NT, 2000, or NetWare server, and you don't have to dedicate an entire PC to the task of sharing modems for remote access.

One of the most popular remote access servers is LanRover, made by Shiva (which is owned by Intel). LanRover is a self-contained remote access server that includes an Ethernet port so that you can connect LanRover to your network and eight serial ports for plug-in modems. Or you can get LanRover Plus, which includes built-in modems. LanRover can use normal modem connections or high-speed ISDN connections for faster connections.

For more information about LanRover, check out Shiva's home page on the Internet at www.shiva.com.

Virtual Private Networking

An alternative to using a dial-up connection to access your office network from home is to use a technique called *Virtual Private Networking,* or *VPN.* VPN lets you create the equivalent of a private connection between two computers or networks using the Internet instead of a separate dial-up connection. For example, suppose you already have an Internet connection at home, either via a dial-up line or with a fast cable or DSL connection, and the network at your office also has an Internet connection. Rather than use dial-up networking to access the office network from home, you could use the Internet to create a VPN connection between your home computer and your office network.

To use VPN, you must first set up a VPN connection on a Windows NT or 2000 Server computer running RAS or a NetWare server with NetWare Connect. (For more information, see the section "Using Remote Access Service" earlier in this chapter.) Then, you can configure a VPN connection on your home computer.

VPN uses a special protocol known as *PPTP,* which stands for *Point-to-Point Tunneling Protocol.* The process of creating a private connection between two computers over an intermediate network such as the Internet is often called tunneling because the connection is similar to a tunnel through the Internet that connects the two computers directly.

Chapter 23

Using Microsoft Office on a Network

. . . .

. . . .

*M*icrosoft Office is far and away the most popular suite of application programs used on personal computers, and it includes the most common types of application programs used in an office: a word processing program (Word), a spreadsheet program (Excel), a presentation program (PowerPoint), and an excellent e-mail program (Outlook). Depending on the version of Office you purchase, you may also get a database program (Access), Web site development program (FrontPage), a desktop publishing program (Publisher), a set of Ginsu knives (KnifePoint), and a slicer and dicer (SalsaMaster).

This chapter describes the networking features of Microsoft Office 2000, the latest and greatest version of Office. Some of these features also work with previous versions of Office as well.

 To get the most from using Office on a network, you should purchase the Microsoft Office Resource Kit. The Office Resource Kit (also known as *ORK*) contains information about installing and using Office on a network and comes with a CD that has valuable tools. If you don't want to purchase the ORK, you can view it online and download the ORK tools from Microsoft's TechNet Web site (technet.microsoft.com). Nanu-nanu.

Installing Office on a Network —
Some Options

You need to make two basic decisions when you prepare to install Microsoft Office on a network. The first is whether you want to copy the Office program files onto each computer's local hard disk or place some or all of the Office program files on a shared server disk. Here are the pros and cons of each option:

- ✔ Installing the Office program files onto each computer's hard disk is usually the best choice. However, this option requires that each computer have enough free disk space to hold the Office program files. Office 2000 can require more than 500MB of disk space if you install all of its components.

- ✔ Placing Office program files on the server frees up disk space on the client computers' hard drives. However, network users will notice that Office runs slower because network files are slower to access than local files. To alleviate this, you can install the most frequently needed Office program files on each computer's local disk and the less frequently used files on the network server.

The second choice to make when installing Office on a network is which of several alternative installation methods to use. Here are the options:

- ✔ Ignore the fact that you have a network, purchase a separate copy of Office for each user on the network, and install Office from the CD on each computer. This option works well if your network is small, if each computer has ample disk space to hold the necessary Office files, and if each computer has its own CD-ROM drive.

- ✔ Buy a separate copy of Office for each computer but install Office onto each computer from a shared CD-ROM drive located on a server computer. This option works well when you have network client computers that do not have their own CD-ROM drives.

- ✔ Copy the entire Office CD into a shared folder on a network server. Then from each network computer, connect to the shared folder and run the Office Setup program to install Office onto each computer on the network.

- ✔ Use the Office Setup program in Administrative Setup mode. This option lets you create a special type of setup on a network server disk, from which you can install Office onto network computers. Administrative Setup enables you to control the custom features selected for each network computer and reduce the amount of user interaction required to install Office onto each computer.

If you choose to use Administrative Setup, you can use the Network Installation Wizard that comes with the Office Resource Kit. The Network Installation Wizard lets you customize settings for installing Office onto client computers. For example, you can choose which Office components to install, provide default answers to yes/no questions that Setup asks the user while installing Office, and select the amount of interaction you want the Setup program to have with the user while installing Office.

No matter which option you choose for installing Office on your network, you must purchase either a copy of Office or a license to install Office for every computer that uses Office. Purchasing a single copy of Office and installing it on more than one computer is illegal.

Accessing Network Files

Opening a file that resides on a network drive is almost as easy as opening a file on a local drive. All Office programs use the File⇨Open command to summon the Open dialog box, as shown in its Excel incarnation in Figure 23-1. (The Open dialog box is nearly identical in other Office programs.)

Figure 23-1:
The Open dialog box in Excel 2000.

To access a file that resides on a network volume that has been mapped to a drive letter, all you have to do is use the Look In drop-down list to select the network drive. If the network volume has not been mapped to a drive, use the Look In drop-down list to select Network Neighborhood and then browse through the network to find the file.

You can map a network drive directly from the Open dialog box by following these steps:

1. **Choose the File➪Open command.**

   This summons the Open dialog box.

2. **Click Tools in the Open dialog box and then choose Map Network Drive.**

   The Map Network Drive dialog box appears, as shown in Figure 23-2.

Figure 23-2:
Mapping a
network
drive.

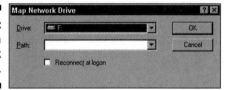

3. **If you don't like the drive letter suggested in the Drive field, change it.**

   Map Network Drive defaults to the next available drive letter — in the case of Figure 23-2, drive F:. If you prefer to use a different drive letter, you can choose any of the drive letters available in the Drive drop-down list.

4. **In the Path field, type the complete network path for the shared drive you want to map.**

   In most cases, the network path is two back slashes, the server name, another back slash, and the shared volume's share name. For example, to map a shared volume named MYDOCS on a server named WALLY, type the following in the Path field:

   `\\WALLY\MYDOCS`

   This type of filename, with the double backslashes, the server name, and the share name, is known as a *UNC name*. (*UNC* stands for *Universal Naming Convention*.)

5. **If you want this drive to be mapped automatically each time you log on to the network, check the Reconnect at Logon option.**

   If you leave this option unchecked, the drive mapping vanishes when you log off the network.

6. **Click OK.**

   You return to the Open dialog box. The Look In field automatically shows the newly mapped network drive, so the Open dialog box lists the files and folders in the network drive.

If you try to open a file that another network user already has opened, Office tells you that the file is already in use and offers to let you open a read-only version of the file. You can read and edit the read-only version, but Office won't let you overwrite the existing version of the file.

Using Workgroup Templates

A *template* is not a place of worship, though an occasional sacrifice to the Office gods may make your computing life a bit easier. Rather, a template is a special type of document file that holds formatting information, boilerplate text, and other customized settings that you can use as the basis for new documents.

Three Office programs — Word, Excel, and PowerPoint — enable you to specify a template whenever you create a new document. When you create a new document in Word, Excel, or PowerPoint by choosing the File⇨New command, you see a dialog box that lets you choose a template for the new document. For example, Figure 23-3 shows the dialog box that appears when you create a new document in Word 2000.

Figure 23-3:
The New dialog box in Word 2000.

Office comes with a set of templates for the most common types of documents. These templates are grouped under the various tabs that appear across the top of the New dialog box.

In addition to the templates that come with Office, you can create your own templates in Word, Excel, and PowerPoint. Creating your own templates is especially useful if you want to establish a consistent look for documents prepared by your network users. For example, you can create a Letter template that includes your company's letterhead or a Proposal template that includes a company logo.

Office enables you to store templates in two locations. The first location, referred to as the User Templates folder, usually resides on the user's local disk drive. The second location, called the Workgroup Templates folder, is usually a folder on a shared network drive. This arrangement lets you store templates that you want to make available to all network users on a network server, but still allows each user to create his or her own templates that are not available to other network users.

When you use both a User Templates folder and a Workgroup Templates folder, Office combines the templates from both folders and lists them in alphabetical order in the New dialog box. For example, suppose that the User Templates folder contains templates called Blank Document and Web Page, and the Workgroup Templates folder contains a template called Company Letterhead. In this case, three templates appear in the New dialog box, in this order: Blank Document, Company Letterhead, and Web Page.

To set the User Templates and Workgroup Templates folders, choose Tools⇨Options in Word to summon the Options dialog box. Then click the File Locations tab to display the file location options, such as those shown in Figure 23-4.

Figure 23-4:
The Options
dialog box.

Although the User Templates and Workgroup Templates settings affect Word, Excel, and PowerPoint, you can change these settings only from Word. The Options dialog boxes in Excel and PowerPoint don't show the User Templates or Workgroup Templates options.

When you install Office, the standard templates that come with Office are copied into a folder on the computer's local disk drive, and the User Templates option is set to this folder. The Workgroup Templates option is left blank. You can set the Workgroup Templates folder to a shared network folder by clicking Network Templates, clicking the Modify button, and specifying a shared network folder that contains your workgroup templates.

Working with Collaboration Features

According to my high school English teacher, Benjamin Franklin turned down an invitation to write the Declaration of Independence because he did not want to write a document that others would edit. Old Ben would have hated the network collaboration features built into Office. Office comes with several features that make it easy for a group of people to work together to create a document. The following sections describe these features.

Routing documents

All the main Office programs — Word, Excel, PowerPoint, and Access — include a document-routing feature that lets you send a document to a list of e-mail recipients. Document routing enables you to choose one of two methods for sending a document to multiple users:

✔ You can send the document to the users on the list one at a time. When the first user receives the document, that person can review it, modify it, and add annotations. Then, the first user forwards the document to the next user in the list. When the last user in the list receives and acts upon the document, that person forwards the document back to you. You can then view all the users' revisions and annotations together.

✔ You can send a separate copy of the document to all the users on the list at once. Then, each user reviews, revises, and annotates the document and sends it back to you. You wind up with multiple versions of the document that you can review independently.

Here's how to route a document to several users:

1. **Create or open the document you want to route.**

2. **Choose the File⇨Send To⇨Routing Recipient command.**

   This summons the Routing Slip dialog box, shown in Figure 23-5.

Figure 23-5:
The Routing
Slip dialog
box.

3. **Click the Address button to summon the Address Book.**

4. **For each person you want to route the document to, click the person's name in your Address Book and then click the To button.**

   Keep adding names until the list is complete.

5. **Click OK to dismiss the Address Book.**

   You return to the Routing Slip dialog box. The names you selected in the Address Book appear in the Routing Slip dialog box.

6. **Type a message in the Message text field.**

   For example, you can say "Please review this by Thursday!" or some other friendly message.

7. **Select One After Another or All at Once as the routing method.**

8. **Check the Return When Done option if you want the document to be returned to you after everyone has reviewed it.**

9. **Check the Track Status option if you want to follow the progress of the document.**

   If you choose the Track Status option, you get an e-mail message each time a user forwards the document to the next person on the list.

10. **Click Route to send the document on its way.**

Tracking changes

Both Word and Excel have a Track Changes feature that lets you keep track of the revisions made to a document or worksheet. This feature enables you to see what changes other users have made to your document and accept or reject the changes based on your own whimsical judgments.

In Word, the Track Changes feature highlights changes to a document by drawing a line through any deleted text and underlining any inserted text. In addition, any text that contains a change — either an insertion or a deletion — is marked with a vertical line in the margin so that you can quickly scan through a document to find changes.

In Excel, each changed cell is marked with a special symbol. Excel allows you to flag all the changes to the worksheet, just those changes made since the worksheet was last saved or since a particular date, or just those changes that you have not yet reviewed.

Both Word and Excel indicate who made each change. As a result, the revision-tracking feature works together with the routing feature. As each routing recipient makes changes to the document, those changes are tracked so that when the document returns to you, you can see the changes that each user proposes.

When a document with changes returns to you, open the document and choose Tools⇨Track Changes⇨Accept or Reject Changes. Word or Excel displays the changes in the document one at a time, along with the name of the person who made the change and the time and date the change was made. You can then accept or reject each change.

Word, Excel, and PowerPoint enable users to insert comments into the document by using the Insert⇨Comment command. In Excel and PowerPoint, the Insert⇨Comment command places a yellow sticky-note comment into the worksheet or presentation. Comments in Word are a little more complicated; they appear in a separate pane at the bottom of the screen rather than right in the document.

Replying to discussions

In addition to simple comments, Office 2000 lets you embed an entire discussion within a document. The Discussions feature allows users to reply to remarks made by other users. For example, one user may post a discussion remark about a particular paragraph in a Word document. Another user may post a reply to the first remark, stating that he or she disagrees with the original remark. When you review the discussion, you can see the original remarks along with the various replies.

Networking an Access Database

If you want to share a Microsoft Access database among several network users, you should be aware of a few special considerations. Here are the more important ones:

- ✔ When you share a database, more than one user may try to access the same record at the same time. This situation can lead to problems if two or more users try to update the record. To handle this, Access locks the record so that only one user at a time can update it. Access uses one of three methods to lock records:

  - **Edited Record:** Locks a record whenever a user begins to edit a record. For example, if a user retrieves a record in a form that allows the record to be updated, Access locks the record while the user edits it so that other users can't edit the record until the first record is finished.

  - **No Locks:** This doesn't really mean that the record isn't locked. Instead, No Locks means that the record is not locked until a user actually writes a change to the database. This method can be confusing to users because it enables one user to overwrite changes made by another user.

  - **All Records:** Locks an entire table whenever a user edits any record in the table.

- ✔ Access lets you split a database so that the forms, queries, and reports are stored on each user's local disk drive, but the data itself is stored on a network drive. This feature can make the database run more efficiently on a network but is a little more difficult to set up. To split a database, use the Tools⇨Database Utilities⇨Database Splitter command.

- ✔ Access includes built-in security features that you should use if you store an Access database on a Windows 95, 98, or Millennium Edition server or on a FAT drive on a Windows NT server. If you store the database on an NTFS volume on an NT server or on a NetWare server, you can use the server's security features to protect the database.

- ✔ Access automatically refreshes forms and datasheets every 60 seconds. That way, if one user opens a form or datasheet and another user changes the data a few seconds later, the first user sees the changes within one minute. If 60 seconds is too long (or too short), you can change the refresh from the Advanced tab of the Options dialog box.

Chapter 24

Networking Older Computers

- -

In This Chapter

▶ Understanding the challenges of networking older computers

▶ Handling older computers in two common ways

▶ Using a DOS network computer

▶ Configuring a network card the old-fashioned way

- -

*W*ouldn't it be great if every computer on your network had a shiny new Pentium III processor, 128MB of RAM, and a 20GB disk drive? Managing a network like this would be a breeze. Everyone could take advantage of the latest networking features of Windows Me or, better yet, Windows 2000, you wouldn't have to worry about incompatible network cards or software conflicts, and the users would never complain about lousy performance (except for the real nerds, who want Pentium *IV* processors).

Unfortunately, few networks in the real world have the luxury of working with only the most current computers. Most networks consist of a hodgepodge of computers, ranging from brand-new Pentium III computers with plenty of RAM and disk space, to older Pentium computers with adequate RAM and disk space, to ancient 486 computers with barely enough RAM and disk space. Some even have prehistoric 386 computers with not enough RAM or disk space. Getting all these computers to work on your network is the topic of this chapter.

Networking Older Computers Presents Challenges

Accommodating older computers on your network presents you with a plethora of challenges to overcome. The following list highlights the major areas of difficulty you face when networking computers that are less than state-of-the-art:

✔ Your client computers may run several different versions of Windows. You may find computers with Windows Millennium Edition (Windows Me), Windows 98 (first and second edition), Windows 95, Windows 3.1, and Windows for Workgroup computers in your network. You may also find Windows NT 4 Workstation and Windows 2000 Professional. Windows 95, 98, and Me as well as Windows NT 4 and Windows 2000 have built-in networking support, but configuring older versions of Windows for networking can be a challenge.

✔ Some of the client computers may not even run Windows. You may have to figure out how to incorporate computers running DOS without Windows into your network.

✔ Older computers are probably very tight on disk space. Not long ago, 650MB of disk space seemed like a lot. Now it's barely enough to hold Windows, let alone any application programs or data files. Users of these computers will crave disk space on your network servers.

✔ Older computers have hardware limitations that make installing and configuring network cards difficult. (For more info, see the section "Configuring a Network Card in an Older Computer," later in this chapter.)

✔ When you mix old computers with new computers on the network, software incompatibilities are bound to arise. For example, some users may use Microsoft Office 2000, while others use older version of Office. Some may even still use DOS versions of WordPerfect and Lotus 1-2-3.

Dealing with Older Computers in Two Ways

The following sections summarize two basic approaches to handling the challenges of networking older computers.

Option 1: Don't include older computers in the network

One option is to simply state a minimum configuration that you will support on your network and refuse even to attempt to network any computer that doesn't meet that minimum. For example, you may say that you won't network any computer that doesn't already run at least Windows 95. Anyone who is still using Windows 3.1 or plain old DOS is out of luck.

Of course, this approach can make a lot of people mad — especially the ones with older computers. To make these people happy, you have two options: upgrade their old computers so that they can run Windows 98, or throw the old computers away and replace them with new computers.

If the computer isn't too old, you may be able to upgrade it to Windows 95 or 98 without much trouble. According to Microsoft, the minimum system requirements for Windows 98 are as follows:

  ✔ A 486 or better processor running at 66 MHz or faster

  ✔ 16MB of RAM

  ✔ 120MB of available disk space

The minimum requirements for Windows 95 are

  ✔ A 486 or better processor running at 25 MHz or faster

  ✔ 4MB of RAM (8MB recommended)

  ✔ 40 to 45MB of free disk space

Most 486-based computers meet the requirements for Windows 95 and can be upgraded easily to meet the Windows 98 requirements by adding more RAM and, if necessary, installing a second disk drive. The computer remains slow, but it works.

The biggest trick is installing and configuring a network card to work in a 486-based computer. For tips on how to do this, see the section "Configuring a Network Card in an Older Computer," later in this chapter.

A computer with a 386 processor (or older) requires a more substantial over-haul to bring it up to Windows 95 or 98 standards. In fact, to upgrade a 386 computer to run Windows 95 or 98, you probably need to replace almost every major component of the computer: the motherboard, disk drive, video card, and maybe even the monitor. By the time you finish, you have spent as much or actually more than a new computer costs. Better to just discard these computers and replace them with new ones.

Although it is possible to run Windows 98 on a 486 computer, I wouldn't try it. By the time you invest the hours it will take to install any needed upgrades, manually configure the network card, install Windows 98 (which will take a long time because of the slow speed of the computer), you'll real-ize that in the long run, replacing the 486 computer with a new computer would be less expensive.

Option 2: Use your network's DOS support

If you have computers that run MS-DOS, with or without old-fashioned Windows 3.1, you can include them in your network by using your network operating system's built-in support for MS-DOS client computers. Both Windows NT/2000 Server and NetWare support MS-DOS client computers. An MS-DOS client computer can access shared network disk drives and printers, but cannot share its own drives or printers with other network users.

For more information about using a DOS computer on a network, see the section "Using a DOS Client Computer," later in this chapter.

Using a DOS Client Computer

Both Windows NT/2000 Server and NetWare enable you to use DOS computers as clients on the network. A DOS client computer cannot share its own disk drives or printers with other network users, but it can access network drives and printers. The following sections describe the basics of using a DOS computer on a network.

Logging on to the network

To use network resources, a DOS client computer must first log on to the network. Usually, the logon process is started automatically by the computer's `AUTOEXEC.BAT` file when you start up your computer. You see a prompt similar to the following:

```
Enter your login name:
```

Type your user ID and press Enter. Then a prompt similar to this one appears:

```
Enter your password:
```

When you type your password, the password doesn't appear on the screen, which prevents someone looking over your shoulder from learning your password, unless of course they watch your fingers while you type.

After the network verifies your user ID and password, a special *login script* runs. The login script sets up your computer so that you can use network drives and printers.

Using a network drive

After you log on to the network, you have access to one or more network drives. Just like local drives, network drives are accessed using drive letters that are assigned to the network drives by the login script.

Every network is set up differently, so I can't tell you what your network drive letters are or what restrictions are in place for accessing your network drives. But you can find out easily enough. If you work on a Windows Server network, just type the following command at an MS-DOS prompt:

```
NET USE
```

This command displays a list of the network drives that are available to you. To see a similar list for a NetWare network, use this command:

```
MAP
```

This displays a list of all mapped network drives.

Network printing with NetWare

If your network is Novell NetWare and you're using NetWare's DOS client software, you set up redirection for a network printer by using the CAPTURE command. This command tells the NetWare software to capture everything sent to a particular printer port and redirect it to a network print queue. You'll probably want to put the CAPTURE command in the computer's AUTOEXEC.BAT file or a login script.

Here's a typical CAPTURE command:

```
CAPTURE Q=LJET TI=10
```

This command redirects any printer output you send to LPT1 to a print queue named LJET. TI=10 sets the time-out value to ten seconds. If your program stops sending output to the printer for ten seconds, NetWare assumes the print job is finished.

If you have a local printer attached to your LPT1 port, you set up LPT2 as a network printer. Here's a CAPTURE command that does that:

```
CAPTURE L=2 Q=LJET TI=10
```

The L=2 tells CAPTURE to redirect LPT2.

Here are some additional important points regarding network printing with NetWare:

- Hopefully, a CAPTURE command is set up in your AUTOEXEC.BAT file, after the LOGIN command. That way, your network printer is set up for you automatically when you start your computer.

- Sometimes, ten seconds isn't long enough for the time-out value. If your reports are being broken apart into several print jobs, try a higher time-out value. If you omit TI altogether, time-out checking is turned off. Then your programs can take as long as they want to create the output.

- To cancel printer redirection, use the ENDCAP command. Good news! ENDCAP doesn't have any parameters, switches, or other adornments! Just say ENDCAP.

- CAPTURE has an AUTOENDCAP option that automatically releases output to the network printer whenever you exit an application. Don't confuse this option with the ENDCAP command, which not only releases any pending printer output to the network, but cancels printer redirection as well.

- Suppose that you have a local printer and two network printers: A laser printer named LASER and an inkjet printer named INKY. To easily switch between these printers, create three batch files named LOCAL.BAT, LASER.BAT, and INKY.BAT. The LOCAL.BAT file should contain this command:

```
ENDCAP
```

LASER.BAT should contain this command:

```
CAPTURE Q=LASER TI=10
```

And INKY.BAT should contain this command:

```
CAPTURE Q=INKY TI=10
```

To switch to the local printer, just type **LOCAL** at the DOS prompt. To switch to a network printer, type **LASER** or **INKY**.

Network printing with Windows NT/2000 Server

If your network is Windows NT or 2000 Server and you use Microsoft MS-DOS client software, you set up printer redirection by using the NET USE command. This command tells the MS-DOS client software to use a particular network printer whenever you send output to a printer.

Here's a typical NET USE command to set up a network printer:

```
NET USE LPT1: \\WARD\LASER
```

This command redirects any printer output that you send to LPT1 to a printer named LASER on the server named WARD.

Here are some additional tips concerning network printing with Windows NT/2000 Server:

- ✔ A NET USE command should be set up in your AUTOEXEC.BAT file. That way, your network printer is set up for you automatically after you start your computer.

- ✔ To cancel printer redirection, use the NET USE /DELETE command, like this:

```
NET USE LPT1: /DELETE
```

- ✔ Suppose that you have a local printer and two network printers: a laser printer named LASER and an inkjet printer named INKY. To easily switch between these printers, create three batch files named LOCAL.BAT, LASER.BAT, and INKY.BAT. The LOCAL.BAT file should contain this command:

```
NET USE LPT1: /DELETE
```

This command disables any network connection for LPT1, so LPT1 reverts to your local printer. LASER.BAT should contain this command:

```
NET USE LPT1: \\WARD\LASER
```

And INKY.BAT should contain this command:

```
NET USE LPT1: \\WARD\INKY
```

To switch to the local printer, just type **LOCAL** at the DOS prompt. To switch to a network printer, type **LASER** or **INKY**.

Logging off the network

When you have finished using the network, you should log off. Logging off the network makes the network drives and printers unavailable, so strangers can't walk up to your computer and access the network.

If you just turn off your computer, you are automatically logged off the network. If you want to log off the network but keep your computer on so that you can continue using it, type the command **LOGOUT** if you use a NetWare network or **NET LOGOFF** if your network uses Windows NT/2000 Server.

Configuring a Network Card in an Older Computer

One of the best features about modern versions of Windows is *Plug and Play*, which makes installing new devices, such as a network interface card, a snap. Plug and Play automatically recognizes your network card, configures it, and installs any special device drivers that the card needs to operate.

To install a network card in a computer that runs Windows 3.1 or plain DOS, you have to configure the card manually. You may have to fiddle with confusing software configuration settings, or, worse yet, you may actually have to make changes on the card itself before you install it into your computer. If that's the case, the following tips should prove helpful:

✔ If possible, use good name-brand network cards (such as Intel or 3Com) for older computers. Name-brand cards may cost more, but they are usually easier to configure, which can be a major plus for older computers.

✔ On some cards, configuration settings are made by changing special switches called *DIP switches* or moving a *jumper block*. Figure 24-1 shows what a DIP switch and jumper block look like. The switch or block must be set *before* you install the card into your computer.

✔ A straightened-out paper clip is the ideal tool for setting DIP switches.

✔ To change a jumper block, you move the *plug* from one set of pins to another. You need fingernails to do it properly. Or a good set of tweezers.

✔ If you're lucky, your network cards have been preconfigured for you with the most likely settings. You need to double-check, though, because *(1)* the factory settings are not always appropriate, and *(2)* sometimes they make mistakes at the factory and configure the cards incorrectly.

Figure 24-1:
A DIP
switch and
a jumper
block.

✔ If you're even luckier, your cards don't use DIP switches or jumper blocks at all. These cards still have to be configured, but the configuration is done with software rather than with a paper clip or your fingernails.

✔ Most network cards have two configuration settings: IRQ number and I/O port address. Some cards also enable you to configure a DMA channel. These settings are described under separate headings in the next few pages. The information is technical and boring, so make sure that you're wide awake.

✔ Network cards that support more than one type of cable connector also have to be configured for the proper cable type. For example, if your card supports both 10baseT and coax connectors, you have to configure the card depending on the type of cable you use.

✔ When you configure a network card, write down the settings you select. You need these settings later when you install the client software. Store your list of network card settings in your network binder.

✔ Adding a joke about DIP switches here would be too easy. Insert your own joke if you're so inclined.

Configuring those irksome IRQ numbers

IRQ stands for *Interrupt ReQuest.* You don't need to know that; I tell you only because I think it's funny that the Q is capitalized in the middle of the word. Each computer has 16 different IRQ numbers, and each I/O device — such as a printer port, modem, mouse, and so on — must be assigned a separate IRQ number. Finding an IRQ number that's not already used isn't always easy. (On old XT computers, only eight IRQ numbers exist. That makes avoiding IRQ conflicts even harder.)

The trick to setting the IRQ number is knowing what IRQ numbers the computer is already using. Table 24-1 shows the usual IRQ settings.

Table 24-1	Typical IRQ Assignments
IRQ Number	*What It's Used For*
IRQ0	The computer's internal timer
IRQ1	The keyboard
IRQ2	Not usable
IRQ3	Serial port COM2, often a mouse or modem

(continued)

Table 24-1 (continued)

IRQ Number	What It's Used For
IRQ4	Serial port COM1, often a mouse or modem
IRQ5	Parallel port LPT2
IRQ6	Floppy disk
IRQ7	Parallel port LPT1
IRQ8	Internal clock
IRQ9-13	Usually available
IRQ14	Hard disk
IRQ15	Usually available

Here is some additional information about IRQ settings:

✔ Some network interface cards support only a few IRQ numbers, such as IRQ3, IRQ4, or IRQ5. IRQ5 is usually a safe choice unless the computer has two printers. However, if you installed a device such as a CD-ROM drive or a scanner, make sure that IRQ5 isn't already in use.

✔ IRQ3 and IRQ4 are used by the serial ports COM1 and COM2. If you have a modem and a serial-port mouse, don't use IRQ3 or IRQ4 for the network card.

✔ If your computer is loaded up with extra devices, check which IRQs are available *before* you buy your network cards. Make sure that the cards you buy can be configured to an IRQ number you can use.

✔ If you're not sure what IRQ numbers are in use and you have DOS Version 6.0 or 6.2 or Windows 3.1, run the MSD program from a DOS prompt. Press Q to display the IRQs that are in use.

Configuring the I/O port address

The I/O port address is a doorway that the network card uses to transfer information to and from the network. The address is usually set to a number such as 300, 310, 320, and so on. The only trick to setting the I/O port is making sure that it doesn't conflict with the port setting used by another device.

Here are some other things you should know about I/O port addresses:

✔ Unlike IRQ lines, I/O port conflicts are less common. You have lots of I/O port addresses to choose from, so avoiding conflicts is easier. The factory I/O port address setting is likely acceptable.

✔ The factory certainly won't ship out a network card with an I/O port setting that conflicts with your printer port, mouse, disk drive, or other common components. You're likely to see a conflict only if you have other stuff attached to your computer, such as a sound card, CD-ROM drive, or scanner. When you configure a network card, just make sure that the I/O port setting isn't the same as the setting you use for some other device.

✔ I/O port addresses are hexadecimal numbers that include the letters A–F along with the digits 0–9. For example, 37C is a valid I/O port address number. Be thankful that you don't have to understand hexadecimal numbering to set the port address correctly; just follow the instructions that come with the card, and the hex monsters won't bite you.

✔ The *h* that's sometimes added to the end of the I/O address — like 300h or 37Ch — is just to remind you that the number is hexadecimal, as if that matters.

Configuring the DMA channel

Some network cards use DMA channels for faster performance. (DMA stands for Direct Memory Access, but that's not important now.) If your card uses a DMA channel, you may have to change the default setting to avoid conflicting with some other add-on card that also may use DMA, such as a CD-ROM adapter or a scanner. Check the manual that came with your card to find out if the card uses DMA.

Chapter 25

Welcoming Macintosh Computers to Your Network

*T*his book dwells on networking PCs as if IBM were the only game in town. To be politically correct, I should at least acknowledge the existence of an altogether different breed of computer: the Apple Macintosh.

Apple prides itself on its ability to include stuff in its Macintosh operating system that Windows users have to purchase separately. Network support is an example. Every Macintosh comes with built-in networking support. All you have to do to network your Macintosh is buy network cable.

Well, you actually discover that networking your Macintosh involves a lot more than that. This chapter presents what you need to know to hook up a Macintosh network, use a Macintosh network, and mix Macintoshes and PCs on the same network. This chapter is not a comprehensive tome on networking Macintoshes, but it should be enough to get you started.

What You Need to Know to Hook Up a Macintosh Network

The following sections present some key things you should know about networking Macintosh computers before you start plugging in cables.

AppleTalk and Open Transport

Every Macintosh ever built, even an original 1984 model, includes networking support. Of course, newer Macintosh computers have better built-in networking features than older Macintosh computers. The newest Macs include built-in 10/100Mbps Ethernet adapters and sophisticated networking support built in to the operating system, similar to the networking features that come with Windows 98 Second Edition or Windows Millennium Edition.

Macintosh computers use a set of networking protocols collectively known as *AppleTalk*. Because AppleTalk is built in to every Mac, it has become an inarguable networking standard among Macintosh users. You don't have to worry about the differences between different network operating systems, because all Macintosh networking is based on AppleTalk.

AppleTalk has gone through several major revisions since it was first introduced back in 1984. Originally, AppleTalk supported only small networks that operated only over low-speed connections. In 1989, Apple enhanced AppleTalk to support larger networks and faster connections.

In 1996, with the release of MacOS System 7.5.3, Apple folded AppleTalk into a grander networking scheme known as Open Transport. The idea behind Open Transport is to bring all the different types of communications software used on Macintoshes under a common umbrella and make them easy to configure and use. Currently, two types of networking are handled by Open Transport:

- ✓ **Open Transport/AppleTalk:** Handles local area networks (LANs) based on the AppleTalk protocols. Open Transport/AppleTalk is a beefed-up version of AppleTalk that's more efficient and flexible.

- ✓ **OpenTransport/TCP:** Handles TCP/IP communications, such as Internet connections.

Open Transport is standard fare on all new Macintosh computers, and old Macintosh computers can be upgraded to Open Transport, provided that they're powerful enough. (The minimum system requirements for Open Transport are a 68030 processor, 5MB RAM, and MacOS System 7.5.3.)

AppleTalk enables you to subdivide a network into *zones,* which are similar to workgroups in Windows for Workgroups. Each zone consists of the network users who regularly share information.

Although basic support for networking is built in to every Macintosh, you still have to purchase cables to connect the computers to one another. You have several types of cables to choose from. You can use AppleTalk with two different cabling schemes that connect to the Macintosh printer port, or you can use AppleTalk with faster Ethernet interface cards.

LocalTalk: The cheap way to network

LocalTalk is an older method of connecting Macintosh computers that don't have built-in network adapters. LocalTalk connects Macintosh computers using special cables that attach to each computer's printer port.

Here are the details:

- ✔ LocalTalk connectors are self-terminating, which means that separate terminators are not required on both ends of the cable segment.

- ✔ Each LocalTalk connector comes with a 2-meter-long LocalTalk cable (that's about 6 ½ feet). You can also purchase 10-meter cables if your computers aren't that close together.

- ✔ LocalTalk uses shielded twisted-pair cable. The shielding protects the cable from electrical interference but limits the total length of a cable that is used in a network segment to 300 feet.

- ✔ No more than 32 computers and printers can be connected to a single segment.

- ✔ A popular alternative to LocalTalk is PhoneNET, made by Farallon Computing. PhoneNET uses inexpensive telephone cable rather than the shielded twisted-pair cable used by LocalTalk.

Ethernet with Macintosh computers

LocalTalk is popular because it's cheap. But LocalTalk has one major problem: It's unbearably slow. LocalTalk uses the Macintosh serial printer ports and therefore transmits data over the network at a paltry 230,400 bits per second (bps). This transmission rate is acceptable for casual use of a network printer and for occasionally copying a small file to or from another computer but not for serious networking.

Fortunately, AppleTalk also supports Ethernet network adapters and cables. With Ethernet, data travels at 10 or 100 megabits per second (Mbps) — much more suitable for real-life networking.

When you use Ethernet, you have access to all the cabling options described in Chapter 10: 10base5 (yellow cable), 10base2 (thinnet), and 10baseT (twisted pair). Fast (100Mbps) Ethernet works as well.

Here are some additional points to ponder when you use Ethernet to network your Macintosh computers:

✔ AppleTalk running on an Ethernet network is sometimes referred to as *EtherTalk*.

✔ Ethernet interface cards for Macintoshes are a bit more expensive than their PC counterparts, mostly because they aren't as widely used. However, most Macs built within the last few years have Ethernet built in, so if your Macs are new, you probably don't need cards. All the current Apple Macintosh computers come with built-in 10/100MHz Ethernet adapters.

✔ Some Macintosh computers that do not have built-in Ethernet adapters have standard PCI expansion slots — the same expansion slots that modern PCs have. That means you can use any PCI Ethernet card in a PCI-equipped Macintosh. (Well, almost any. The manufacturer of the card must supply a Macintosh driver for the card, and some manufacturers don't.)

✔ Some older Macintosh computers used a special interface for Ethernet cards called the *Ethernet cabling system*. When the Ethernet cabling system is used, the network cards themselves don't have coax or 10baseT connectors. Instead, they have a special type of connector called an *Apple Attachment Unit Interface* (AAUI). You must plug a device called a transceiver into the AAUI connector so that you can attach the computer to a coax or twisted-pair cable. Newer Macintosh computers with built-in Ethernet adapters use standard RJ-45 connectors.

✔ You can use a router to connect a LocalTalk network to an Ethernet network. This arrangement often connects a small group of Macintosh users to a larger network or connects an existing LocalTalk network to an Ethernet network.

AppleShare

AppleShare turns any Macintosh computer that runs the Mac OS 9 operating system into a dedicated file server. AppleShare can support up to 250 users connected to the server simultaneously using AppleTalk or 500 users with TCP/IP.

The current version of AppleShare, called AppleShare IP 6.3, offers the following features:

- ✔ File server using AppleTalk's standard file protocol, AFP
- ✔ Print server
- ✔ Mail server
- ✔ Web server
- ✔ FTP server
- ✔ Support for both AppleTalk and TCP/IP protocols

You need to purchase AppleShare only if you want to set up a Macintosh computer to act as a dedicated file server. All Macintosh computers come with the ability to connect to a network, access network printers and drives, and share their own printers and disk drives with other network users.

Mac OS X Server

Apple also offers a dedicated network operating system known as Mac OS X Server (the *X* is pronounced "Ten," not "Ex"), which is designed for PowerMac G3 computers. Mac OS X Server is based on a UNIX operating system kernel known as Mach. As a result, Mac OS X Server can handle many network server tasks as efficiently as any other network operating system, including Windows 2000, NetWare, and UNIX.

The Mac OS X Server includes the following features:

- ✔ Apache Web server
- ✔ NetBoot, a feature that simplifies the task of managing network client computers
- ✔ File services using AFP
- ✔ WebObjects, a high-end tool for creating Web sites
- ✔ QuickTime Streaming Server, which lets the server broadcast multimedia programs over the network

What You Need to Know to Use a Macintosh Network

Here are some of the most common questions that come up after you install the network cable. Note that the following sections assume that you're working with AppleTalk networking using MacOS 9. The procedures may vary somewhat if you're using Open Transport networking or an earlier version of the Macintosh Operating System.

Configuring a Mac for networking

Before you can access the network from your Mac, you must configure your Mac for networking by activating AppleTalk and assigning your network name and password.

Activating AppleTalk

After all the cables are in place, you have to activate AppleTalk. Here's how:

1. **Choose the Chooser desk accessory from the Apple menu.**

2. **Click the Active button.**

3. **Close the Chooser.**

That's all there is to it.

Assigning your name and password

Next, assign an owner name, a password, and a name for your computer. This process allows other network users to access your Mac. Here's how:

1. **Choose the File Sharing control panel from the Apple menu (Apple⇨Control Panels⇨File Sharing).**

2. **Type your name in the Owner Name field.**

3. **Type a password in the Owner Password field.**

   Don't forget what the password is.

4. **Type a descriptive name for your computer in the Computer Name field.**

   Other network users will know your computer by this name.

5. **Click the Close button.**

Piece of cake, eh?

Accessing a network printer

Accessing a network printer with AppleTalk is no different than accessing a printer when you don't have a network. If more than one printer is available on the network, you use the Chooser to select the printer you want to use. Chooser displays all the available network printers — just pick the one you want to use. And keep the following points in mind:

✔ **Be sure to enable Background Printing for the network printer.** If you don't, your Mac is tied up until the printer finishes your job — that can be a long time if someone else sent a 500-page report to the printer just before you. When you enable Background Printing, your printer output is captured to a disk file and then sent to the printer later while you continue with other work.

To enable Background Printing:

   1. Choose Apple⇨Chooser desk accessory.

   2. Select the printer you want to use from the Chooser.

   3. Click the Background Printing On button.

✔ **Do not enable Background Printing if a dedicated print server has been set up.** In that case, print data is automatically spooled to the print server's disk so that your Mac doesn't have to wait for the printer to become available.

Sharing files with other users

To share files on your Mac with other network users, you must set up a shared resource. You can share an entire disk or just individual folders and restrict access to certain users, if you want.

Before you can share files with other users, you must activate the AppleTalk file-sharing feature. Here's how:

   1. Choose the File Sharing control panel from the Apple Menu.

   2. Click the Start button in the File Sharing section of the control panel.

   3. Click the Close button.

To share a file or folder, click the file or folder once. Then open the File menu, choose Get Info, and then choose Sharing from the submenu that appears. You can also use the Sharing section of the Info window to set access privileges to restrict access to the file or folder.

Accessing shared files

To access files on another Macintosh, follow this procedure:

1. **Choose the Chooser from the Apple menu.**

2. **Click the AppleShare icon from the Chooser window.**

3. **Click the name of the computer you want to access. (If your network has zones, you must first click the zone you want to access.)**

4. **Click OK.**

   A login screen appears.

5. **If you have a user account on the computer, click the Registered User button and enter your user name and password. Otherwise, click the Guest button and then click OK.**

   A list of shared folders and disks appears.

6. **Click the folders and disks you want to access.**

   A check box appears next to each item on the list. If you check this box, you connect to the folder or disk automatically each time you start your computer.

7. **Click OK.**

With Mac OS 8.5 and later, you can also use the Network Browser, found in the Apple menu, to access network drives or folders. Just open the Network Browser from the Apple menu, double-click the server that contains the shared disk or folder, and then double-click the drive or folder you want to use.

What You Need to Know to Network Macintoshes with PCs

Life would be too boring if Macs lived on one side of the tracks and PCs lived on the other. If your organization has a mix of both Macs and PCs, odds are you eventually want to network them together. Fortunately, you have several ways to do so:

✔ If your network has an AppleShare server, you can use the Windows client software that comes with AppleShare to connect any version of Windows to the AppleShare server. Doing so enables Windows users to access the files and printers on the AppleShare server.

✔ If you have Windows NT/2000 Server, you can use a feature called Services for Macintosh to allow Macintosh computers to access files and printers managed by the Windows NT/2000 Server without having to install special client software on the Macintosh computers.

✔ If you use NetWare, you must purchase separate NetWare client software for your Macintosh computers. After you install this client software, the Macs can access files and printers managed by your NetWare servers.

The biggest complication that occurs when you mix Macintosh and Windows computers on the same network is that the Mac OS and Windows have slightly different rules for naming files. For example, Macintosh filenames are limited to 31 characters, but Windows filenames can be up to 255 characters. And although a Macintosh filename can include any characters other than a colon, Windows filenames can't include backslashes, greater than or less than signs, and a few other oddball characters.

The best way to avoid filename problems is to stick with short names (under 31 characters) and limit your filenames to letters, numbers, and common symbols such as the hyphen or pound sign. Although you can translate any filenames that violate the rules of the system being used into a form that is acceptable to both Windows and the Macintosh, doing so sometimes leads to cryptic or ambiguous filenames.

Chapter 26

Using a Linux Server

● ●

In This Chapter

▶ Finding out about Linux and how it differs from Windows

▶ Choosing which version of Linux to use for your server

▶ Installing Linux

▶ Configuring Linux network settings and user accounts

▶ Running a Web server

▶ Using Samba to create a file server

▶ Creating a Linux firewall

● ●

*L*inux, the free operating system based on UNIX, is becoming more and more popular as an alternative to expensive server operating systems such as Windows 2000 Server and NetWare. In fact, by some estimates, there are more computers now running the Linux operating system than there are running the Macintosh operating system. You can use Linux as a Web server for the Internet or for an intranet, and you can use it as a firewall or a file and print server on your local area network.

Linux was started in 1991 by a Linus Torvalds, who was at the time an undergraduate student at the University of Helsinki in Finland. Linus thought it would be fun to create his own operating system for his brand-new PC, based on UNIX. In the nearly ten years since Linux was first conceived, Linux has become a full-featured operating system that is fast and reliable.

In this chapter, you find out the basics of setting up a Linux server on your network and using it as a file server, as a Web server for the Internet or an intranet, as an e-mail server, and as a router and firewall to help connect your network to the Internet.

Linux is a complicated operating system. Learning how to use it can be a daunting task, especially if your only prior computer experience is with Windows. Fortunately, IDG Books Worldwide has a plethora of *For Dummies* books that make learning Linux less painful. Check out *Linux For Dummies,* 2nd Edition by Jon "maddog" Hall, *Linux For Dummies Quick Reference,* 2nd Edition by Phil Hughes, and *Linux Administration For Dummies* by Michael Bellomo.

Comparing Linux with Windows

If your only computer experience is with Windows, you are in for a steep learning curve when you first start working with Linux. There are many fundamental differences between the Linux operating system and Windows. Here are some of the more important differences:

✔ **Linux is a multiuser operating system**. That means that more than one user can log on and use a Linux computer at the same time. Two or more users can log on to a Linux computer from the same keyboard and monitor by using virtual consoles, which let you switch from one user session to another with a special key combination. Or, users can log on to the Linux computer from a terminal window running on another computer on the network.

In contrast, most versions of Windows are single-user systems. Only one user at a time can log on to a Windows computer and run commands. (Windows 2000 can be configured as a multiuser system with terminal services.)

✔ **Linux does not have a built-in graphical user interface (GUI) as Windows does.** Instead, the GUI in Linux is provided by an optional component called *X Window System*. You can run Linux without X Window, in which case you interact with Linux by typing commands. If you prefer to use a GUI, you must install and run X Window.

X Window is split into two parts: a server component, called an *X server,* which handles the basic chores of managing multiple windows and providing graphics services for application programs, and a user interface component, called a *window manager,* which provides user interface features such as menus, buttons, toolbars, a taskbar, and so on. Several different window managers are available, each with a different look and feel. With Windows, you are stuck with the user interface that Microsoft designed. With Linux, you can use the user interface of your choosing.

✔ **Linux cannot run Windows programs.** That means you cannot run Microsoft Office on a Linux system; instead, you must find a similar program that is written specifically for Linux. Many Linux distributions come with an office suite called StarOffice, which provides word processing, spreadsheet, presentation, graphics, database, e-mail, calendar, and scheduling software. Thousands of other programs are available for Linux. (There are Windows emulator programs — the best known is Wine — that can run some Windows programs on Linux. But the emulators can run only some Windows programs, and it runs them slower than they would run on a Windows system.)

✔ **Linux doesn't do Plug and Play like Windows does.** Although the major Linux distributions come with configuration programs that can automatically detect and configure the most common hardware components,

Linux does not have built-in support for Plug-and-Play hardware devices. As a result, you're more likely to run into a hardware configuration problem with Linux than with Windows.

✔ **Linux uses a different system for accessing disk drives and files than Windows does.** For an explanation of how the Linux file system works, see the sidebar "I can't see my C drive!" later in this chapter.

✔ **Linux runs better on older hardware than the current incarnations of Windows do.** Linux is an ideal operating system for an older Pentium computer with at least 32MB of RAM and 2GB of hard disk. However, with a bit of juggling, you can get Linux to run well even on a 486 computer with as little as 4MB of RAM and a few hundred MB of disk space.

I can't see my C drive!

Linux and Windows have a completely different method of referring to your computer's disk drives and partitions. The differences can take some getting used to for experienced Windows users.

Windows uses a separate letter for each drive and partition on you system. For example, if you have a single drive formatted into three partitions, Windows identifies the partitions as drives C, D, and E. Each of these drives has its own root directory, which can in turn contain additional directories used to organize your files. As far as Windows is concerned, drives C, D, and E are completely separate drives, even though the drives are actually just partitions on a single drive.

Linux does not use drive letters. Instead, Linux combines all the drives and partitions into a single directory hierarchy. In Linux, one of the partitions is designated as the *root* partition. The root is roughly analogous to the C drive on a Windows system. Then, the other partitions can be *mounted* on the root partition and treated as if they were directories on the root partition. For example, you might designate the first partition as the root partition and then mount the second partition as /user and the third partition as

/var. Then, any files stored in the /user directory would actually be stored in the second partition, and files stored in the /var directory would be stored on the third partition.

The directory which a drive mounts to is called the drive's *mount point.*

Notice that Linux uses regular forward slash characters (/) to separate directory names rather than the backward slash characters (\) used by Windows. Typing backslashes instead of regular slashes is one of the most common mistakes made by new Linux users.

While we're on the subject, Linux uses a different convention for naming files, too. In Windows, file names end in a three-letter extension that is separated from the rest of the file name by a period. The extension is used to indicate the file type. For example, files that end in .exe are program files, but files that end in .doc are word processing documents.

Linux doesn't use file extensions, but periods are often used in Linux file names to separate different parts of the name and the last part often indicates the file type. For example, ldap.conf, and pine.conf are both configuration files.

Choosing a Linux Distribution

Because the kernel (that is, the core operating functions) of the Linux operating system is free, several companies have created their own *distributions* of Linux, which include the Linux operating system along with a bundle of packages to go along with it, such as administration tools, Web servers, and other useful utilities, as well as printed documentation. These distributions are inexpensive — ranging from $25 to $100 — and are well worth the small cost.

The following are some of the more popular Linux distributions:

- **Red Hat** is by most counts the most popular Linux distribution. Red Hat comes in three versions: Red Hat Standard Edition ($29.95), which includes the basic Linux operating system and tools; Deluxe Edition ($79.95), which adds a collection of workstation tools and additional printed documentation; and Professional Edition ($179.95), which adds advanced server and e-commerce tools. If you prefer, you can also download Red Hat Linux free from the Red Hat Web site. For more information, see www.redhat.com.

  All of the examples in this chapter are based on Red Hat Linux.

- **Linux-Mandrake** is another popular Linux distribution, one that is often recommended as the easiest for first-time Linux users to install.

- **SuSE** (pronounced "Soo-zuh," like the famous composer of marches) is a popular Linux distribution that comes on six CD-ROM disks and includes more than 1,500 Linux application programs and utilities, including everything you need to set up a network, Web, e-mail, or electronic commerce server. You can find more information at www.suse.com.

- **Caldera OpenLinux** emphasizes Linux's role as an electronic commerce server for the Internet with its OpenLinux distributions. With Caldera, you get just about everything you need to set up an online Web store. Check out www.caldera.com for more information.

- **Slackware**, one of the oldest Linux distributions, is still popular especially among Linux old-timers. A full installation of Slackware gives you all the tools you need to set up a network or Internet server. See www.slackware.com for more information.

- **Corel** offers not only the Corel Linux distribution but also a Linux version of its office suite, WordPerfect Office 2000. Although Corel Linux was designed with desktop users in mind, it comes with Web, mail, and news servers so you can use it as an Internet or intranet server. You can find more information about Corel Linux at linux.corel.com.

All distributions of Linux include the same core components — the Linux kernel, an X Server, popular windows managers such as GNOME and KDE, compilers, Internet programs such as Apache, Sendmail, and so on. However, not all Linux distributions are created equal. In particular, the manufacturer of each distribution creates it own installation and configuration programs to install and configure Linux.

The installation program is what makes or breaks a Linux distribution. All the distributions I list in this section have easy-to-use installation programs that automatically detect the hardware that is present on your computer and configure Linux to work with that hardware, eliminating most if not all manual configuration chores. The installation programs also let you select the Linux packages you want to install and let you set up one or more user accounts besides the root account.

The most enjoyable installation program overall comes with the Caldera distribution: It lets you play PacMan while it copies files from the CD-ROM disk to your hard disk!

Installing Linux

All the Linux distributions described in the section "Choosing a Linux Distribution" include an installation program that simplifies the task of installing Linux on your computer. The installation program asks you a series of questions about your hardware, what components of Linux you want to install, and how you want to configure certain features. Then it copies the appropriate files to your hard disk and configures your Linux system.

If the thought of installing Linux gives you hives, you can buy computers with Linux preinstalled, just as you can buy computers with Windows already installed.

Before you begin to install Linux, you should make a list of all the hardware components on your computer and how they are configured. Be as specific as you can: Write down each component's manufacturer and model number as well as configuration information such as the component's IRQ and I/O address, if appropriate.

Next, decide how you want to partition your hard disk for Linux. Although Windows is usually installed into a single disk partition, Linux installations typically require three or more hard disk partitions:

  ✔ **A boot partition:** This should be small — 16MB is recommended. The boot partition contains the operating system kernel and is required to start Linux properly on some computers.

  ✔ **A swap partition:** This should be about twice the size of your computer's RAM. For example, if the computer has 64MB of RAM, allocate a 128MB swap partition. Linux uses this partition as an extension of your computer's RAM.

✔ **A root partition:** This, in most cases, uses up the remaining free space on the disk. The root partition contains all the files and data used by your Linux system.

You can also create additional partitions if you wish. The installation program includes a disk-partitioning feature that lets you set up your disk partitions and indicate the mount point for each partition. (For more information about disk partitions, see the sidebar "I can't see my C drive!" earlier in this chapter.)

Linux is happy to share your hard disk with another operating system, such as Windows. However, you may have to repartition your disk to install Linux without erasing your existing operating system. If you need to repartition your hard drive, I recommend you pick up a copy of PowerQuest's PartitionMagic (www.powerquest.com) or a similar partitioning program, which will allow you to juggle your partitions without losing your existing operating system.

You'll also need to decide which optional Linux packages to install along with the Linux kernel. If you have enough drive space, I recommend you install all the packages that come with your distribution. That way, if you decide you need to use a package, you won't have to figure out how to install the package outside of the installation program. If you're tight on space, make sure that you at least install the basic network and Internet server packages, including Apache, Sendmail, FTP, and Samba.

Finally, you'll need to set the password for the root account and, in most distributions, choose whether or not to create one or more user accounts. I suggest you create at least one user account during installation, so you can log on to Linux as a user rather with the root account. That way, you can experiment with Linux commands without accidentally deleting or corrupting an important system file

Managing User Accounts

After you get your Linux server up and running, it will probably chug along for days, weeks, or even months at a time without any attention from you. However, on occasion you will have to put on your Network Administrator cap and perform some basic Linux system management chores. One of the most common network administration tasks is adding a user account.

Each Linux user account has the following information associated with it:

✔ **User name:** The name the user types to log on to the Linux system.

✔ **Full name:** The user's full name.

✔ **Home directory:** The directory which the user will be placed in when he or she logs in. In Red Hat Linux, the default home directory is

/home/username. For example, if the user name is blowe, the home directory will be /home/blowe.

✔ **Shell:** The program used to process Linux commands. Several shell programs are available. In most distributions, the default shell is /bin/bash.

✔ **Group:** You can create group accounts, which make it easy to apply identical access rights to groups of users.

✔ **User ID:** The internal identifier for the user.

You can add a new user by using the useradd command. For example, to create a user account named slowe and using default values for the other account information, type this command:

```
# useradd slowe
```

The useradd command has many optional parameters you can use to set account information such as the user's home directory and shell.

Fortunately, most Linux distributions come with special programs that simplify routine system management tasks. For example, Figure 26-1 shows the linuxconf program, which comes with the Red Hat Linux distribution. From this one program, you can manage network settings, user accounts, file system rights, and other system configuration options. Other Linux distributions include similar programs.

Figure 26-1:
Using
linuxconf
to manage a
Red Hat
Linux server.

In Linux, the user ID for the system administrator account is called root. You set the password for the root account when you install Linux. The root account is a very powerful account, as it has unrestricted access to all the files, directories, and programs on your Linux system. When you are logged on with the root account, be careful that you don't accidentally delete or modify any important system files.

Do not get into the habit of logging on to your Linux system using the root account! Instead, log on with your normal user account. Then, when you need to perform some type of system administration, use the `su` command (with no arguments) to switch to the root user. (`su` stands for Switch User.) The `su` command asks you to enter the root user password and then temporarily switches you to the root user account. When you are finished performing your administrator duties, type **exit** to return to your regular user account.

Configuring Linux Network Settings

In most cases, the installation program for your Linux distribution will automatically detect your network interface card and install the necessary drivers for the card. Linux refers to your Ethernet card as device `eth0`. (If you have more than one Ethernet card, the second card is `eth1`, the third card is `eth2`, and so on.)

You can check to see if your Ethernet card is working properly by using the `ifconfig` command. If your Ethernet card is working, `ifconfig` will display something similar to the following:

```
eth0      Link encap:Ethernet  Hwaddr 00:20:78:16:7C:16
          inet addr:192.168.1.103  Bcast:192.168.1.255
                Mask:255.255.255.0
          UP BROADCAST RUNNING MULTICAST  MTU:1500  Metric:1
          RX packets:3441 errors:0 dropped:0 overruns:0
            frame:0
          TX packets:2622 errors:0 dropped:0 overruns:0
            carrier:0
          collisions:0 txqueuelen:100
          Interrupt:9 Base addr:0x600

10        Link encap:Local Loopback
          inet addr:127.0.0.1  Mask:255.0.0.0
          UP LOOPBACK RUNNING  MTU:3924  Metric:1
          RX packets:44 errors:0 dropped:0 overruns:0 frame:0
          TX packets:44 errors:0 dropped:0 overruns:0
            carrier:0
          collisions:0 txqueuelen:100
```

The first section shows information for your Ethernet card (device `eth0`), such as the card's IP address (`192.168.1.103`) and the number of packets it has received (3,441). The second section shows information for an internal loopback device, which is used for testing and diagnostic purposes.

If `ifconfig` does not show an IP address for your card and you want to manually configure an address, you can do so by using an `ifconfig` command similar to this one:

```
ifconfig eth0 192.168.1.103
```

The `ifconfig` command has numerous arguments that let you set other network options besides the IP address. Fortunately, the system configuration program included with most Linux distributions provides an easier way to configure network settings. For example, Figure 26-2 shows one of several network configuration screens displayed by the `linuxconf` program that comes with Red Hat Linux.

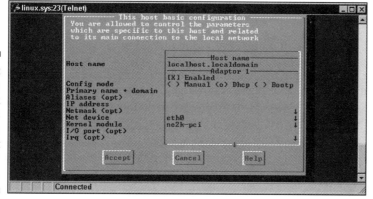

Figure 26-2:
Configuring
network
settings
using the
Red Hat
`linuxconf`
program.

A basic test to see if your network is up and running is to use the `ping` command to see if your Linux computer can contact other computers on the network, and vice-versa. All you need to know is the IP address of the computer you want to contact. Here is an example of a `ping` session attempting to contact a computer whose IP address is 192.168.1.1:

```
# ping 192.168.1.1 -c 5
PING 192.168.1.1 (192.168.1.1) from 192.168.1.103 : 56(84)
            bytes of data.
64 bytes from 192.168.1.1: icmp_seq=0 ttl=64 time=1.2 ms
64 bytes from 192.168.1.1: icmp_seq=1 ttl=64 time=1.0 ms
64 bytes from 192.168.1.1: icmp_seq=2 ttl=64 time=1.0 ms
64 bytes from 192.168.1.1: icmp_seq=3 ttl=64 time=1.0 ms
64 bytes from 192.168.1.1: icmp_seq=4 ttl=64 time=1.0 ms
--- 192.168.1.1 ping statistics ---
5 packets transmitted, 5 packets received, 0% packet loss
round-trip min/avg/max = 0.9/1.0/1.2 ms
```

In this example, I used a `ping` command to ping the computer at
192.168.1.1 five times. The output from the `ping` command shows that
each of the five attempts to contact 192.168.1.1 were successful. If any of
the `ping` attempts failed, an error message would be displayed.

Running the Apache Web Server

All the popular Linux distributions come with Apache, the most popular Web
server on the Internet today. In most cases, Apache is installed and configured automatically when you install Linux. Then, setting up a Web server for
the Internet or an intranet is simply a matter of tweaking a few Apache configuration settings and copying your HTML document files to Apache's home
directory.

An easy way to find out if Apache is up and running is to try to display the
default home page shipped with Apache from another computer on your network. You can do that by firing up a Web browser such as Internet Explorer
and typing the IP address of your Linux server in the Address bar. If Apache
is running on the server, a page such as the one shown in Figure 26-3 will be
displayed.

Figure 26-3:
The default
page
displayed by
Apache.

Apache should run fine using the default configuration settings made when you install it. However, you can change various configuration settings either by editing the Apache configuration files or by using your distribution's configuration program. For example, Figure 26-4 shows some of the Apache configuration settings available from Red Hat's `linuxconf` program.

Figure 26-4:
Apache
configuration
options.

From this screen, you can change the following Apache settings:

- ✔ The e-mail address of the server administrator
- ✔ The IP address of the server
- ✔ The server's name
- ✔ The location of the server's HTML documents
- ✔ The location of the server's log files
- ✔ CGI settings
- ✔ The TCP/IP port number

If you prefer, you can configure your Apache server by directly editing the configuration files. Apache's configuration settings are found in three separate configuration files, named `httpd.conf`, `srm.conf`, and `access.conf`. These files are located in `/etc/httpd/conf` in Red Hat Linux, but might be in a different location in other Linux distributions. Be sure to study the Apache documentation before you start messing with these files!

For more information about running Apache, see *Apache Server For Dummies* by Ken A.L. Coar, published, of course, by IDG Books Worldwide.

Running the Sendmail Mail Server

Sendmail, which comes with all of the Linux distributions mentioned in this chapter, is one of the most popular mail server programs on the Internet. You can also use Sendmail as an alternative to expensive mail server programs such as Microsoft Exchange Server to provide email services for your LAN.

Red Hat's linuxconf program has several screens that let you configure Sendmail settings. Figure 26-5 shows the basic Sendmail configuration screen, where you can set such options as the name of the mail server, the name of a mail gateway to forward outgoing mail to, and other basic options. Other distributions include similar configuration programs.

Figure 26-5:
Configuring
Sendmail in
Red Hat
Linux.

For more control over Sendmail configuration, you can edit special configuration macro files that contain detailed configuration settings. You must first run the configuration macro files through a program called m4 before Sendmail can use them.

Spam artists — unscrupulous marketers who clutter the Internet with tens of thousands of unsolicited e-mails — are constantly on the prowl for unprotected Sendmail servers, which they can use to launch their spam campaigns. If you don't protect your server, sooner or later a spammer will coax your computer into spending almost all its time sending out the spammer's e-mail. To protect your server from becoming an indentured spam servant, you can configure it to refuse any mail that merely wants to use your computer to relay messages to other computers.

Doing the Samba Dance

Until now, you probably thought of Samba as a Brazilian dance with intricate steps and fun rhythms. But in the Linux world, Samba refers to a file and printer sharing program that allows Linux to mimic a Windows file and print server so that Windows computers can use shared Linux directories and printers. If you want to use Linux as a file or print server in a Windows network, you'll have to learn how to dance the Samba.

Why did Samba's developers choose to call their program *Samba?* Simply because the protocol that Windows file and print servers use to communicate with one another is called *SMB,* which stands for *Server Message Block.* Add a couple of vowels to *SMB* and you get *Samba.* One way to describe Samba is to say that Samba is a Linux implementation of SMB.

You can configure Samba by editing the `smb.conf` file located in `/etc` in Red Hat installations. (Different distributions may place this file elsewhere.) Or, you can use a configuration program such as Red Hat's `linuxconf` to configure Samba settings. Figure 26-6 shows the `linuxconf` screen used to configure basic Samba settings. You can use this screen to set basic options such as the server name, the workgroup name, and a brief description of the server.

Figure 26-6:
Configuring
Samba with
Red Hat's
`linuxconf`
program.

Red Hat's `linuxconf` program also makes it easy to share directories on your Samba server. Figure 26-7 shows the screen you use to share a directory.

Figure 26-7:
Sharing a
Linux
directory
using
linuxconf.

On this screen, you supply the following information:

✔ The share name, which other users will use to access the directory.

✔ Whether or not to enable the share. If you leave this option unchecked, the shared directory will not be accessible by network users.

✔ Whether or not the share should be browsable. If the share is browsable, users can access it via Network Neighborhood or My Network Places. If not, users must know the share name to access the directory.

✔ The directory to be shared.

✔ Access controls, which enable you to restrict access to certain users, make the share read-only, prevent certain users from accessing the share, and so on.

Using Linux as a Firewall

If your network is connected to the Internet, you should use some type of firewall to protect your LAN from unauthorized access from unfriendly Internet users. You can purchase special firewall devices for this purpose, or you can create your own inexpensive firewall using Linux.

A Linux firewall is a type of router that performs two functions:

✔ The firewall selectively allows certain TCP/IP packets to pass from the Internet to your LAN and prevents other packets from passing through. This is known as *packet filtering*.

✔ The firewall hides all knowledge of the individual computers that are on your network by representing all your computers to the Internet using a single IP address. This is known as *IP masquerading*.

Fortunately, packet filtering and IP masquerading are standard features of Linux.

To create a Linux firewall, the Linux computer must have two network interfaces: an Ethernet card to connect to your LAN and a modem or other type of high-speed connection (such as cable or DSL) to connect to the Internet. The firewall computer must have two IP addresses: one for its connection to the Internet and the other for its connection to your LAN.

The first step in setting up a Linux firewall is to install Linux on the firewall computer and get both the network interfaces up and running. Then, setting up the firewall is a matter of telling Linux what types of TCP/IP packets to block and which types to let through and instructing Linux how to handle IP masquerading. Both tasks are performed using the ipchains command.

Unfortunately, the details of using ipchains to set up a Linux firewall are complicated enough to make most normal people either scream or cry. To do it properly, you must create a script containing perhaps dozens of ipchains commands, each one setting up a rule that blocks or allows a particular type of TCP/IP packet.

If you are a TCP/IP expert, you can probably set up the necessary ipchains commands yourself. Fortunately, the good folks at Red Hat have created a script that you can download and customize to create a basic firewall. You can find the firewall script at the following Web page:

```
www.redhat.com/support/docs/tips/firewall/firewallservice.html
```

Read the script over carefully (it has lots of comments) and then modify it carefully to suit your firewall needs.

Part VI
The Part of Tens

The 5th Wave   By Rich Tennant

"I DON'T KNOW — SOME PARTS OF THE NETWORK SEEM JUST FINE, AND OTHER PARTS SEEM TO BE COMPLETELY OUT OF CONTROL."

In this part . . .

*I*f you keep this book in the bathroom, the chapters in this section are the ones that you'll read most. Each chapter consists of ten (more or less) things that are worth knowing about various aspects of networking. Without further ado, here they are, direct from the home office in Fresno, California.

Chapter 27

Ten Big Network Mistakes

· ·

In This Chapter

▶ Skimping on cable

▶ Turning off or restarting a server while users are logged on

▶ Deleting important files on the server

▶ Copying a file from the server, changing it, and then copying it back

▶ Sending something to the printer again just because it didn't print the first time

▶ Unplugging a cable while the computer is on

▶ Assuming that the server is safely backed up

▶ Thinking you can't work just because the network is down

▶ Always blaming the network

· ·

*J*ust about the time you figure out how to avoid the most embarrassing computer mistakes, such as folding a 5¼-inch disk in half to make it fit in a 3½-inch drive, the network lands on your computer. Now you have a whole new list of dumb things you can do, mistakes that can give your average computer geek a belly laugh because they seem so basic to him. Well, that's because he's a computer geek. Nobody had to tell him not to fold the disk — he was born with an extra gene that gave him an instinctive knowledge of such things.

Here's a list of some of the most common mistakes made by network novices. Avoid these mistakes and you deprive your local computer geek of the pleasure of a good laugh at your expense.

Skimping on Cable

If your network consists of more than a few computers or has computers located in different rooms, you should invest in a professional-quality cable installation, complete with wall-mounted jacks, patch panels, and high-quality hubs. It is tempting to cut costs by using the cheapest hubs and by stringing inexpensive cable directly from the hubs to each computer on the network. But in the long run, that approach will actually prove to be more expensive than investing in a good cable installation in the first place.

Here are just a few of the reasons it pays to do the cabling right in the first place:

- A good cable installation will last much longer than the computers it services. A good cable installation can last 10 or 15 years, long after the computers on your network have been placed on display in a computer history museum.

- Installing cable is hard work. No one enjoys going up in the attic, poking his or her head up through ceiling panels, or fishing cables through walls. If you're going to do it, do it right so that you don't have to do it again in just a few years. Build your cable installation so that it lasts.

- Your network users may be satisfied with 10BaseT networking now, but it won't be long before they demand 100BaseT. And a few years after that, they'll want Gigahertz speed. If you cut costs by using Category 3 instead of Category 5 cable or by installing less than Cat 5 patch panels or modular jacks, you'll have to replace them later.

- You might be tempted to skip the modular wall jacks and patch cables and instead just run the cable down the wall, out through a hole, and the directly to the computer or hub. That's a bad idea because the wires inside the network cable are solid wire, which is designed to last for a long time, provided it doesn't get handled much. If you run solid-wire cable directly to a computer, the wire will be stressed each time someone unplugs the cable. Even just dusting behind the computer (which some people actually do) can jostle the cable. Sooner or later, one of the wires inside the cable will break. Patch cables are made with stranded rather than solid wire, so they can tolerate a lot of handling without breaking.

For more information about professional touches for installing cable, see Chapter 10.

Turning Off or Restarting a Server Computer While Users Are Logged On

The fastest way to blow your network users to kingdom come is to turn off a server computer while users are logged on. Restarting it by pressing its reset button can have the same disastrous effect.

If your network is set up with a dedicated file server, you probably won't be tempted to turn it off or restart it. But if your network is set up as a true peer-to-peer network, where each of the workstation computers — including your own — also doubles as a server computer, be careful about the impulsive urge to turn your computer off or restart it. Someone may be accessing a file or printer on your computer at that very moment.

Before turning off or restarting a server computer, find out whether anyone is logged on. If so, politely ask him or her to log off.

Deleting Important Files on the Server

Without a network, you can do anything you want to your computer, and the only person you can hurt is yourself. Kind of like the old "victimless crime" debate. Put your computer on a network, though, and you take on a certain amount of responsibility. You must find out how to live like a responsible member of the network society.

That means you can't capriciously delete files from a network server just because you don't need them. They may not be yours. You wouldn't want someone deleting your files, would you?

Be especially careful about files that are required to keep the network running. For example, Windows e-mail uses a folder named `wgpo0000` as a workgroup post office. Delete this folder and your e-mail is history.

Copying a File from the Server, Changing It, and Then Copying It Back

Sometimes working on a network file is easier if you first copy the file to your local hard drive. Then you can access it from your application program more efficiently because you don't have to use the network. This is especially true for large database files that have to be sorted to print reports.

You're asking for trouble, though, if you copy the file to your PC's local hard drive, make changes to the file, and then copy the updated version of the file back to the server. Why? Because somebody else may be trying the same thing at the same time. If that happens, the updates made by one of you — the one who copies the file back to the server first — are lost.

Copying a file to a local drive is an okay thing to do, but not if you plan on updating the file and copying it back.

Sending Something to the Printer Again Just Because It Didn't Print the First Time

What do you do if you send something to the printer and nothing happens? *Right answer:* Find out why nothing happened and fix it. *Wrong answer:* Send it again and see whether it works this time. Some users keep sending it over and over again, hoping that one of these days, it'll take. The result is rather embarrassing when someone finally clears the paper jam and then watches 30 copies of the same letter print.

Unplugging a Cable While the Computer Is On

Bad idea! If for any reason you need to unplug a cable from behind your computer, turn your computer off first. You don't want to fry any of the delicate electronic parts inside your computer, do you?

If you need to unplug the network cable, you should wait until all the computers on the network are off. This is especially true if your network is wired with thinnet coax cable; it's not such a big deal with twisted-pair cable.

Note: With thinnet cable, you can disconnect the T connector from your computer as long as you don't disconnect the cable itself from the T connector.

Assuming That the Server Is Safely Backed Up

Some users make the unfortunate assumption that the network somehow represents an efficient and organized bureaucracy worthy of their trust. Far from the truth. Never assume that the network jocks are doing their jobs backing up the network data every day. Check up on them. Conduct a surprise inspection one day: Burst into the computer room wearing white gloves and demand to see the backup tapes. Check the tape rotation to make sure that more than one day's worth of backups are available.

If you're not impressed with your network's backup procedures, take it upon yourself to make sure that you never lose any of your data. Back up your most valued files to floppy disks frequently or, better yet, a Zip disk or some other high-capacity removable disk.

Thinking You Can't Work Just Because the Network Is Down

A few years back, I realized that I can't do my job without electricity. Should a power failure occur and I find myself without electricity, I can't even light a candle and work with pencil and paper because the only pencil sharpener I have is electric.

Some people have the same attitude about the network: They figure that if the network goes down, they may as well go home. That's not always the case. Just because your computer is attached to a network doesn't mean that it won't work when the network is down. True — if the wind flies out of the network sails, you can't access any network devices. You can't get files from network drives, and you can't print on network printers. But you can still use your computer for local work: accessing files and programs on your local hard drive and printing on your local printer (if you're lucky enough to have one).

Always Blaming the Network

Some people treat the network kind of like the village idiot who can be blamed whenever anything goes wrong. Networks do cause problems of their own, but they aren't the root of all evil.

If your monitor displays only capital letters, it's probably because you pressed the Caps Lock key. Don't blame the network.

If you spill coffee on the keyboard, well, that's your fault. Don't blame the network.

Your toddler sticks Play-Doh in the floppy drive — hey, kids will be kids. Don't blame the network.

Get the point?

Chapter 28

Ten Networking Commandments

*"B*lessed is the network manager who walks not in the council of the ignorant, nor stands in the way of the oblivious, nor sits in the seat of the greenhorn, but delights in the Law of the Network and meditates on this Law day and night."

—Networks 1:1

And so it came to pass that these Ten Networking Commandments were passed down from generation to generation, to be worn as frontlets between the computer geeks' eyes and written upon their doorposts. Obey these commandments and it shall go well with you, with your children, and with your children's children.

I. Thou Shalt Back Up Thy Hard Drive Religiously

Prayer is a wonderful thing, but when it comes to protecting the data on your network, nothing beats a well-thought-out schedule of backups followed religiously.

II. Thou Shalt Protect Thy Network from Infidels

Remember Colonel Flagg from *M*A*S*H,* who hid in trashcans looking for Commies? You don't exactly want to become him, but on the other hand, you don't want to ignore the possibility of getting zapped by a virus or your network being invaded by hackers. Make sure that your Internet connection is properly secured, and do not allow the use of modems to access the Internet unless you have provided adequate security.

As for virus threats, start by making sure that every user realizes that any floppy disk from the outside can be infected, and after one computer on the network is infected, the entire network is in trouble. Then show the users how easily they can scan suspicious disks before using them.

If possible, install an antivirus program on every computer on the network and show your users how to use it.

Also, make sure your users are aware of the danger posed by viruses that can infiltrate your network via e-mail attachments.

III. Thou Shalt Keepeth Thy Network Drive Pure and Cleanse It of Old Files

Don't wait until your 40GB network drive is down to just one cluster of free space before thinking about cleaning it up. Set up a routine schedule for disk housekeeping, where you wade through the files and directories on the network disk to remove old junk.

IV. Thou Shalt Not Tinker with Thine Network Configuration Files Unless Thou Knowest What Thou Art Doing

Networks are finicky things. After yours is up and running, don't mess around with it unless you know what you're doing. And be especially careful if you think you know what you're doing. It's people who think they know what they're doing who get themselves into trouble!

V. Thou Shalt Not Covet Thy Neighbor's Network

Network envy is a common malady among network managers. If your network uses plain old Windows 98 and it works, nothing can be gained by coveting someone else's network. If you run NetWare 4.2, resist the urge to upgrade to 5 unless you have a really good reason. And if you run Windows NT Server, fantasizing about Windows 2000 Enterprise Server is a venial sin.

You're especially susceptible to network envy if you're a gadget freak. There's always a better hub to be had or some fancy network protocol gizmo to lust after. Don't give in to these base urges! Resist the devil, and he will flee!

VI. Thou Shalt Schedule Downtime before Working upon Thy Network

As a courtesy, try to give your users plenty of advance notice before you take down the network to work on it. Obviously, you can't predict when random problems strike. But if you know you're going to add a new computer to the network on Thursday morning, you earn points if you tell everyone about the inconvenience two days before rather than two minutes before.

VII. Thou Shalt Keep an Adequate Supply of Spare Parts

There's no reason that your network should be down for two days just because a cable breaks. Always make sure that you have at least a minimal supply of network spare parts on hand. As luck would have it, Chapter 29 suggests ten things you should keep in your closet.

VIII. Thou Shalt Not Steal Thy Neighbor's Program without a License

How would you like it if Inspector Clouseau barged into your office, looked over your shoulder as you ran Lotus 1-2-3 from a network server, and asked, "Do you have a liesaunce?"

"A liesaunce?" you reply, puzzled.

"Yes of course, a liesaunce, that is what I said. The law specifically prohibits the playing of a computer program on a network without a proper liesaunce."

You don't want to go against the law, do you?

IX. Thou Shalt Train Thy Users in the Ways of the Network

Don't blame the users if they don't know how to use the network. It's not their fault. If you're the network administrator, your job is to provide training so that the network users know how to use the network.

X. Thou Shalt Write Down Thy Network Configuration upon Tablets of Stone

If you cross the river Jordan, who else will know diddly-squat about the network if you don't write it down somewhere? The back of a napkin won't cut it. Write down everything and put it in an official binder labeled *Network Bible* and protect the binder as if it were sacred.

Your hope should be that 2,000 years from now, when archaeologists are exploring caves in your area, they find your network documentation hidden in a jar and marvel at how meticulously the people of our time recorded their network configurations.

They'll probably draw ridiculous conclusions such as we offered sacrifices of burnt data packets to a deity named TCP/IP, but that makes it all the more fun.

Chapter 29

Ten Things You Should Keep in Your Closet

*W*hen you first networkize your office computers, you need to find a closet where you can stash some network goodies. If you can't find a whole closet, shoot for a shelf, a drawer, or at least a sturdy cardboard box.

Here's a list of what stuff to keep on hand.

Tools

Make sure that you have at least a basic computer toolkit, the kind you can pick up for $15 from just about any office supply store. You also should have wire cutters, wire strippers, and cable crimpers that work for your network cable type.

Extra Cable

When you buy network cable, never buy exactly the amount you need. In fact, buying at least twice as much cable as you need isn't a bad idea, because half the cable is left over in case you need it later. You will. Something will go wrong, and you'll suspect a cable problem, so you'll need extra cable to replace the bad cable. Or you may add a computer or two to the network and need extra cable.

If your network is glued together with preassembled 25-foot lengths of thinnet coax cable, having at least one 25-foot segment lying around in the closet is a good idea.

Extra Connectors

Don't run out of connectors, either. If you use twisted-pair cabling, you'll find that connectors go bad more often than you'd like. Buy the connectors 25, 50, or 100 at a time so that you have plenty of spares lying around.

If you use thinnet cable, keep a few spare BNC connectors handy, plus a few T connectors and a few terminators. Terminators have been known to mysteriously disappear. Rumor has it that they are sucked through some kind of time vortex into the distant future, where they're refabricated and returned to our time in the form of Arnold Schwarzenegger.

Patch Cables

If you wired your network the professional way, with wall jacks in each office, keep a few patch cables of various lengths in the closet. That way, you won't have to run to the store every time you need to change a patch cable.

Twinkies

If left sealed in their little individually wrapped packages, Twinkies keep for years. In fact, they'll probably outlast the network itself. You can give 'em to future network geeks, ensuring continued network support for generations to come.

Extra Network Cards

Ideally, you want to use identical network cards in all your computers. But if the boss's computer is down, you'd probably settle for whatever network card the corner network street vendor is selling today. That's why you should always keep at least one spare network card in the closet. You can rest easy knowing that if a network card fails, you have an identical replacement card sitting on the shelf, just waiting to be installed — and you won't have to buy one from someone who also sells imitation Persian rugs.

Obviously, if you have only two computers on your network, justifying spending the money for a spare network adapter card is hard. With larger networks, it's easier to justify.

The Complete Documentation of the Network on Tablets of Stone

I've mentioned several times in this book the importance of documenting your network. Don't spend hours documenting your network and then hide the documentation under a pile of old magazines behind your desk. Put the binder in the closet with the other network supplies so that you and everyone else always know where to find it. And keep backup copies of the Word, Excel, or other documents that make up the network binder in a fireproof safe or at another site.

Don't you dare chisel passwords into the network documentation, though. Shame on you for even thinking about it!

If you do decide to chisel the network documentation in stone tablets, consider using sandstone. It's attractive, inexpensive, and easy to update (just rub out the old info and chisel in the new). Keep in mind, however, that sandstone is subject to erosion from spilled Jolt Cola or Snapple. Oh, and make sure that you store it on a reinforced shelf.

The Network Manuals and Disks

In the land of Oz, a common lament of the Network Scarecrow is "If I only had the manual." True, the manual probably isn't a Pulitzer-prize candidate, but that doesn't mean you should toss it in a landfill, either. Put the manual where it belongs: in the closet with all the other network tools and artifacts.

Likewise, the disks. You may need them someday, so keep them with the other network stuff.

Ten Copies of This Book

Obviously, you want to keep an adequate supply of this book on hand to distribute to all your network users. The more they know, the more they stay off your back. Sheesh, 10 copies may not be enough — 20 may be closer to what you need.

Chapter 30

Ten Network Gizmos Only Big Networks Need

*P*eople who compile statistics on things, such as the ratio of chickens to humans in Arkansas and the likelihood of the Mets losing when the other team shows up, report that more than 40 percent of all networks have fewer than ten computers and that this percentage is expected to increase in coming years. A Ross Perot-style pie chart would be good here, but my editor tells me I'm running long, so I have to pass on that.

The point is that if you're one of the lucky 40 percent with fewer than ten computers on your network, you can skip this chapter altogether. Here, I briefly describe various network gizmos that you may need if your network is really big. How big is big? There's no hard-and-fast rule, but the soft-and-slow rule is that you should look into this stuff when your network grows to about 25 computers.

The exceptions to the soft-and-slow rule are as follows: *(1)* Your company has two or more networks that you want to hook together, and these networks were designed by different people who refused to talk to each other until it was too late; *(2)* your network needs to connect computers that are more than a few hundred yards apart, perhaps in different buildings or via the Internet.

Repeaters

A *repeater* is a gizmo that gives your network signals a boost so that the signals can travel farther. It's kind of like the Gatorade stations in a marathon. As the signals travel past the repeater, they pick up a cup of Gatorade, take a sip, splash the rest of it on their heads, toss the cup, and hop in a cab when they're sure that no one is looking.

You need a repeater when the total length of a single span of network cable is larger than the maximum allowed for your cable type:

Cable	*Maximum Length*
Thick coax (yellow stuff)	500 meters or 1,640 feet
Thin coax (cheaper net)	185 meters or 606 feet
10/100baseT (twisted sister)	100 meters or 328 feet

For coax cable (thick and thin), the preceding cable lengths apply to cable segments, not individual lengths of cable. A segment is the entire run of cable from one terminator to another and may include more than one computer. In other words, if you have ten computers and you connect them all with 25-foot lengths of thin coax cable, the total length of the segment is 225 feet. (Made you look! Only nine cables are required to connect ten computers — that's why it's not 250 feet.)

For 10baseT or 100baseT cable, the 100-meter length limit applies to the cable that connects a computer to the hub or the cable that connects hubs to each other when hubs are daisy-chained with twisted-pair cable. In other words, you can connect each computer to the hub with no more than 100 meters of cable, and you can connect hubs to each other with no more than 100 meters of cable.

Figure 30-1 shows how you can use a repeater to connect two groups of computers that are too far apart to be strung on a single segment. When you use a repeater like this, the repeater divides the cable into two segments. The cable length limit still applies to the cable on each side of the repeater.

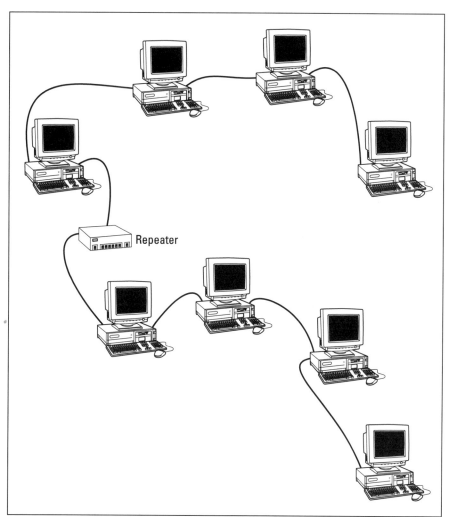

Figure 30-1:
Using a
repeater.

Here are some points to ponder when you lie awake tonight wondering about repeaters:

✔ Repeaters are used only with Ethernet networks wired with coax cable. 10/100baseT networks don't use repeaters.

Actually, that's not quite true: 10/100baseT does use repeaters. It's just that the repeater isn't a separate device. In a 10/100baseT network, the hub is actually a multiport repeater. That's why the cable used to attach each computer to the hub is considered a separate segment.

✔ Some 10/100baseT hubs have a BNC connector on the back. This BNC connector is a thinnet repeater that enables you to attach a full 185-meter thinnet segment. The segment can attach other computers, 10baseT hubs, or a combination of both.

✔ A basic rule of Ethernet life is that a signal cannot pass through more than three repeaters on its way from one node to another. That doesn't mean you can't have more than three repeaters or hubs, but if you do, you have to carefully plan the network cabling so that the three-repeater rule isn't violated.

✔ A two-port thinnet repeater costs about $200.

✔ Repeaters are legitimate components of a by-the-book Ethernet network. They don't extend the maximum length of a single segment; they just enable you to tie two segments together. Beware of the little black boxes that claim to extend the segment limit beyond the standard 185-meter limit for thinnet or 500-meter limit for the yellow stuff. These products usually work, but playing by the rules is better.

Managed Hubs

A *managed hub* is a 10baseT or 100baseT hub that allows you to monitor and control various aspects of the hub's operation from a remote computer. Here are some of the benefits of managed hubs:

✔ Managed hubs can keep network usage and performance statistics, so you can find out which parts of your network are heavily used and which are not.

✔ A managed hub can alert you when something goes wrong with your network. In fact, the management software that controls the hub can even be configured to send you e-mail or dial your pager when a network error occurs.

✔ You can reconfigure a managed hub from any computer on the network, without having to actually go to the hub.

Inexpensive hubs, which can be purchased for as little as $5 per port, do not include management features. An unmanaged hub is fine for a small network, but for larger networks, you should invest in managed hubs. A typical managed hub can cost two or three times as much as an equivalent unmanaged hub, but for larger networks, the benefits of hub management are well worth the additional cost.

Switches

A *switch* is similar to a hub but provides much better performance. The difference between a hub and a switch is that when a hub receives data from one of its ports, it automatically rebroadcasts that data on each of its other ports. In contrast, when a switch receives data from one of its ports, it forwards the data only to the port that is connected to the computer to which the data is being sent.

In other words, a switch is able to create a separate internal connection (called a *segment*) between any two of the switch's ports. Each of these connections operates at a full 10MHz, or in the case of a 100MHz switch, at 100MHz.

Switches have become so popular that many networks now use switches exclusively instead of hubs. Switches have all but replaced bridges except for unusual applications. A switch typically costs about twice as much as an equivalent hub. You can purchase unmanaged switches for as little as $10 per port. Managed switches can cost as much as $50 to $100 or more per port.

Bridges

A bridge is a device that connects two networks so that they act as if they are one network. Bridges are used to partition one large network into two smaller networks for performance reasons. You can think of a bridge as a kind of smart repeater. Repeaters listen to signals coming down one network cable, amplify them, and send them down the other cable. They do this blindly, paying no attention to the content of the messages they repeat.

In contrast, a bridge is a little smarter about the messages that come down the pike. For starters, most bridges have the capability to listen to the network and automatically figure out the address of each computer on both sides of the bridge. Then the bridge can inspect each message that comes from one side of the bridge and broadcast it on the other side of the bridge only if the message is intended for a computer that's on the other side.

This key feature enables bridges to partition a large network into two smaller, more efficient networks. Bridges work best in networks that are highly segregated. For example (humor me here — I'm a Dr. Seuss fan), suppose that the Sneetches networked all their computers and discovered that, although the Star-Bellied Sneetches' computers talked to each other frequently and the Plain-Bellied Sneetches' computers also talked to each other frequently, rarely did a Star-Bellied Sneetch computer talk to a Plain-Bellied Sneetch computer.

A bridge can partition the Sneetchnet into two networks: the Star-Bellied network and the Plain-Bellied network. The bridge automatically learns which computers are on the Star-Bellied network and which are on the Plain-Bellied network. The bridge forwards messages from the Star-Bellied side to the Plain-Bellied side (and vice versa) only when necessary. The overall performance of both networks improves, although the performance of any network operation that has to travel over the bridge slows down a bit.

Here are a few additional things to consider about bridges:

✔ As I mentioned, some bridges also have the capability to translate the messages from one format to another. For example, if the Star-Bellied Sneetches build their network with Ethernet and the Plain-Bellied Sneetches use Token Ring, a bridge can tie the two together.

✔ You can get a basic bridge to partition two Ethernet networks for about $500 from mail-order suppliers. More sophisticated bridges can cost as much as $5,000 or more.

✔ If you've never read Dr. Seuss's classic story of the Sneetches, you should.

✔ If you're not confused yet, don't worry. Read on.

Routers

A *router* is like a bridge, but with a key difference. Bridges can tell the address of the network node to which each message is sent, and can forward the message to the appropriate segment. But routers have the extra ability to actually peek inside the message to see what type of information is being sent. In contrast, bridges are completely ignorant of the content of network messages.

You can think of a router as a super-intelligent bridge. Bridges know the addresses of all the computers on each side of the bridge and can forward messages accordingly. But routers know even more about the network. A router knows not only the addresses of all the computers but also other routers on the network and can decide the most efficient path to send each network message. In fact, the router knows everything about you and your little network.

One key difference between a bridge and a router is that a bridge is essentially transparent to the network. In contrast, a router is itself a node on the network, with its own address. That means that messages can be directed to a router, which can then examine the contents of the message to determine how it should handle the message.

You can configure a network with several routers that can work cooperatively together. For example, some routers are able to monitor the network to determine the most efficient path for sending a message to its ultimate destination. If a part of the network is extremely busy, a router can automatically route messages along a less-busy route. In this respect, the router is kind of like a traffic reporter up in a helicopter. The router knows that 101 is bumper-to-bumper all the way through Sunnyvale, so it sends the message on 280 instead.

Here is some additional information about routers:

✔ Routers aren't cheap. But for big networks, they're worth it.

✔ The functional distinctions between bridges and routers — and switches and hubs, for that matter — get blurrier all the time. As bridges, hubs, and switches become more sophisticated, they're able to take on some of the chores that used to require a router, thus putting many routers out of work.

✔ Some routers are nothing more than computers with several network interface cards and special software to perform the router functions. In fact, NetWare comes with a router program that lets a NetWare server act as a router, and Windows NT Server has a similar feature.

✔ Routers can also connect networks that are geographically distant from one another via a phone line (using modems) or ISDN. You can't do that with a bridge.

✔ You can also use a router to join your LAN to the Internet. You can get inexpensive (under $500) routers that are specially designed for this purpose.

✔ If you're confused about the distinction between bridges, switches, and routers, join the club. The technical distinction has to do with the OSI Reference Model network layer where the devices operate. Bridges operate at the MAC layer (MAC stands for Media Access Control), whereas routers operate at the next level up: the network layer.

Firewalls

A *firewall* is a security-conscious router that sits between your network and the rest of the world in an effort to prevent "them" from getting to "us."

It's also Pat Buchanan's favorite computer component.

Firewalls are often used when you're providing Internet access to your network, and they're a must if you create a World Wide Web (WWW) site, which enables Internet users all around the world to access files on your network. Naturally, you want to limit the files that Internet users can access. A firewall is the best way to do that.

There are two ways to build a firewall. The first is to set up a server computer to act as your firewall. The firewall server will have two network cards, one connected to your LAN, the other to the Internet. The firewall server then runs special software that filters data as it travels between the Internet and your LAN and protects your LAN from intruders.

The other way to build a firewall is to purchase a firewall router, which is a special type of router that has built-in firewall features.

For more information about firewalls, refer to Chapters 18 and 26.

Gateways

No, not the Bill Gates way. This kind of gateway is a super-intelligent router, which is a super-intelligent bridge, which is a super-intelligent repeater. Notice a pattern here?

Gateways are designed to connect radically different types of networks together. They do this by translating messages from one network's format to another's format, much like the Universal Translator that got Kirk and Spock out of so many jams. (Ever notice how all those planets with gorgeous females never seemed to have a word for *kiss,* so Kirk had to demonstrate?)

Gateways usually connect a network to a mainframe or minicomputer. If you don't have a mainframe or minicomputer, you probably don't need a gateway.

Keep the following points in mind:

- ✔ Gateways are necessary only because of the mess that computer manufacturers got us into by insisting on using their own proprietary designs for networks. If computer manufacturers had talked to each other 20 years ago, we wouldn't have to use gateways to make their networks talk to each other today.

- ✔ Gateways come in several varieties. My favorite is ornamental wrought iron.

It's a RAID!

In most small networks, it's a hassle if a disk drive goes south and has to be sent to the shop for repairs. In some large networks, a failed disk drive is more than a hassle: It's an outright disaster. Big companies don't know how to do anything when the computer goes down. Everyone just sits around, looking at the floor, silently keeping vigil 'til the computers come back up.

A *RAID system* is a fancy type of disk storage that hardly ever fails. It works by lumping several disk drives together and treating them as if they were one humongous drive. RAID uses some fancy techniques devised by computer nerds at Berkeley. These computer nerds guarantee that if one of the disk drives in the RAID system fails, no data is lost. The disk drive that failed can be removed and repaired, and the data that was on it can be reconstructed from the other drives.

Here are a few additional thoughts on RAID:

- RAID stands for Redundant Array of Inexpensive Disks, but that doesn't matter. You don't have to remember that for the test.

- A RAID system is usually housed in a separate cabinet that includes its own RAID disk controller. It's sometimes called a disk subsystem.

- In the coolest RAID systems, the disk drives themselves are *hot swappable*. That means that you can shut down and remove one of the disk drives while the RAID system continues to operate. Network users won't even know that one of the disks has been removed because the RAID system reconstructs the data that was on the removed disk using data from the other disks. After the failed disk has been replaced, the new disk is brought online without a hitch.

Superservers

A funny thing happened to personal computers when networks became popular. They turned into mainframe computers.

As networks grew and grew, some organizations found that they had to have dozens of PCs functioning as dedicated file servers. Some networks had 50 or 100 dedicated servers! You can imagine the network management nightmares you'd have to contend with on a network that large.

To ease the burdens of managing a gaggle of file servers, some network managers are turning to superservers, unbelievably high-powered computers that can single-handedly take on the duties of half a dozen or more mere mortal computers. These superservers have huge cabinets that can hold stacks of disk drives, specialized high-speed disk controllers, room for more memory than Colonel Hathi, and — get this — more than one CPU.

Superservers aren't cheap — they sell for tens of thousands of dollars. But they're often less expensive than an equivalent number of ordinary computers, they're more efficient, and they're easier to manage.

One common argument against the use of superservers is the old "don't put all your eggs in one basket" line. What if the superserver breaks? The counter to this argument is that superservers are loaded with state-of-the-art fault-tolerance gizmos that make it unlikely that they'll ever break. In contrast, if you use ten separate file servers, you actually increase the likelihood that one of them will fail, probably sooner than you'd like.

Server Farms

Large networks with multiple servers often have their servers bunched together in one room, known as a *server farm*. If you have more than two or three servers, you might want to consider some or all of the following methods of dealing with them:

- ✔ You can use inexpensive wire shelving to hold your servers. You can get special wire shelves designed to hold keyboards, monitors, and processors, providing easy access to cabling. For a more professional look, you can get customized LAN management furniture that is designed to hold multiple server computers in just about any configuration you need.

- ✔ If you have limited space, you can use a device known as a *KVM Switch* to connect several server computers to a single keyboard, monitor, and mouse. (*KVM* stands for Keyboard, Video, and Mouse.) That way, you can control any of the servers from the same keyboard, monitor, and mouse by turning the dial on the KVM switch.

- ✔ To save even more space, you can get rack-mounted servers instead of servers built in standard computer cases. Rack-mounted servers can be attached to the same standard 19-inch racks that rack-mounted hubs and patch panels mount to.

Gigabit Ethernet

Most small networks operate just fine with standard 10baseT or 100baseT Ethernet connections. However, if your network is large enough to merit a high-speed backbone connection, you may want to look into Gigabit Ethernet. Gigabit Ethernet is a relatively new version of Ethernet, which runs at 1000Mbps instead of 10 or 100Mbps.

Gigabit Ethernet, also known as 1000baseX, was initially designed to operate over fiber-optic cables but will eventually be able to work over Category 5 UTP cable as well. That's one of the reasons you should take care to install only top-quality Category 5 cable and keep the cable lengths under 100 meters.

Of course, Gigabit Ethernet is more expensive than 10baseT or 100baseT. A Gigabit Ethernet switch can cost several thousand dollars, and you need one at each end of the backbone.

Chapter 31

Ten Layers of the OSI Model

*O*SI sounds like the name of a top-secret government agency you hear about only in Tom Clancy novels. What it really stands for, as far as this book is concerned, is Open System Interconnection, as in the Open System Interconnection Reference Model, affectionately known as the OSI model.

The OSI model breaks the various aspects of a computer network into seven distinct layers. These layers are kind of like the layers of an onion: Each successive layer envelopes the layer beneath it, hiding its details from the levels above. The OSI model is also like an onion in that if you start to peel it apart to have a look inside, you're bound to shed a few tears.

The OSI model is not itself a networking standard in the same sense that Ethernet and Token Ring are. Rather, the OSI model is a framework into which the various networking standards can fit. The OSI model specifies what aspects of a network's operation can be addressed by various network standards. So, in a sense, the OSI model is sort of a standard's standard.

Although the OSI model contains seven layers, the bottom two are the layers that have the most practical impact on smaller networks. Networking standards like Ethernet and Token Ring are layer-1 and layer-2 standards. The higher layers of the OSI model haven't resulted in widespread standards.

Layer 1: The Physical Layer

The bottom layer of the OSI model is the physical layer. It addresses the physical characteristics of the network: the types of cables used to connect devices, the types of connectors used, how long the cables can be, and so on. For example, the Ethernet standard for 10baseT cable specifies the electrical characteristics of the twisted-pair cables, the size and shape of the connectors, the maximum length of the cables, and so on.

Another aspect of the physical layer is the electrical characteristics of the signals used to transmit data over the cables from one network node to another. The physical layer doesn't define any meaning to those signals other than the basic binary values 0 and 1. The higher levels of the OSI model must assign meanings to the bits that are transmitted at the physical layer.

Layer 2: The Data Link Layer

The data link layer is the layer at which meaning is assigned to the bits that are transmitted over the network. A standard for the data link layer must address things such as the size of each packet of data to be sent, a means of addressing each packet so that it's delivered to the intended recipient, and a way to ensure that two or more nodes don't try to transmit data on the network at the same time.

The data link layer also provides basic error detection and correction to ensure that the data sent is the same as the data received. If an uncorrectable error occurs, the data link standard must specify how the node is to be informed of the error so that it can retransmit the data.

Layer 3: The Network Layer

The network layer addresses the interconnection of networks by routing packets from one network to another. The network layer is most important when you use a router to link two different types of networks, such as an Ethernet network and a Token Ring network. Because the network layer is one step above the data link layer, whether the two networks use different standards at the data link and physical layers doesn't matter.

Layer 4: The Transport Layer

The transport layer is the basic layer at which one network computer communicates with another network computer. The transport layer identifies each node on the computer with a unique address and manages connections between nodes. The transport layer also breaks large messages into smaller messages and reassembles the messages at the receiving node.

The transport layer and the OSI layers above it are implemented differently by various network operating systems. You can thank the OSI model for the capability to run NetWare, LANtastic, Windows for Workgroups, or just about any other network operating system on a standard Ethernet network. Ethernet addresses the lower layers of the OSI model. As long as the network operating system's transport layer is able to interface with Ethernet, you're in business.

Layer 4a: The Lemon-Pudding Layer

The lemon-pudding layer is squeezed in between the rather dry and tasteless transport and session layers to add flavor and moistness.

Layer 5: The Session Layer

The session layer establishes *sessions* between network nodes. A session must be established before data can be transmitted over the network. The session layer makes sure that these sessions are properly established and maintained.

Layer 6: The Presentation Layer

The presentation layer is responsible for converting the data sent over the network from one type of representation to another. For example, the presentation layer can apply sophisticated compression techniques so that fewer bytes of data are required to represent the information when it's sent over the network. At the other end of the transmission, the transport layer then uncompresses the data.

The presentation layer also can scramble the data before it's transmitted and unscramble it at the other end, using a sophisticated encryption technique that even Sherlock Holmes would have trouble breaking.

Layer 7: The Application Layer

The highest layer of the OSI model, the application layer deals with the techniques that application programs use to communicate with the network. The name of this layer is a little confusing. Application programs like Lotus 1-2-3 and WordPerfect aren't a part of the application layer. Rather, the network operating system itself works within the application layer.

Chapter 32

Ten Hot Network Buzzwords Guaranteed to Enliven a Cocktail Party

*T*ired of boring cocktail parties where everyone talks about the latest prime time game show or who's going to play Anakin Skywalker in the next Star Wars movie? Here are some conversation topics guaranteed to liven things up a bit or get you thrown out. Either way, they work. Try 'em.

Intranet

What it means: I've grown weary of the Internet, and now I want to create my own little private Internet on my LAN. An intranet uses the tools of the Internet: TCP/IP, HTTP, HTML, and Web-server software, but it isn't connected to the Internet. Intranets are used to create "internal" home pages that can be accessed from the company LAN but not from outside the company.

Used in a sentence: I won't be home for supper tonight, honey. I've got to finish uploading the third-quarter results to the company intranet!

Extranet

What it means: Connecting two or more networks, usually at different locations, either using a private backbone connection or via the Internet. If the Internet is used to make the extranet connection, special precautions such as firewalls must be used to make sure the connection is private.

Used in a sentence: We've got a great network at our home office in Cincinnati, and another great network at our sales office in Cleveland, and we finally got the two to talk to each other over the Internet by setting up an extranet.

Client/Server

What it means: A computer system in which part of the work happens on a client computer, and part of it happens on a server computer. To be a true client/server application, real work must be done on the server. Any server-based network can be loosely called client/server, but in a true client/server system, at least part of the real work — not just file access — is done on the server. For example, in a true client/server database, a database query is processed on the server computer, and just the results of the query are sent back to the client computer. If you want to know more, get a copy of my very own book, *Client/Server Computing For Dummies,* 3rd Edition (IDG Books Worldwide, Inc.).

Used in a sentence: I heard that it took your company five years to replace your old mainframe invoicing system to client/server! You should have gotten a copy of *Client/Server Computing For Dummies,* 3rd Edition, by that fabulous author Doug Lowe.

Enterprise Computing

What it means: The complete computing needs of a business enterprise. In the past, computing was too often focused on the individual needs of small departments or workgroups. The result was a hodgepodge of incompatible systems: Marketing had a minicomputer, sales had a NetWare network, and accounting had an abacus. Enterprise computing views the computing needs of the organization as a whole. Very smart.

Used in a sentence: Our Enterprise computing effort is sailing along at warp 9; I hear you guys are still stuck at one-quarter impulse. Fascinating.

Interoperability

What it means: Fitting round pegs into square holes. Literally, linking estranged networks together so that they work well together. This one is so hot that a whole trade show called Interop is devoted to making different networks work together.

Used in a sentence: We've finally solved our interoperability problems — we fired the guy who bought the stuff that wasn't interoperable.

Fiber Optics

What it means: The fastest form of network cable, where signals are transmitted by light rather than by electricity. Fiber optics are typically used to form the backbone of large networks or to link networks in separate buildings, where the 500-meter limit of yellow cable just won't do. Fiber-optic cables hum along at a cool 100 Mbps or 1,000 Mbps.

Used in a sentence: What am I going to do now that I've linked three buildings on the campus using a fiber-optic backbone? I'm going to Disneyland!

SNA

What it means: IBM's grand scheme of old to dominate the networking business. SNA is found wherever IBM mainframes are found. SNA stands for Systems Network Architecture and is pronounced *snaw* by mainframers.

Used in a sentence: After we get the link between SNA and Ethernet worked out, our mainframe users will be able to access the advanced computing power of our PCs.

E-commerce

What it means: Conducting business over the Internet — that is, actually selling products or services, collecting the money via the Internet, and possibly even delivering the product via the Net.

Used in a sentence: Our profitability has shot up so much since we put in our e-commerce system that we've decided to retire and move to Vail.

TCP/IP

What it means: TCP/IP is the protocol for the Internet. It stands for Transmission Control Protocol/Internet Protocol.

Used in a sentence: Don't worry, after you get TCP/IP up and running, you'll be on the Internet soon enough.

Broadband

What it means: Broadband is a networking technology that allows more than one signal to travel over a cable at the same time. One use of broadband is on those new cable TV systems that can send more than just TV: They can also handle your phone lines and an Internet connection. Broadband cable is lightning fast. In fact, an Internet connection over broadband cable is just as fast as an Ethernet connection on a local area network.

Used in a sentence: No, uh, I don't have broadband yet. Boy, weird weather we've been having lately, don't you think?

Appendix

Glossary

● ●

10base2: The type of coax cable most often used for Ethernet networks. Also known as *thinnet* or *cheapernet*. The maximum length of a single segment is 185 meters (600 feet).

10base5: The original Ethernet coax cable, now used mostly as the backbone for larger networks. Also known as *yellow cable* or *thick cable*. The maximum length of a single segment is 500 meters (1,640 feet).

10baseT: Twisted-pair cable, commonly used for Ethernet networks. Also known as *UTP, twisted pair,* or *twisted sister* (just kidding!). The maximum length of a single segment is 100 meters (330 feet). Of the three Ethernet cable types, this one is the easiest to work with.

100baseFX: The Ethernet standard for high-speed fiber-optic connections.

100baseTX: The leading standard for 100Mbps Ethernet, which uses two-pair Category-5 twisted-pair cable.

100baseT4: An alternative standard for 100Mbps Ethernet using four-pair Category-3 cable.

100VG AnyLAN: A standard for 100Mbps Ethernet that isn't as popular as 100baseT. Like 100baseT, 100VG AnyLAN uses twisted-pair cable.

1000baseT: A new standard for 1,000Mbps Ethernet using four-pair Category-5 unshielded twisted pair cable. 1000baseT is also known as *Gigabit Ethernet.*

802.2: The forgotten IEEE standard. The more glamorous 802.3 standard relies upon 802.2 for moral support.

802.3: The IEEE standard known in the vernacular as *Ethernet.*

8088 processor: The microprocessor chip around which IBM designed its original PC, marking the transition from the Bronze Age to the Iron Age.

80286 processor: *Computo-habilis,* an ancient ancestor of today's modern computers.

80386 processor: The first 32-bit microprocessor chip used in personal computers, long since replaced by newer, better designs but still used by far too many people.

80486 processor: The last of Intel's CPU chips to have a number instead of a name. Replaced years ago by the Pentium processor.

AAUI: *Apple Attachment Unit Interface,* a type of connector used in some Apple Ethernet networks.

access rights: A list of rights that tell you what you can and can't do with network files or directories.

account: You can't get into the network without one of these. The network knows who you are and what rights you have on the network by virtue of your account.

acronym: An abbreviation made up of the first letters of a series of words.

Active Server Pages: An Internet feature from Microsoft that enables you to create Web pages with scripts that run on the server rather than on the client. Also known as *ASP.*

adapter card: An electronic card that you can plug into one of your computer's adapter slots to give it some new and fabulous capability, such as displaying 16 million colors, talking to other computers over the phone, or accessing a network.

address book: In an e-mail system, a list of users with whom you regularly correspond.

administrator: The big network cheese who is responsible for setting things up and keeping them running. Pray that it's not you. Also known as the *network manager.*

AFP: *Apple Filing Protocol,* a protocol for filing used by Apple. (That helps a lot, doesn't it?)

AGP: *Advanced Graphics Port,* a high-speed graphics interface used on most new computer motherboards.

allocation unit: Windows allocates space to files one allocation unit at a time; the allocation unit is typically 2,048 or 4,096 bytes, depending on the size of the disk. Also known as *cluster.* NetWare and Windows NT/2000 can use allocation schemes that are more efficient than standard Windows.

antivirus program: A program that sniffs out viruses on your network and sends them into exile.

Apache: The most popular Web server on the Internet. It comes free with most versions of Linux.

AppleTalk: Apple's networking system for Macintoshes.

application layer: The highest layer of the OSI reference model, which governs how software communicates with the network.

archive bit: A flag that's kept for each file to indicate whether the file has been modified since it was last backed up.

ARCnet: A slow but steady network topology developed originally by Datapoint. ARCnet uses a token-passing scheme similar to Token Ring.

Athlon: A competitor to Intel's Pentium CPU chip manufactured by AMD.

attributes: Characteristics that are assigned to files. DOS alone provides four attributes: system, hidden, read-only, and archive. Networks generally expand the list of file attributes.

AUI: *Attachment Unit Interface,* the big connector found on older network cards and hubs that's used to attach yellow cable via a transceiver.

AUTOEXEC.BAT: A batch file that DOS executes automatically every time you start your computer.

AUTOEXEC.NCF: A batch file that NetWare executes automatically every time you load the server software.

backbone: A trunk cable used to tie sections of a network together. The backbone is often 100Mbps Fast Ethernet.

BackOffice: A suite of Microsoft programs designed to run on server computers based on Windows NT/2000 Server.

backup: A copy of your important files made for safekeeping in case something happens to the original files; something you should make every day.

banner: A fancy page that's printed between each print job so that you can easily separate jobs from one another.

batch file: In DOS, a file that contains one or more commands that are executed together as a set. You create the batch file by using a text editor (like the DOS EDIT command) and run the file by typing its name at the command prompt.

benchmark: A repeatable test you use to judge the performance of your network. The best benchmarks are the ones that closely duplicate the type of work you routinely do on your network.

bindery: The big database where user accounts and other related info are stored on a NetWare 3 server. Replaced in NetWare 4 by NetWare Directory Services.

BNC connector: The connector that's used with 10base2 cable.

bottleneck: The slowest link in your network, which causes work to get jammed up. The first step in improving network performance is identifying the bottlenecks.

bridge: Not the popular card game, but a device that enables you to link two networks together. Bridges are smart enough to know which computers are on which side of the bridge, so they only allow those messages that need to get to the other side to cross the bridge. This device improves performance on both sides of the bridge.

buffer: An area of memory that holds data en route to somewhere else. For example, a disk buffer holds data as it travels between your computer and the disk drive.

bus: A type of network topology in which network nodes are strung out along a single run of cable called a *segment.* 10base2 and LocalTalk networks use a bus topology. *Bus* also refers to the row of expansion slots within your computer.

cache: A sophisticated form of buffering in which a large amount of memory is set aside to hold data so that it can be accessed quickly.

CAPTURE: The NetWare command used to redirect printer output to a network printer. CAPTURE is usually run in a batch file or login script.

Category-3: An inexpensive form of unshielded twisted pair that is suitable only for 10Mbps networks (10baseT). Avoid using Category-3 cable for new networks.

Category-5: The higher grade of 10baseT cable that is suitable for 100Mbps networks (100baseTX) and gigabit Ethernet (1000baseT).

CD-R drive: A CD drive that can read and write CDs.

CD-ROM: A high-capacity disc that uses optical technology to store data in a form that can be read but not written over.

CD-RW drive: A CD drive that can read, write, and then rewrite CDs.

Certified NetWare Engineer: Someone who has studied hard and passed the official exam offered by Novell. Also known as *CNE.*

Certified Network Dummy: Someone who knows nothing about networks but nevertheless gets the honor of installing one. Also known as *CND*.

CGA: *Crayon Graphics Adapter,* a crude type of graphics display used on early IBM computers. (Actually, *CGA* stands for *Color Graphics Adapter*.)

chat: What you do on the network when you talk *live* with another network user.

Chaucer: A dead English dude.

cheapernet: See *10base2*.

CHKDSK: A DOS command that checks the record-keeping structures of a DOS disk for errors.

click: What you do in Windows to get things done.

client: A computer that has access to the network but doesn't share any of its own resources with the network. See *server*.

client/server: A vague term meaning roughly that the work load is split between a client and server computer.

Clouseau: The most dangerous man in all of France. Some people say he only plays the fool.

cluster: See *allocation unit*.

coaxial cable: A type of cable that contains two conductors. The center conductor is surrounded by a layer of insulation, which is then wrapped by a braided-metal conductor and an outer layer of insulation.

COM1: The first serial port on a computer.

CompuServe: An online information network that you can access to talk with other users about issues such as NetWare, Windows NT/2000, politics, and the latest reality-based TV show.

computer name: A unique name assigned to each computer on a network.

CONFIG.SYS: A file on every DOS computer that contains configuration information. CONFIG.SYS is processed every time you start your computer.

console: In NetWare, the file server's keyboard and monitor. Console commands can be entered only at the server console.

console operator: In NetWare, a user working at the file server's console.

Control Panel: In Windows, an application that enables you to configure various aspects of the Windows operating system.

conventional memory: The first 640KB of memory on a DOS-based computer.

CPU: The *central processing unit,* or brains, of the computer.

crimp tool: A special tool used to attach connectors to cables. No network manager should be without one.

CSMA/CD: *Carrier Sense Multiple Access with Collision Detection,* the traffic management technique used by Ethernet.

daisy-chain: A way of connecting computer components in which the first component is connected to the second, which is connected to the third, and so on. In 10baseT and 100baseT Ethernet, you can daisy-chain hubs together.

DAT: *Digital audiotape,* a type of tape often used for network backup.

data-link layer: The second layer of the OSI model, responsible for transmitting bits of data over the network cable.

dedicated server: A computer used exclusively as a network server.

delayed write: A disk-caching technique in which data written to disk is placed in cache memory and actually written to disk later.

differential backup: A type of backup in which only the files that have changed since the last full backup are backed up.

digitized sound: A file containing a sound that you can play if the computer has a sound card. See *Clouseau.*

DIP switch: A bank of switches used to configure an old-fashioned adapter card. Modern cards configure themselves automatically, so DIP switches aren't required. See *jumper block*.

directory hash: A popular breakfast food enjoyed by NetWare managers.

disk: A device that stores information magnetically on a disk. A hard disk is permanently sealed in an enclosure and has a capacity usually measured in thousands of megabytes. Also known as *gigabytes*. A *floppy disk* is removable and can have a capacity of 360KB, 720KB, 1.2MB, 1.44MB, or 2.88MB.

DMA channel: A direct pipeline for I/O that's faster than normal I/O. Network cards use DMA for fast network access.

DNS: See *Domain Name System*.

domain: (1) In a Windows NT/2000 network, one or more network servers that are managed by a single network directory. (2) In the Internet, a name assigned to a network.

Domain Name System (DNS): The naming system used on the Internet, in which a network is given a domain name and individual computers are given host names.

DOS: *Disk Operating System,* the original operating system for IBM and IBM-compatible computers. DOS isn't used as much now that Windows 9*x*/Me have taken over.

dot-matrix printer: A prehistoric type of printer that works by applying various-colored pigments to the walls of caves. Once the mainstay printer for PCs, dot-matrix printers have given way to laser printers and inkjet printers. High-speed matrix printers still have their place on the network, though, and matrix printers have the advantage of being able to print multipart forms.

DriveSpace: A disk compression feature of Windows 9*x*/Me (and MS-DOS 6.2). DriveSpace compresses file data so that files require less disk space. This compression increases the effective capacity of the disk, often by a factor of 2:1 or more.

dumb terminal: Back in the heyday of mainframe computers, a monitor and keyboard attached to the central mainframe. All the computing work occurred at the mainframe; the terminal only displayed the results and sent input typed at the keyboard back to the mainframe.

DVD drive: A new type of CD-ROM drive with much higher storage capacity than a standard CD-ROM drive — as much as 17GB on a single disk compared to the 600MB capacity of a standard CD.

Eddie Haskell: The kid who's always sneaking around, poking his nose into other people's business, and generally causing trouble. Every network has one.

editor: A program for creating and changing text files. DOS 5 and later versions come with a basic editor called EDIT. Other editors are available, but EDIT is good enough for most network needs.

EGA: The color monitor that was standard with IBM AT computers, based on 80286 processors. Now obsolete, but some are still in use.

EISA bus: *Extended Industry Standard Architecture,* an improved I/O bus that is compatible with the standard ISA bus but provides advanced features. Computers with an EISA bus were often used as file servers until the PCI bus became more popular. See *ISA bus* and *PCI*.

e-mail: An application that enables you to exchange notes with other network users.

emoticon: A shorthand way of expressing emotions in e-mail and chats by combining symbols to create smiles, frowns, and so on.

ENDCAP: The NetWare command you use to stop network printer redirection.

enterprise computing: A trendy term that refers to a view of an organization's complete computing needs, rather than just a single department's or group's needs.

ESDI: An older style of disk drive that's not often used nowadays.

Ethernet: The World's Most Popular Network Standard.

EtherTalk: What you call Ethernet when you use it on a Macintosh.

ETLA: *Extended Three-Letter Acronym,* an acronym with four letters. See *TLA*.

expanded memory: An ancient technique for blasting past the 640KB limit that was a problem with first-generation PCs.

extended memory: Memory beyond the first 640KB in a DOS computer. The term isn't used with Windows 9*x*/Me or Windows NT/2000; memory is just memory.

Farallon: The company that popularized PhoneNET as a cheaper and more flexible alternative to LocalTalk, Apple's cabling scheme for networking Macintoshes.

Fast Ethernet: 100Mbps Ethernet. Also known as 100baseT or 100baseTX.

FAT: *File allocation table,* a record-keeping structure that DOS uses to keep track of the location of every file on a disk.

FAT32: An improved way of keeping track of disk files that can be used with Windows 98 and later.

FDDI: *Fiber Distributed Data Interface,* a 100Mbps network standard used with fiber-optic backbone. When FDDI is used, FDDI FDDI/Ethernet bridges connect Ethernet segments to the backbone.

ferrule: The outer metal tube that you crimp on to attach a BNC connector to the cable.

fiber-optic cable: A blazingly fast network cable that transmits data using light rather than electricity. Fiber-optic cable is often used as the backbone in large networks, especially where great distances are involved.

file rights: The ability of a particular network user to access specific files on a network server.

file server: A network computer containing disk drives that are available to network users.

firewall: A special type of router that connects a LAN to the Internet while preventing unauthorized Internet users from accessing the LAN.

FTP: *File Transfer Protocol,* a method for retrieving files from the Internet.

full backup: A backup of all the files on a disk, whether or not the files have been modified since the last backup. See ***differential backup***.

fulminic acid: An unstable acid (CNOH) that forms explosive salts of some metals, especially mercury. Used to punish users who write their passwords on stick-on notes stuck on their monitors.

gateway: A device that connects dissimilar networks. Gateways often connect Ethernet networks to mainframe computers or to the Internet.

GB: *Gigabyte,* roughly a billion bytes of disk storage (1,024MB to be precise). See ***KB***, ***MB***, and ***TB***.

generation backup: A backup strategy in which several sets of backup disks or tapes are retained; sometimes called grandfather-father-son.

generation gap: What happens when you skip one of your backups.

glass house: The room where the mainframe computer is kept. Symbolic of the mainframe mentality, which stresses bureaucracy, inflexibility, and heavy iron.

group account: A grouping of user accounts that share common access rights.

groupware: A relatively new category of application programs that are designed with networks in mind to enable and even promote collaborative work.

guru: Anyone who knows more about computers than you do.

HTML: *Hypertext Markup Language,* the language used to compose pages that can be displayed via the World Wide Web.

HTTP: *Hypertext Transfer Protocol,* the protocol used by the World Wide Web for sending HTML pages from a server computer to a client computer.

hub: In Ethernet, a device that is used with 10baseT and 100baseT cabling to connect computers to the network. Most hubs have from 5 to 24 ports. See also ***switch***.

IACI: *International Association of the Computer Impaired.*

IDE: *Integrated Drive Electronics*, the most common type of disk interface in use today, popular because of its low cost and flexibility. For server computers, SCSI is the preferred drive interface. See *SCSI*.

IEEE: *Institute of Electrical and Electronic Engineers*, where they send computer geeks who've had a few too many parity errors.

incremental backup: A type of backup in which only the files that have changed since the last backup are backed up. Unlike a differential backup, an incremental backup resets each file's archive bit as it backs it up. See *archive bit*, *differential backup*, and *full backup*.

inkjet printer: A type of printer that creates full-color pages by spraying tiny jets of ink onto paper.

Internet: A humongous network of networks that spans the globe and gives you access to just about anything you could ever hope for, provided that you can figure out how to work it.

Internet Explorer: Microsoft's popular Web browser.

interoperability: Providing a level playing field for incompatible networks to work together, kind of like NAFTA.

intranet: A network that resembles the Internet but is accessible only within a company or organization. Most intranets use the familiar World Wide Web interface to distribute information to company employees.

intranetWare: A funny name that Novell used for NetWare when the term *intranet* was the hottest buzzword.

I/O port address: Every I/O device in a computer — including network interface cards — must be assigned a unique address. In the old days, you had to configure the port address using DIP switches or jumpers. Newer network cards automatically configure their own port addresses so that you don't have to mess with switches or jumper blocks.

IP address: A string of numbers used to address computers on the Internet. If you enable TCP/IP on your network, you must provide an IP address for each computer on the network.

IPX: The transport protocol used by NetWare.

IPX.COM: The program file that implements IPX.

IRQ: *Interrupt ReQuest*, network interface cards must be configured for the proper IRQ in order to work. In olden times, you had to use DIP switches or jumper blocks to set the IRQ. Nowadays, network cards configure themselves.

ISA bus: *Industry Standard Architecture,* the most popular type of expansion bus for accommodating adapter cards. See *EISA bus* and *PCI.*

ISDN: A digital telephone connection that lets you connect to the Internet at about twice the speed of a regular phone connection.

ISO: *International Standards Organization,* whom we can thank for OSI.

ISP: *Internet service provider,* a company that provides access to the Internet for a fee.

Java: A programming language popular on the Internet.

JavaScript: A popular scripting language that can be used on Web pages.

JetDirect: A device made by Hewlett-Packard that enables printers to connect directly to the network without the need for a separate print server computer.

jumper block: A device used to configure an old-fashioned adapter card. To change the setting of a jumper block, you remove the jumper from one set of pins and place it on another.

KB: *Kilobytes,* roughly one thousand bytes (1,024 to be precise). See *GB, MB,* and *TB.*

LAN: *Local area network,* what this book is all about.

LAN Manager: An obsolete network operating system that Microsoft used to sell. Microsoft long ago put all its networking eggs in the Windows NT/2000 basket, so LAN Manager exists only on isolated islands along with soldiers who are still fighting World War II.

LAN Server: IBM's version of LAN Manager.

LANcache: The disk caching program that comes with LANtastic.

LANtastic: A peer-to-peer network operating system that was once the most popular choice for small networks, before the built-in Windows for Workgroups and Windows 9*x*/Me came along.

laser printer: A high-quality printer that uses lasers and photon torpedoes to produce beautiful output.

lemon-pudding layer: A layer near the middle of the OSI reference model that provides flavor and moistness to an otherwise dry and tasteless fruitcake.

Linux: A public domain version of the UNIX operating system that is becoming popular as a network server.

LLC sublayer: The *logical link sublayer* of layer 2 of the OSI model. The LLC is addressed by the IEEE 802.2 standard.

local area network: See *LAN*.

local bus: A fast expansion bus found on 486 and Pentium computers that operates at a higher speed than the old ISA bus and allows 32-bit data transfers. Two types are commonly found: VESA and PCI. Many 486 computers include several VESA local bus slots, but newer Pentium computers use PCI slots. For best network performance, all servers should have VESA or PCI disk I/O and network interface cards.

local resources: Disk drives, printers, and other devices that are attached directly to a workstation rather than accessed via the network.

LocalTalk: Apple's scheme for cabling Macintosh networks by using the Mac's printer ports. PhoneNET is a cabling scheme that's compatible with LocalTalk but less expensive.

log in: Same as *log on*.

log on: The process of identifying oneself to the network (or a specific network server) and gaining access to network resources.

log out: The process of leaving the network. When you log out, any network drives or printers you were connected to become unavailable to you.

LOGIN: The NetWare command used to log on to a NetWare network.

LOGIN **directory:** In NetWare, a network directory that's mapped to the workstation before the user has logged on. The LOGIN directory contains commands and programs that are accessible to every computer on the network, regardless of whether a user has logged on. Chief among these commands is the LOGIN command.

logon name: In a Windows network, the name that identifies a user uniquely to the network. Same as *user name* or *user ID*.

logon script: A file of NetWare commands that is executed when a user logs in.

LOGOUT: In NetWare, the command you use to log out.

LPT1: The first printer port on a PC. If a computer has a local printer, it more than likely is attached to this port. That's why you should set up printer redirections using LPT2 and LPT3.

Mac OS 9: The latest and greatest operating system for Macintoshes.

Mac OS X Server: Apple's most powerful server operating system for Macintosh computers.

MAC sublayer: The *media access control* sublayer of layer 2 of the OSI model. The MAC is addressed by the IEEE 802.3 standard.

Macintosh: A cute little computer that draws great pictures and comes with built-in networking.

mail server: The server computer on which e-mail messages are stored. This same computer also may be used as a file and print server, or it may be dedicated as a mail server.

mainframe: A huge computer housed in a glass house on raised floors and cooled with liquid nitrogen. The cable that connects the disk drives to the CPU weighs more than most PCs.

mapping: Assigning unused drive letters to network drives or unused printer ports to network printers. See *redirection*.

MB: *Megabytes,* roughly one million bytes (1,024K to be precise). See *GB*, *KB*, and *TB*.

memory: The electronic storage where your computer stores data that's being manipulated and programs that are running. See *RAM*.

metaphor: A literary construction suitable for Shakespeare and Steinbeck but a bit overused by writers of computer books.

modem: A device that converts signals the computer understands into signals that can be accurately transmitted over the phone to another modem, which converts the signals back into their original form. Computers use modems to talk to each other. *Modem* is a combination of *modulator-demodulator.*

monochrome: Monitors that display only one color, usually green or amber against a dark background. Monochrome monitors are often used on NetWare server computers, where flashy color displays would be wasted on an empty closet.

mouse: The obligatory way to use Windows. When you grab it and move it around, the cursor moves on the screen. After you get the hand-eye coordination down, using it is a snap. *Hint:* Don't pick it up and talk into it like Scotty did in *Star Trek IV.* Very embarrassing, especially if you've traveled millions of miles to get here.

Mr. McFeeley: The nerdy-looking mailman on *Mr. Rogers' Neighborhood.* He'd make a great computer geek. Speedy delivery!

MSD: *Microsoft Diagnostics,* a program that comes with DOS 6 and 6.2 and Windows 3.1. MSD gathers and displays useful information about your computer's configuration. In Windows 9*x*/Me, you can get similar information from a program called Microsoft System Information.

My Network Places: An icon on a Windows 2000 and Window Millennium desktop that enables you to access network servers and resources. In Windows 95 and 98, this icon is known as *Network Neighborhood.*

NE2000: The standard by which network interface cards are judged. If your card is NE2000 compatible, you can use it with just about any network.

NETBIOS: *Network basic input output system,* a high-level networking standard developed by IBM and used by most peer-to-peer networks. It can be used with NetWare as well.

Netscape: The company that makes Navigator, a popular program for browsing the World Wide Web.

NetWare: A popular network operating system, the proud child of Novell, Inc.

NetWare Directory Services: A feature of NetWare first introduced with Version 4, in which the resources of the servers are pooled together to form a single entity.

NetWare Loadable Module: A program that's loaded at the file server. Also known as *NLM.* NLMs extend the functionality of NetWare by providing additional services. Btrieve runs as an NLM, as do various backup, antivirus, and other utilities.

network: What this book is about. For more information, see Chapters 1 through 32.

network drive: A drive that resides somewhere out in the network rather than on your own computer.

network interface card: An adapter card that lets the computer attach to a network cable. Also known as *NIC.*

network layer: One of the layers somewhere near the middle of the OSI reference model. It addresses the interconnection of networks.

network manager: Hope that it's someone other than you.

Network Neighborhood: An icon on a Windows 95 or 98 desktop that enables you to access network servers and resources. In Windows 2000 and Windows Millennium, this icon is known as *My Network Places.*

network operating system: An operating system for networks, such as NetWare or Windows 2000 Server. Also known as *NOS*.

network resource: A disk drive, printer, or other device that's located in a server computer and shared with other users, in contrast with a *local resource,* which is located in a user's computer.

newsgroup: Internet discussion groups in which people leave messages which can be read and responded to by other Internet users.

NIC: See *network interface card*.

NLM: See *NetWare Loadable Module*.

node: A device on the network, typically a computer or printer. A router is also a node.

Norton Utilities: A big box chock-full of useful utilities, all for one affordable price. Get it.

NOS: See *network operating system*.

Novell: The folks you can thank or blame for NetWare, depending on your mood.

NTFS: A special type of disk format that you can use on Windows NT/2000 Server disk drives for improved performance and security.

offline: Not available on the network.

online: Available on the network.

operator: A user who has control over operational aspects of the network, but doesn't necessarily have the power to grant or revoke access rights, create user accounts, and so on.

OSI: The agency Lee Majors worked for in *The Six Million Dollar Man*. Also, the *Open System Interconnection* reference model, a seven-layer fruitcake framework upon which networking standards are hung.

packets: Data is sent over the network in manageable chunks called *packets,* or *frames*. The size and makeup of a packet is determined by the protocol being used.

parallel port: A port normally used to connect printers, sometimes called a *printer port*. Parallel ports send data over eight "parallel" wires, one byte at a time. See *serial port*.

partition: A division of a single disk drive into several smaller units that are treated by the operating system as if they were separate drives.

password: The only thing protecting your files from an impostor masquerading as you. Keep your password secret, and you'll have a long and happy life.

patch cable: A short cable used to connect a computer to a wall outlet, or one running from a patch panel to a hub.

PCI: *Peripheral Component Interconnect,* the high-speed bus design found in modern Pentium computers.

PCONSOLE: The NetWare command you use from a DOS command prompt to manage network printing.

peer-to-peer network: A network in which any computer can be a server if it wants to be. Kind of like the network version of the Great American Dream. You can easily construct peer-to-peer networks by using Windows 95, 98, Millennium, or 2000 Professional.

permissions: In Windows NT/2000, rights that have been granted to a particular user or group of users enabling them to access specific files.

PhoneNET: An alternative cabling scheme for Macintosh networks, cheaper than Apple's LocalTalk cables.

physical layer: The lowest layer of the OSI reference model (whatever that is). It refers to the parts of the network you can touch: cables, connectors, and so on.

pocket protector: A status symbol among computer geeks.

port: A connector on the back of your computer that you can use to connect a device such as a printer, modem, mouse, and so on.

PPP: *Point to Point Protocol,* the most common way of connecting to the Internet for World Wide Web access.

presentation layer: The sixth layer of the OSI reference model, which handles data conversions, compression, decompression, and other menial tasks.

print job: A report, letter, memo, or other document that has been sent to a network printer but hasn't printed yet. Print jobs wait patiently in the queue until a printer agrees to print them.

Print Manager: In old-style Windows (Windows 3.1 and Windows for Workgroups), the program that handles print spooling.

print queue: The line that print jobs wait in until a printer becomes available.

print server: A computer that handles network printing or a device such as a JetDirect, which enables the printer to attach directly to the network.

PRN: The DOS code name for the first parallel port. Also known as *LPT1*.

protocol: (1) The droid C-3PO's specialty. (2) The rules of the network game. Protocols define standardized formats for data packets, techniques for detecting and correcting errors, and so on.

punch-down block: A gadget for quickly connecting a bunch of wires, used in telephone and network wiring closets.

QIC: *Quarter-inch cartridge,* the most popular and least expensive form of tape backup. Now known as *Travan drives.* See ***DAT*** and ***Travan***.

queue: A list of items waiting to be processed. The term usually refers to the list of print jobs waiting to be printed, but networks have lots of other types of queues as well.

RAID: *Redundant Array of Inexpensive Disks,* a bunch of disk drives strung together and treated as if they were one drive. The data is spread out over several drives, and one of the drives keeps checking information so that if any one of the drives fails, the data can be reconstructed.

RAM: *Random access memory,* your computer's memory chips.

redirection: One of the basic concepts of networking, in which a device, such as a disk drive or printer, appears to be a local device but actually resides on the network. The networking software on your computer intercepts I/O requests for the device and redirects them to the network.

registry: The file where Windows keeps its configuration information.

repeater: A device that strengthens a signal so that it can travel on. Repeaters are used to lengthen the cable distance between two nodes. A *multiport repeater* is the same as a *hub.*

resource: A disk drive, disk directory, printer, modem, CD-ROM, or other device that can be shared on the network.

ring: A type of network topology in which computers are connected to one another in a way that forms a complete circle. Imagine the Waltons standing around the Thanksgiving table holding hands, and you have the idea of a ring topology.

RJ-45: The kind of plug used by 10baseT and 100baseT networks. It looks kind of like a modular phone plug, but it's bigger.

router: A device that works kind of like a bridge but can handle different protocols. For example, a router can link Ethernet to LocalTalk or a mainframe.

Samba: A program that runs on a Linux server, allowing the Linux computer to work as a file and print server in a Windows network.

ScanDisk: A Windows command that examines your hard disk for physical defects.

scheduling software: Software that schedules meetings of network users. Works only if all network users keep their calendars up-to-date.

SCSI: *Small computer systems interface,* a connection used mostly for disk drives but also suitable for CD-ROM drives, tape drives, and just about anything else. Also winner of the Acronym Computer Geeks Love to Pronounce Most award.

segment: A single-run cable, which may connect more than two computers, with a terminator on each end.

serial port: A port normally used to connect a modem or mouse to a DOS-based computer, sometimes called a communications port. See *parallel port*.

server: A computer that's on the network and shares resources with other network users. The server may be dedicated, which means that its sole purpose in life is to provide service for network users, or it may be used as a client as well. See *client*.

session layer: A layer somewhere near the middle of the beloved OSI reference model that deals with sessions between network nodes.

SFT: *System Fault Tolerance,* a set of networking features designed to protect the network from faults, such as stepping on the line (known as a *foot fault*).

share name: A name that you assign to a network resource when you share it. Other network users use the share name to access the shared resource.

shared folder: A network server disk drive or a folder on a server drive that has been shared so that other computers on the network can access it.

shared resource: A resource, such as a disk or printer, that is made available to other network users.

shielded twisted pair: Twisted-pair cable with shielding, used mostly for Token Ring networks. Also known as *STP*. See *twisted pair*.

smiley: A face made from various keyboard characters; often used in e-mail messages to convey emotion. : -)

SNA: *Systems Network Architecture,* a networking standard developed by IBM that dates from the mid-Mainframerasic Period, approximately 65 million years ago. Used by fine IBM mainframe and AS/400 minicomputers everywhere.

sneakernet: The cheapest form of network, in which users exchange files by copying them to disks and walking them between computers.

SNMP: *Simple Network Management Protocol,* a standard for exchanging network management information between network devices that is anything but simple.

spooling: A printing trick in which data that is intended for a printer is actually written to a temporary disk file and later sent to the printer.

ST-506: An old type of disk drive interface that's obsolete but still found on far too many computers.

star: A type of network topology in which each node is connected to a central wiring hub. This gives the network a star-like appearance.

SUPERVISOR: The top-dog account in NetWare. Log in as SUPERVISOR, and you can do just about anything.

switch: An efficient type of hub that sends packets only to the port that is connected to the packet's recipient rather than sending packets to all of the ports, as a simple hub does.

SYS: The volume name of the system volume on most NetWare servers.

system fault tolerance: See *SFT.*

tape drive: The best way to back up a network server. Tape drives have become so inexpensive that even small networks should have one.

task: For a technically accurate description, enroll in a computer science graduate course. For a layperson's understanding of what a task is, picture the guy who used to spin plates on *The Ed Sullivan Show.* Each plate is a task. The poor guy had to frantically move from plate to plate to keep them all spinning. Computers work the same way. Each program task is like one of those spinning plates; the computer must service each one periodically to keep it going.

TB: *Terrazzo bytes,* imported from Italy. Approximately one trillion bytes (1,024GB to be precise). (Just kidding about *terrazzo bytes.* Actually, TB stands for *terabytes.* It won't be long before you can buy disk drives that can hold a terabyte or more.)

TCP/IP: *Transmission Control Protocol/Internet Protocol,* the protocol used by the Internet.

terminator: The little plug you have to use at each end of a segment of thin coax cable (10baseT).

thinnet: See *10base2*.

three-letter acronym: See *TLA*.

time sharing: A technique used on mainframe computers to enable several users to access the computer at the same time.

time-out: How long the print server waits while receiving print output before deciding that the print job has finished.

TLA: *Three-letter acronym,* such as FAT (File Allocation Table), DUM (Dirty Upper Memory), and HPY (Heuristic Private Yodel).

token: The thing that gets passed around the network in a Token Ring topology. See *Token Ring*.

Token Ring: A network that's cabled in a ring topology in which a special packet called a token is passed from computer to computer. A computer must wait until it receives the token before sending data over the network.

topology: The shape of the network; how its computers and cables are arranged. See *bus*, *star*, and *ring*.

transceiver: A doohickey that connects a network interface card (NIC) to a network cable. A transceiver is always required to connect a computer to the network, but 10base2 and 10baseT NICs have built-in transceivers. Transceivers were originally used with yellow cable. You can also get transceivers that convert an AUI port to 10baseT.

transport layer: One of those layers somewhere near the middle of the OSI reference model that addresses the way data is escorted around the network.

Travan: A newer technology for inexpensive tape backup that can record up to 800MB on a single tape cartridge. See *QIC* and *DAT*.

trojan horse: A program that looks interesting but turns out to be something nasty, like a hard-disk reformatter.

trustee rights: In NetWare, rights that have been granted to a particular user or group of users enabling them to access specific files.

twisted pair: A type of cable that consists of one or more pairs of wires that are twisted in a certain way to improve the cable's electrical characteristics. See *unshielded twisted pair* and *shielded twisted pair*.

uninterruptible power supply: See *UPS*.

unshielded twisted pair: Twisted-pair cable that doesn't have a heavy metal shield around it. Used for 10baseT networks. Also known as *UTP*. See **twisted pair**.

UPS: *Uninterruptible power supply,* a gizmo that switches to battery power whenever the power cuts out. The *Enterprise* didn't have one of these, which is why the lights always went out until Spock could switch to auxiliary power.

URL: *Uniform Resource Locator,* a fancy term for an Internet address. URLs are those familiar "dot" addresses, such as "www-dot-microsoft-dot-com" or "www-dot-idgbooks-dot-com."

USB: A high-speed serial interface that is found on most new computers. USB can be used to connect printers, scanners, mice, keyboards, network adapters, and other devices.

user ID: The name by which you're known to the network.

user profile: The way Windows keeps track of each user's desktop settings, such as window colors, wallpaper, screen savers, Start menu options, favorites, and so on.

user rights: Network actions that a particular network user is allowed to perform after he or she has logged on to the network. See **file rights**.

users' group: A local association of computer users, sometimes with a particular interest, such as networking.

UTP: *Unshielded twisted pair.* See **10baseT**.

vampire tap: (1) A whirligig that enables you to tap into a 10base5 cable to attach a transceiver. (2) What Dracula orders from when he goes to a bar.

VBScript: A scripting language that can be used to add fancy features to Web pages or to create macros for Microsoft Office programs.

VGA: *Video Graphics Array,* the current standard in video monitors. Most VGA adapters these days are actually super VGA adapters, which are compatible with VGA adapters but have extra bells and whistles.

Vines: A network operating system made by Banyan, comparable to NetWare or Windows NT/2000 Server.

virus: An evil computer program that slips into your computer undetected, tries to spread itself to other computers, and may eventually do something bad like trash your hard drive.

volume name: In NetWare, each disk volume has a name. Most NetWare servers have a volume named SYS.

Web browser: A program that enables you to display information retrieved from the Internet's World Wide Web.

Windows: The world's most popular operating system.

Windows 2000: The newest version of Windows NT. Available in four versions: Windows 2000 Professional for desktop users, and Windows 2000 Server, Windows 2000 Advanced Server, and Windows 2000 Datacenter Server for server computers.

Windows 95: A version of Windows that became available in — you guessed it — 1995. Windows 95 was the first version of Windows that did not require DOS.

Windows 98: The successor to Windows 95 introduced in 1998. Windows 98 includes a new user interface that makes the Windows desktop resemble the World Wide Web.

Windows for Workgroups: Microsoft's first network-aware version of Windows, now pretty much defunct.

Windows Millennium Edition: The successor to Windows 98, designed especially for home users and featuring a Home Networking Wizard that simplifies the task of setting up a home network.

Windows NT: The predecessor to Windows 2000. Windows NT is available in two versions: Windows NT Client for desktop computers and Windows NT Server for server computers.

wiring closet: Large networks need a place where cables can congregate. A closet is ideal.

workstation: See *client*.

World Wide Web: A graphical method of accessing information on the Internet.

WWW: See *World Wide Web*.

yellow cable: See *10base5*.

Index

• D •

• E •

• J •

• K •

• *X–Z* •

Notes

Notes

Notes

Notes

Notes

Notes

Notes

Notes

FOR DUMMIES
BOOK REGISTRATION

Register This Book and Win!

We want to hear from you!

Visit **dummies.com** to register this book and tell us how you liked it!

- ✔ Get entered in our monthly prize giveaway.

- ✔ Give us feedback about this book — tell us what you like best, what you like least, or maybe what you'd like to ask the author and us to change!

- ✔ Let us know any other *For Dummies* topics that interest you.

Your feedback helps us determine what books to publish, tells us what coverage to add as we revise our books, and lets us know whether we're meeting your needs as a *For Dummies* reader. You're our most valuable resource, and what you have to say is important to us!

Not on the Web yet? It's easy to get started with *Dummies 101: The Internet For Windows 98* or *The Internet For Dummies* at local retailers everywhere.

Or let us know what you think by sending us a letter at the following address:

For Dummies Book Registration
Dummies Press
10475 Crosspoint Blvd.
Indianapolis, IN 46256

BESTSELLING BOOK SERIES